PROJECT EAGLE

PROJECT EAGLE

THE AMERICAN CHRISTIANS OF NORTH KOREA IN WORLD WAR II

Robert S. Kim

POTOMAC BOOKS *An imprint of the University of Nebraska Press*

Library of Congress Control Number: 2017933717

Set in Lyon by Rachel Gould.
Designed by N. Putens.

To my grandfather and grandmother,
Pak Doo Jae (1909–50) and Chu Yong Ai (1911–2004),
who lived through the events that this book describes.

CONTENTS

ILLUSTRATIONS

PREFACE

On September 20, 1884, a young physician from the United States arrived in the little-known country of Korea, which was ending a long period of isolation and opening itself to foreigners for the first time in centuries. He was the first of hundreds of American Christian missionaries who served in Korea for over half a century, establishing a special relationship between Americans and Koreans at a time when few in the United States had ever heard of Korea. They spread Christianity throughout Korea, established its first universities and hospitals, and brought Western ideas and science. They began the process that made South Korea the modern, successful, and technologically advanced society that it is today.

Sixty years later, during the final months of the Second World War, an army of Koreans in exile was poised to return to Korea to start the liberation of their country from the empire of Japan. It was the product of the first alliance between the United States and Korea, made between the Korean government in exile and the U.S. intelligence service, the Office of Strategic Services (OSS). Called Project Eagle, it united OSS officers who were sons of the first American missionaries in Korea with a Korean liberation movement led by Christians inspired by American ideals, brought to Korea by the missionaries.

Memory of this first American alliance with the people of Korea is nonexistent in the United States. Other than a few Korean Americans, no one remembers that Americans once had a special relationship with

Koreans over a century ago. Project Eagle disappeared into the classified records of the Central Intelligence Agency soon after the Second World War, completely forgotten by the time that the United States began to pay attention to Korea during the Korean War. Even during the wave of Second World War remembrance from the 1990s onward, Project Eagle escaped notice, as its last participants faded and passed away. Americans' historical memory of Korea essentially commences with the Korean War of 1950–53, overlooking several generations of shared experience.

The role of Pyongyang as the virtual capital of American Christians in Korea has been especially forgotten. Pyongyang and other cities in what is now North Korea were the main centers of Christianity in Korea a century ago, the hotbeds of the movement that made Korea the heavily Christian nation that it is today. At a time of widespread debate about the eventual fate of North Korea and of work to rescue and reach out to people in North Korea by Korean Christians, the forgotten American heritage in North Korea has taken on a new relevance that demands remembrance.

This book resurrects the lost history of these six decades of common experience between Koreans and Americans. The main vehicle for describing it is the story of three lives, one Korean and two American, spanning the entire period and all of its main events. The Korean is Kim Ku, the foremost leader of the Korean struggle for independence from Imperial Japan. He emerged from humble origins to lead a movement of exiled Korean patriots who kept the dream of Korean independence alive. The Americans are Clarence Weems and George McCune, leading Christian missionaries in what is now North Korea who lived and raised families there for over three decades. Their sons, also named Clarence Weems and George McCune, then became the leading minds behind the U.S.-Korean alliance of the Second World War as wartime intelligence officers in the OSS.

NOTE ON TERMINOLOGY

This book uses current place-names and romanizations, except in a few instances where an older name or romanization will be clearer for a Western reader. For example, the names Beijing and Shenzhen are used in place of wartime references to Peiping (Peking) and Canton. On the other hand, the wartime spelling Chungking is used instead of the modern romanization, Chongqing, and the historical name Mukden is used instead of the current name Shenyang. Similarly, romanization of Korean names will use the revised system officially adopted in Korea in 2000 instead of the older McCune-Reischauer system, except where names under the older system or nonstandard names are in general use in English-speaking countries. Two such names are those of Kim Ku and Syngman Rhee, the two leading figures of the Korean independence movement.

ACKNOWLEDGMENTS

Reconstructing little-known events from seventy years earlier is a difficult task, and numerous individuals in the United States and Korea were essential to this instance of it. Members of the Weems and McCune families generously offered their family histories and personal memories from Korea, without which telling the stories of Clarence Weems and George McCune would have been impossible. They include, but are not limited to, Peter Weems, Jonathan Weems, Helen McCune Lawless, Antoinette McCune Bement, and Heather McCune Thompson. Robert Sargent, son of Clyde Sargent, contributed invaluable memories and photographs of his father in China, especially his involvement in Project Eagle. Kim Dong Jin, founder of the Hulbert Memorial Society, provided essential insight and access to people and resources in Korea. The staffs of the National Archives and Records Administration in College Park, Maryland, the Presbyterian Historical Society in Philadelphia, and the United Methodist Archives and History Center at Drew University in Madison, New Jersey, patiently responded to my many requests for information over the course of several years. Last but far from least, my colleagues in the U.S. government over the years have taught me numerous lessons on how military and civilian organizations of the U.S. government work overseas in wartime, without which properly understanding the events described in this book could not occur.

PROJECT EAGLE

PART 1

Jerusalem of the East

1

Genesis, 1882–1919

Korea Opens to the United States

Americans and Koreans have a shared history that began far earlier than the Korean War of 1950–53 or the emergence of modern Korea at the end of the Second World War in 1945. Few Americans know that the United States has been connected to Korea since 1882, when the two countries signed a treaty that ended the period of isolation that caused Korea to become known as the "hermit kingdom." Korea had existed as a unified state since 668 AD, and in the 1880s it was in a period of isolation that had begun as a way to protect the country after devastating invasions from Japan and China during the sixteenth and seventeenth centuries. Korea ended its isolation by reaching out to the United States during a period of crisis.

The 1882 treaty followed two decades in which Korea fought imperial powers attempting to pry open the country. The troubles began in 1866, when one European power and then another sent a naval expedition to Korea's shores, beginning an era in which foreign empires fought Korea and each other for influence. The first was from Imperial Russia, which in 1860 had established an outpost on the Pacific Ocean at Vladivostok, only a hundred miles from Korea. Russian ships appeared on the east coast of Korea in January 1866, demanding trade and residency rights. They left without any hostilities, but the next European expedition in October 1866 did not. It was a French fleet that sailed from Tianjin, China (then called Tientsin), to punish Korea for executing French

Catholic missionaries earlier that year. The French force of six ships and approximately eight hundred men seized and for a month occupied Gangwha Island, which commands the entrance to the Han River, the sea approach to the capital at Seoul.[1] Korea continued its isolation after the Russian and French expeditions, but they showed that Korea was in danger of sharing the fate of China, which had been defeated by Great Britain in the Opium Wars of 1839–42 and 1856–60 and fallen into a humiliating period of domination by European colonial empires.

The United States unintentionally entered the situation in Korea in 1866 with a visit by a merchant ship that ended in disaster. In August 1866, only a few weeks before the French naval assault on Korea, a voyage to Korea by the *General Sherman* went badly awry.[2] The *General Sherman* was a former Confederate blockade runner that had been captured and used by the U.S. Navy during the Civil War, then sold to a British firm in Tianjin. Whether the *General Sherman* should be considered American is questionable, because it was a commercial vessel, not a U.S. Navy ship, and its owners were British. The *General Sherman* sailed from Tianjin to Pyongyang with an American captain and chief petty officer and a crew of sixteen Chinese and Malay sailors, in an attempt to meet with Korean officials and negotiate a trade agreement. The *General Sherman*, armed with cannons, attempted to force its way up the Taedong River to Pyongyang against the orders of the local governor. The ship was doomed when it ran aground in a shallow part of the river, enabling Koreans to set it on fire with flaming boats and kill everyone on board.

The sinking of the *General Sherman*, forgotten in the United States, lives on a century and a half later in North Korea as part of the mythology of the ruling family of Kim Il Sung. After the division of Korea, propagandists in North Korea created a fictional history in which an ancestor of Kim Il Sung led the sinking of the *General Sherman*, a story that has no evidence to support it. North Korea has further connected the story to the modern era by using the site where the *General Sherman* is believed to have burned as the mooring place for the USS *Pueblo*, a U.S. Navy intelligence ship captured off North Korea in 1968.[3] For Americans, the *General Sherman* incident is the first act in a history of Americans in

Korea that has been completely forgotten, or perhaps better described as never actually known in the first place so that it could be forgotten.

An official U.S. mission to Korea followed five years later, when a U.S. Navy expedition sailed to Korea in 1871 to determine the fate of the *General Sherman* and deliver a diplomatic mission to establish political and trade relations. The U.S. Asiatic Squadron, with five ships and 1,230 sailors and marines, sailed from Shanghai to Korea bearing the U.S. minister to China. The expedition ended up repeating the experience of the French in 1866, however. The squadron arrived at the mouth of the Han River on June 1 and attempted to sail to the capital at Seoul, but it found itself fired upon from Korean forts on Gangwha Island. The sailors and marines, mostly veterans of the American Civil War and armed with modern breech-loading rifles and artillery, succeeded in storming and capturing the forts, at a cost of three Americans and over three hundred Koreans killed.[4] The tactical victory did not lead to any contact with the Korean government, and after waiting for a month, the squadron weighed anchor and departed on July 3. No further U.S. attempts to contact Korea occurred for the remainder of the decade.

By the beginning of the 1880s, Korea's situation had changed dramatically, and its monarchy began to abandon its centuries-old policy of isolation. Always surrounded by larger and more powerful states, Korea was now especially vulnerable after falling behind the economic and military development of the industrialized powers. Korea became the first target for the imperial ambitions of Japan, industrializing and building a modern army and navy after the Meiji Restoration of 1868. Gunboat diplomacy by Japan, including another attack on Gangwha Island in 1875, resulted in Korea agreeing in 1876 to an unequal treaty opening the country to trade with Japan and giving extraterritorial rights to its subjects. The 1876 treaty exposed Korea's weakness as decisively as Commodore Perry's mission had done for Japan in 1854. It caused the Korean monarchy to consider reopening the country in order to learn from the Western powers and modernize, to preserve national security during an age of imperialism.

The second U.S. attempt to establish relations with Korea came in peace and succeeded in concluding a treaty after two years of patient negotiations. Rear Adm. Robert Shufeldt, acting as the U.S. envoy to Korea, sailed into Pusan twice in April and May 1880 to initiate treaty discussions but was rejected. Relocating to Tianjin, he initiated negotiations with Korean representatives through the Chinese viceroy, culminating in the signing of a treaty in Inchon on May 22, 1882. Called the Treaty of Peace, Amity, Commerce and Navigation, it was the first treaty between Korea and a Western power. Similar treaties followed with Britain and Germany in 1883, Italy and Russia in 1884, and France in 1886. The first U.S. diplomatic representative to Korea, Lucius Foote, presented his credentials to King Kojong of Korea on May 20, 1883. A naval attaché, Ens. George Foulk, followed in December 1883.

For Koreans, the new relationship with the United States was a historic opportunity. King Kojong and his advisers saw the United States as the one major power with no territorial or political ambitions in Korea and therefore uniquely suited to assist in the modernization of the country and the preservation of its independence. Excitement was so high that the king reportedly "danced for joy" when Foote arrived.[5] The king soon issued a request for the United States to provide high-ranking advisers to be placed in Korea's army and foreign ministry, which Foote sent to the secretary of state in Washington on October 19, 1883.[6] Through Foote and his own emissaries, the king reached out to Admiral Shufeldt, who had impressed his Korean counterparts during the negotiation of the treaty, and persuaded him to return to Korea as an adviser. Korea also placed an order for four thousand modern breech-loading rifles from the United States. The presence of these American advisers and weapons would have given the United States considerable influence over the foreign affairs and armed forces of Korea.

The U.S. government far away in Washington showed no interest in fulfilling this modest request, however, not even bothering to send a reply for over a year. The secretary of state, Frederick Theodore Frelinghuysen, finally wrote a response to Foote on November 6, 1884; it did not arrive in Seoul until January 1885. It explained that Foote's dispatch from October 1883 had been mislaid, delaying the secretary's response, and thanked Foote for his efforts without approving the request.[7] With this total indifference, Washington ignored the first invitation by Koreans to intervene and serve as a positive influence on their country.[8] It set the pattern for what the U.S. government would do in Korea for the next six decades.

The U.S. diplomatic mission in Korea soon degenerated into a farce. In July 1884 Congress downgraded the diplomatic position in Seoul from minister plenipotentiary to minister resident, causing Foote to resign when he learned of the demotion. Without informing the State Department, Foote appointed Ensign Foulk as the chargé d'affaires and departed on the day after Christmas in 1884. In this way, a twenty-eight-year-old holding the lowest officer rank in the Navy became the official representative of the United States in Seoul, alone with only an interpreter. He had no official funds because Foote had taken them away with him, and the State Department would not authorize sending its funds to a military officer. Foulk stayed on the job for over a year before the State Department sent a new minister in June 1886. The new minister turned out to be chronically drunk, and the State Department made Foulk return to Korea, where he continued to serve until January 1887. Ill health from overwork and the loss of years from his Navy career caused Foulk to resign his commission and settle down in Japan, where he died six years later at the age of thirty-seven.

U.S. military advisers finally came to Korea in April 1888, with the arrival of a short-lived training mission led by William McEntyre Dye. A veteran of Indian campaigns on the frontier, Dye became a brevet brigadier general of volunteers in the Union army during the Civil War, then resigned his commission and went to Egypt in 1873, where he served as a colonel in the Egyptian Army. Returning to the United States in 1878, he served in senior civilian positions, including superintendent of the Metropolitan Police of Washington DC and head of the Army and Navy Division of the Pension Bureau. In 1888 Dye and a team of three retired officers attempted to create and train a modern Korean army, but the mission ended and disbanded the following year. Having gained the trust of the Korean royal family, Dye stayed in Korea for another ten years, serving as a military adviser training the royal palace guard until 1899. During the 1890s he would witness the darkest days of the end of Korean independence.

Death of the Korean Monarchy

While the United States stumbled through its arrival on the stage in Korea, the monarchy of Korea became engulfed in a long state of crisis that ended with the destruction of the Korean state and the start of half a century of foreign occupation by Imperial Japan.

The royal house that had opened diplomatic relations with the Western powers and invited U.S. advisers split into factions that set traditionalists against modernizers, with China and Japan contending for influence by intervening in the power struggle. King Kojong had assumed the throne in 1873 seeking to modernize the country following the example of Japan. The majority of the ruling family and the upper class (the *yangban*) were opposed to the entry of foreign influences, however, and they supported maintaining Korea's traditional close relationship with China. They included Kojong's father, who had preceded Kojong as Taewongun (regent) until forced to step down, and the influential family of Kojong's wife, Queen Min. Divided against itself, the Korean monarchy was doomed.

An armed rebellion and an attempted coup in Seoul brought intervention by Chinese and Japanese troops at the same time that the United States sent its first diplomatic representatives and then ignored them. In July 1882 Koreans soldiers mutinied over favoritism toward a newly formed elite unit, killing its Japanese military adviser and attacking the Japanese legation in Seoul. After a conservative faction exploited the turmoil by calling for the restoration of the Taewongun to power, China sent three thousand troops who established forts at the royal palace and other strategic points around the city. Japan sent four warships and an infantry battalion to protect the Japanese legation. In December 1884 a group of reformist officials, educated in Japan, attempted a coup at a time when China had withdrawn half of its force in Seoul for a war with France in Indochina. Called the Gapsin Coup, it failed when Japan did not provide military support and the remaining Chinese troops crushed it. The coup plotters were given refuge by the Japanese legation and went into exile.

China and Japan finally went to war over Korea a decade later. The Sino-Japanese War began in July 1894 after China and Japan each dispatched troops to Korea during a peasant revolt, called the Tonghak Rebellion after the religious movement that the rebels followed. Japan's modern Western-style army drove China's troops out of Korea and invaded Manchuria, while its small but well-trained navy destroyed the Chinese fleet in the Battle of the Yalu River. Japan had finally eclipsed China as the great power in Northeast Asia and displaced it as the dominant power in Korea.

The Sino-Japanese War also brought about the entrance of the final great power to become involved in the contest for control over Korea. Russia was a recent arrival in the Far East, having established its first permanent presence on the Pacific Ocean when it founded Vladivostok in 1860. Russian interests in Asia were precariously distant from the center of Russian power in Europe, but Russia was working to connect them, beginning construction of the Trans-Siberian Railroad in 1891. Russia began to contest Japanese influence in Manchuria and Korea immediately after Japan's victory over China in 1895, and for a decade Korea would be a battleground in the rivalry between these two great powers.

Imperial Japan set about dominating Korea through a group of reformist officials, some of them leaders of the 1884 Gapsin Coup returned from exile. To preside over the government, Japan installed the Taewongun, who was now useful to them as an opponent of his own son. From 1894 to 1897 they passed a series of laws known as the Kabo Reforms. They first ended Korea's centuries-old tributary relationship with China, then addressed a wide range of issues including creating a modern education system, establishing a modern judicial system, eliminating the privileges of the yangban class, and abolishing slavery and child marriage. The Taewongun and the reformist cabinet, supervised by Japanese advisers in every cabinet meeting, reduced King Kojong to a puppet. As a symbol of the new order in Korea, in January 1895 Kojong went through an elaborate Japanese-directed ceremony in which he announced to his ancestors the advent of a new era and swore to follow the new laws created by Japan.

Although it brought reforms, Japan also was bringing a regime of great brutality, which showed itself just after midnight on October 8, 1895. That night Japanese agents and hired Korean thugs following the orders of the Japanese minister to Korea, Viscount Miura Goro, stormed into the Gyeongbokgung Palace, killed the palace guards at the main gate, and murdered Queen Min and her ladies-in-waiting in the royal residence. After hacking the women to death, the assassins identified Queen Min's body and desecrated it by setting it on fire.[9] The murder of the queen was so appalling that reports in American and European newspapers led to a wave of international outrage toward Japan, which felt compelled to recall Viscount Miura and place him and fifty-five others on trial. A Japanese court acquitted them all, however, and Japan's policies aimed at dominating Korea continued uninterrupted.

The barbaric assassination signaled the end of Korea's monarchy. Kojong and then his son would continue to occupy the throne until 1910, but in reality they were powerless in the face of Japanese military power and influence. Kojong, living like a prisoner in his palace, took refuge in the Russian legation in Seoul under the protection of Russian troops for an entire year, from February 1896 to February 1897. When he reemerged and returned to his own palace, he did it with Russian soldiers guarding him. Kojong took on the grand new title of emperor in October 1897, intended to signify his independence and equality with the emperors of China and Japan, but he was an emperor who had lost sovereignty over his own country. Dominated by Japan, and protected only by Russia in furtherance of its own ambition for influence in the Far East, the Korean monarchy had become a pawn of two competing empires.

When Japan defeated Russia in the Russo-Japanese War of 1904–5, the end came quickly, despite Korean pleas for support from the United States and other foreign powers. In November 1905, with victorious Japanese troops occupying the country, Korea signed a treaty that yielded control over its foreign affairs, making itself a protectorate of Japan. Kojong attempted to appeal for U.S. support by invoking the 1882 treaty and dispatching envoys to Washington led by Homer Hulbert, an American who had become a trusted adviser to the Korean royal family, but the State Department would not listen to Hulbert and refused the request.[10] When Kojong continued to resist Japanese domination by sending Hulbert to the Hague Conference on World Peace in the summer of 1907, Japan forced him to abdicate, installed his weak son on the throne, and imposed a treaty giving Japan control over Korea's domestic government through a Japanese resident-general. On August 22, 1910, Korean independence completely disappeared when Japan formally annexed Korea.

Homer Hulbert has gone down in history as the first American scholar of Korea and advocate for Korea during the late nineteenth and early twentieth centuries. He came to Korea in 1886, at the age of twenty-three, and he soon became a prominent teacher and scholar. Hulbert first taught children of the Korean royal family and nobility at the Royal English College established by King Kojong, then became a significant influence on the beginning of Korea's education system when Kojong placed him in charge of creating a Western-style middle school and commissioned him to prepare textbooks and train teachers. He wrote a history of Korea that became the standard text in the United States for half a century.[11] Japan expelled Hulbert from Korea after the Hague Peace Conference in 1907, but he continued to campaign for Korea in the United States into the 1940s. For his contributions to defending the independence of Korea, the postwar government of independent Korea awarded him one of its highest awards, the Order of Merit for National Foundation.[12]

The U.S. government stood aside as these events occurred, acquiescing to Japan's protectorate and annexation of Korea. President Theodore Roosevelt had already decided to recognize Japanese domination of Korea, and in July 1905 Secretary of War William Howard Taft, acting as Roosevelt's personal representative, reached an agreement with Prime Minister Katsura Taro of Japan in which each country recognized the other's sphere of influence in Asia. Without a formal treaty or any official agreement, Taft acknowledged a Japanese protectorate over Korea while Katsura disclaimed any interest in the Philippines, an informal pact called the Taft-Katsura Agreement or Memorandum.[13] The United States closed its legation in Korea after Japan established its protectorate in November 1905, and except for consular activities on behalf of American citizens, U.S. government involvement in Korea ceased until the end of the Second World War.

With the final acts of 1905–10, the first decade of the twentieth century saw the end of more than 1,200 years of Korea as an independent country. Korea had survived invasions by China, the Mongols, and Japan for twelve centuries since its unification in 668 AD, but it could not survive the onslaught of the industrialized great powers during the age of imperialism.

Rise of the Korean People

While the Korean state dissolved at the end of the nineteenth century, the Korean people were beginning a journey that would raise them from backwardness and foreign domination to being one of the leading economic powers in the world a century later. It began with a growing understanding that their social order was failing. Korean society had become a tinderbox over the course of the nineteenth century, with numerous groups organizing to fight crippling taxation, abuse by landlords, and other injustices. As Imperial Japan, China, and Russia fought over Korea, movements arose with widely differing ideas on what should be done to end the decline of the country and save it from foreign rule. Their struggles would continue for half a century until the liberation of Korea in 1945 and would define the future character of Korea when it emerged again as an independent nation.

The first movement to surface was the Tonghak (Eastern Learning) movement, whose rebellion in 1894 had precipitated the Sino-Japanese War. Tonghak began in the 1860s as a religious movement seeking to reform and revive the traditional Confucian ideals of Korea, with a new emphasis on human equality, while rejecting Christianity and other "Western learning." It spread rapidly among people angered by abuses by the monarchy and the yangban class and opposed to the influx of foreign commerce and ideas. Tonghak followers formed an underground guerilla army that numbered in the tens of thousands by the early 1890s. The Tonghak Rebellion in July 1894 fought the Korean royal army and Japanese troops but faded later that year.

By 1905 the Tonghak movement had evolved into a new form called Cheondogyo (Heavenly Way). It continued the traditionalism and Korean nationalism of Tonghak, leaving behind the rebellion and violent resistance that had brought persecution by the Korean monarchy. It drew many followers in the early twentieth century and has continued on a small scale in both South and North Korea.

As Imperial Japan expanded its influence in Korea and Japanese agents carried out the brutal murder of Queen Min, another armed force emerged to fight—the Righteous Armies (Uibyeong). A hallowed Korean tradition dating back a thousand years, the Righteous Armies were militias that rose whenever Korea faced an invasion that the state could not resist on its own. The first Righteous Armies emerged during a series of invasions of Korea by the Mongol Khitan people from 993 to 1019. Righteous Armies rose again to defend Korea from invasion by the Mongols (1231–59), Japan (1592–98), and Manchu China (1627 and 1637).

The finest hour of the Righteous Armies had been the war against the first Japanese invasion of Korea in 1592–93. When an invading Japanese army quickly shattered the Korean royal army and captured Seoul in April 1592 and then Pyongyang in July, Righteous Armies rose to fight under the leadership of army officers, local yangban, scholars, and Buddhist monks. They denied the Japanese forces of control over the country, defending fortresses and fighting a guerilla war. Their resistance bought time for rebuilding the Korean army and for Chinese military intervention, which together forced the Japanese to withdraw. Histories of the war usually emphasize the role of the Korean navy under Adm. Yi Sun-Shin, which won numerous battles against superior Japanese naval power and blocked Japanese maritime supply lines. But victory would have been impossible without the contributions of the Righteous Armies on land against the Japanese invasion force.

In 1895 Righteous Armies again rose to defend Korea against Japan. Their ranks swelled after the murder of Queen Min, which inspired outrage throughout Korea. They attacked Japanese troops, pro-Japanese Koreans, and Japanese living in Korea. One was a nineteen-year-old former Tonghak rebel named Kim Changahm, who killed a Japanese man whom he found in an inn in Chihapo, in southern Korea, claiming that the man was a Japanese agent who had participated in the assassination of Queen Min. Kim Changahm later took on the name Kim Ku, and the story of killing a Japanese assassin of Queen Min would become part of the legend of his life.

Without modern weapons or military training and organization, the Righteous Armies could not fight the Imperial Japanese forces directly, and they resisted for over two decades but could not stop the destruction of their country. One Righteous Army attempted to enter Seoul and expel Japanese forces from the capital in 1907, but it was easily defeated by the Imperial Japanese Army. By the annexation of Korea by Japan in 1910, all that was left of the Righteous Armies were a few small bands of guerillas hiding in the mountains or across the border in China.

A third force emerged soon after the rise of the Righteous Armies. It was inspired by American ideals and led by So Chaepil, who had taken on the Westernized name Philip Jaisohn. Born into an aristocratic family, Jaisohn had been one of the organizers of the 1884 Gapsin Coup. When he went into exile, he chose to go to the United States, where he spent ten years attending preparatory school, Columbia University, and the George Washington University medical school. He became the first Korean-born American citizen in 1890 and the first Korean physician in the United States in 1892, and in 1894 he married a niece of former president James Buchanan. Jaisohn returned to Korea in January 1896, at the age of thirty-one, determined to bring civil rights, democracy, and independence to his native country.

Calling themselves the Independence Club, Jaisohn and his movement sought to implement a far-reaching program to create the foundation for a civil society, economic progress, and democratic rule in Korea. They looked first and foremost to education, following Western ideas and examples, and they helped in the creation of a new social class in Korea. Coming of age in the late nineteenth century, they were converts to Christianity, some of them aristocratic by birth and educated in the traditional Confucian classics, but with Western ideas learned in American-organized Christian schools. The schools that were their incubators were the work of American missionaries who came to Korea to spread the gospel but unintentionally helped to create the basis for modern Korean nationalism.

The American Missions in Korea

American missionary work in Korea began in 1884 with the arrival of two Presbyterian missionaries soon after the United States and Korea established diplomatic relations. The first conversions of Koreans to Christianity had occurred during the eighteenth century, and French Catholic priests had been the first Western missionaries to arrive in Korea in 1836. Catholicism spread despite persecution by the Korean monarchy, which killed thousands of converts, including 103 later canonized by the Catholic Church in 1984. Protestant mission work began in Korea in the late 1870s, when a Scottish Presbyterian named John Ross sought converts in northern Korea from his mission in Manchuria. Soon after Americans arrived in 1884, they became the predominant missionaries in the country. By 1910, more than four hundred Americans had served as missionaries, most of them Presbyterians and Methodists.

The American missionaries led an explosive growth of Christianity in Korea during the late nineteenth and early twentieth centuries. When they arrived in 1884, there were already small groups of Korean Catholics and Protestants and Koreans who had embraced Christianity and were waiting to be officially baptized and linked to an established church.[14] In 1900 there were 21,000 Protestants in Korea out of a total of over 60,000 Christians. Ten years later, Korean Protestants had increased almost sevenfold to over 144,000. Christians of all denominations totaled over 218,000, with Protestants outnumbering Catholics by almost two to one.[15] The predominance of Presbyterians and Methodists began in the early twentieth century and continues today.

Pyongyang and the regions that are now in North Korea led the growth of Christianity in Korea. They were the starting points of two great revival movements that drew thousands of new members to the churches. The first began in 1903 in the port city of Wonsan, created on the east coast of Korea for trade with Imperial Japan after the unequal treaty of 1876. A far larger revival began in 1907 in Pyongyang. It began with a joint Presbyterian/Methodist Bible conference that drew thousands of Koreans seeking a new path, at a time when foreign armies had fought across Korea for the second time in recent memory, the country had fallen under foreign rule, and society was in disarray after more than a decade of upheavals. Called the Great Pyongyang Revival, it produced mass conversions that soon expanded throughout Korea as Koreans spread the word around the country. By 1910 Pyongyang and its surrounding area counted 60,736 members in the Presbyterian Church alone.[16] They made the Pyongyang region the most heavily Christian in Korea.

The work of the American Protestant missionaries helped to make Christianity a native religion rather that one brought by westerners, as the missions in Korea were unique in following the methods laid down by Dr. John Nevius, a Presbyterian missionary in China who in 1885–86 published a series of writings advocating a new type of independent, self-supporting mission. The Nevius method called for overseas missions to become self-supporting, self-governing entities in which local members would run the churches and support their own church activities, no longer relying on support and leadership from their parent churches in the United States. American missionaries would found churches and travel around the countryside to reach the people, leaving the security of their mission compounds, and they would turn over leadership as soon as possible to local clergy whom they had educated. As a result, Koreans gradually took over leadership of the churches after the first ordination of a Korean as a Protestant clergyman occurred in 1907.

Koreans in turn transformed the Protestant churches brought by the Americans. The churches came to Korea as separate organizations reflecting divisions within American society, as the Methodists and Presbyterians had each split into separate Northern and Southern churches during the Civil War era over the issue of slavery, with the Methodists not reuniting until 1939 and the Presbyterians not until 1983. The churches divided Korea into separate territories for missionary work.[17] The Korean Methodist Church that formed in 1930 united all Korean Methodists while the American parent churches remained divided, and the Korean Presbyterian Church did the same for all Korean Presbyterians in 1934. Ordination of women also began in the Korean Methodist Church in 1930, long before in the United States, at the insistence of Koreans who demanded equality within their church.[18] In a society with extreme divisions between social classes and between men and women, the early Christians of Korea quietly brought about a social revolution, creating a community that ended traditional social divisions and began to create the far more equal society that exists in South Korea today.

Spreading the new religion outside of Korea as well as within it soon became a priority for the earliest Korean Christians. In 1912, only five years after the ordination of the first Korean Protestant minister, Koreans began their first foreign mission, with the Presbyterians sending three Korean pastors to China.[19] It was the start of Korean foreign missionary work that by the end of the twentieth century would send more missionaries abroad than any country other than the United States.

Equal in importance to bringing religion, the missions were the first source of formal education for most Koreans. American missionaries founded numerous schools that opened education—previously available only to upper-class families—to the common people, including to women. The first opened in Seoul in 1886: Paejae, a school for boys founded by Methodist missionary Henry Appenzeller, and Ewha, a school for girls started by a missionary wife, Mary Scranton, in her living room. Ewha expanded into Korea's leading university for women, whose graduates would become Korea's first female physician, lawyer, doctorate holder, Constitutional Court justice, and prime minister. Homer Hulbert created a middle school system at the request of King Kojong in 1897. The founding of these schools began to create the access to education that made Korea into one of the world's best-educated nations by the end of the twentieth century.

Western medical science also came to Korea through the missions. The first hospital practicing Western medicine in Korea opened in Seoul in 1885, founded by Dr. Horace Allen, a Presbyterian who had arrived in 1884 as the first American missionary in Korea. Arriving under an appointment as physician to the U.S. diplomatic legation to avoid the Korean monarchy's hostility toward Christians, Allen became a trusted physician to King Kojong after saving the life of a royal family member wounded during the Gapsin Coup. The hospital started a training program for physicians the following year, creating the beginnings of Korea's first medical school. Renamed Severance Hospital in 1904, after a wealthy Standard Oil executive who donated funds to the hospital and other Presbyterian missions, the hospital added a medical school and nursing school during the same year.

Pyongyang became the center of Presbyterianism in Korea and throughout Asia, leading to the city receiving the nickname "The Jerusalem of the East." The first mission station in Pyongyang opened in 1895, and by the 1900s an array of churches, schools, and other institutions had grown in the city to serve the rapidly growing Christian community. They included the Lula Wells Industrial School for vocational training of widows and abandoned wives, the Presbyterian Theological Seminary, Union Christian Hospital, and Union Christian College, also called the Sungshil School, founded in 1897 as a private instruction program, made into a formal four-year high school in 1900, and expanded into a college in 1905.[20] They made Pyongyang the main hub for Presbyterian mission work in Asia, serving the largest Christian community in Northeast Asia and also American missionaries in China, many of whom sent their children to boarding schools in Pyongyang for their educations.[21] They also made Pyongyang a center of interdenominational work. Union Christian College and Union Christian Hospital received their names to signify that they were unified efforts of the Presbyterian and Methodist Churches, which cooperated in Pyongyang even though they worked separately in Korea.

Some of the American missionaries established deep roots in Korea that would last far into the twentieth century. They created an enduring

American presence that continued unaffected by the withdrawal of the U.S. government from Korean affairs, continuing their work until war between the United States and Imperial Japan compelled them to depart in 1940–41.

The best known of the American missionary families was the Underwoods. The first to arrive was Horace Grant Underwood, brother of John Underwood, who had founded the Underwood Typewriter Company and made it the largest typewriter manufacturer in the world. With the family fortune supporting his missionary work, Horace Underwood arrived in Korea on Easter Sunday of 1885, on the same boat as Henry Appenzeller. He began as an instructor at Horace Allen's medical school and then started his own mission work, founding a church in Seoul and numerous schools. With Appenzeller he worked on the committee that translated the New Testament into Korean. In 1915 he founded Chosun Christian College, which later merged with Severance Hospital Medical School to become Yonsei University, one of Korea's leading universities. His son, grandson, and great-grandson would each grow up and live in Korea. The family affiliation with Yonsei University continued for almost a century until the passing of his grandson, Horace Grant Underwood II, in 2004.

American missionaries generally attempted to stay out of political issues and maintain neutrality in conflicts between Koreans and Japan, but their religious and educational work inevitably influenced Korean resistance against Japanese rule. Concerned with keeping the permission of the Japanese authorities for their work, missionaries and Korean church leaders kept the churches out of politics, following the biblical injunction to "render unto Caesar the things that are Caesar's, and unto God the things that are God's," often excluding members of political movements from church offices and in some cases even excommunicating them. The churches and their schools became magnets for idealistic young Koreans, however, and they would produce a significant number of the future leaders of Korea.

The young Koreans educated in the mission schools became a new social class in Korea, an intelligentsia that sought to defend their Korean identity in the face of Japanese oppression while incorporating into their society the modern Western ideas that they had learned. They would become most of the leaders of the Korean independence movement. They included a young Methodist convert named Yi Sung Man, twenty-one years of age in 1896, later known as Syngman Rhee. Educated at the Paejae School, he stood out at an early age as an orator on the Korean nationalist cause, and he became an early member of Philip Jaisohn's Independence Club. Half a century later he became the first president of the Republic of Korea. Another was Kim Hyong Jik, a man born in 1894 in northern Korea outside of Pyongyang. He attended the Sungshil School in Pyongyang and later married the daughter of a Presbyterian minister and had a son named Kim Song Ju in 1912. The son would change his name to Kim Il Sung and become the founder of the Democratic People's Republic of Korea, installing his family as the totalitarian rulers of North Korea.

The March First Movement of 1919

The Western-influenced program of Philip Jaisohn began literally as a one-man crusade and expanded into a nationwide movement. Jaisohn started by wandering the streets of Seoul by himself, observing the habits of a country that he had not seen firsthand for a dozen years, and orating on the streets in front of surprised people whenever he witnessed injustices or bad behavior. In April 1896 Jaisohn founded Korea's first newspaper and began delivering guest lectures at the Paejae School at the request of his friend Henry Appenzeller. July saw the formal creation of the Independence Club, with regular open public meetings for discussing political issues. By the end of 1896, the Independence Club had as many as 2,000 members and a rapidly growing student following, and it had begun to exert political influence. A landmark event was its organization of the first mass demonstration in modern Korea on March 10, 1898, bringing out eight thousand people to protest Russian influence in Korea.

Politics doomed the Independence Club, however, and it soon disappeared as an organized movement. Imperial Russian officials viewed the Independence Club as an obstacle to their interests. Korean conservatives and the dying Korean monarchy, living under the protection of Russian troops, regarded the movement's goal of establishing democratic rule to be a threat. In May 1898 the Korean government sent Philip Jaisohn back to the United States, and in December 1898 it arrested many Independence Club leaders, including Syngman Rhee. Most were soon released, but Syngman Rhee remained in prison until 1904 after continuing to organize an opposition movement. The arrests brought the Independence Club to an end.

The disbanding of the Independence Club did not end the work of Korean nationalists, who continued to educate the people and organize resistance to Japanese rule. A patriotic enlightenment movement spread around the country, teaching modern Western ideas to young Koreans. The Protestant churches became rallying points in this struggle against Japanese authority. Mass meetings to pray for Korea became common after 1905, with many becoming demonstrations against Japanese rule, and some ending in fights with the police. These efforts became more intense as Japan forced treaties on Korea ceding control to Japan in 1905 and 1907, then annexed Korea in 1910.

By 1919, discontent with Japanese rule inspired a revolution that has gone down in Korean history as the March First Movement or Three One Movement. In January 1919 word reached Korea of President Woodrow Wilson's proclamation of his Fourteen Points, promising self-determination for nations, at the Paris Peace Conference on January 8, 1919. The deposed King Kojong died in Seoul on January 21, amid rumors that Japanese agents had poisoned him. The death of the last ruler of independent Korea symbolized the end of an era, and with his funeral scheduled for March 3, 1919, a group of Korean nationalists planned to precede it with a dramatic gesture for Korean independence. At 2:00 p.m. on March 1, 1919, thirty-three activists met in a restaurant in downtown Seoul and signed a Declaration of Independence, followed immediately by nationwide demonstrations for independence.

The thirty-three activists who proclaimed Korea's independence showed the influence of thirty-five years of American missionary work in Korea. In a country where only a small percentage of the population had embraced Christianity, sixteen were Christians, fifteen were followers of the Cheondogyo nationalist religion, and two were Buddhists. Among the sixteen Christians, several were Korean clergymen, and ten were born in the heavily Christian northwest that is now in North Korea. Christian, Cheondogyo, and Buddhist groups collaborated in planning the declaration, with a Cheondogyo-affiliated printer surreptitiously printing 35,000 copies of the Declaration of Independence during the night of February 27 and an interfaith network distributing them nationwide the next day. To prepare for their action on March 1, the thirty-three activists met during the night of February 28 in the basement prayer hall of Seung Dong Presbyterian Church in Seoul, which was founded in 1893 and still exists over a century later.

The March First Movement that ensued was a milestone in world history, a nonviolent revolution against colonial rule a decade before Gandhi's Salt March in India. In Seoul a student read the just-signed declaration to a crowd assembled in Pagoda Park, and a march through the city began. Throughout the country, delegates from the independence movement simultaneously read copies of the declaration at 2:00 p.m. An estimated 2 million of Korea's population of 20 million participated in more than 1,500 demonstrations during the ensuing months. The demonstrations spread beyond Korea, to Korean communities in Manchuria and Russia, and Philip Jaisohn organized a campaign to inform the American public. In all demonstrations, participants were under strict instructions not to engage in any violence or threaten Japanese officials, police, or civilians. They would only demonstrate for independence, waving the *taegukgi* flag that is the national flag of the Republic of Korea today, and shouting, "*Taehan tongnip mansei!*" (Long live the independence of Korea!)

Americans who witnessed the March First Movement realized that they were witnessing an unprecedented event, a sign of the rapid revival of a people who only a few years earlier had fallen into decline and become one of many conquered nations during the age of imperialism. A missionary's report on the demonstrations stated,

We are beholding the sudden and startling awakening of a people, almost in a single day, as it were. The propaganda that has been painstakingly carried on for the past twenty years, and to which good men have sometimes lent themselves, inculcating the idea that the Koreans have no future as a people, that their best days are in the past, and that they are a decadent and degenerate race, has met its refutation—a refutation not by words but by deeds. Seldom, if ever, have a people changed so suddenly and to such a marked degree. We who have been here many years and had an intimate acquaintance with them have known that the statements made to their disparagement were largely untrue, but even we have been surprised at the suddenness of the change that has taken place before our eyes. They have shown qualities of leadership, of heroism, of sacrifice, of patience and self-control and endurance that would do credit to any people. A new spirit has taken hold of them, from the highest to the lowest, the young and the old. Whatever the attempts to fetter them, though their bodies may be bound, their thoughts and minds now range freely over the whole world—to China, Palestine, Germany, Paris, and America. The Koreans are *awake*.

Whatever the immediate or more distant future may hold for them politically, they are going to take their place as a people, and do the work for which Providence has assigned to them as a race among other peoples of the Orient. And in all our planning for the coming days we shall do well to consider wisely and to adjust our plans to this changed spirit."[22]

The Japanese authorities, caught by surprise on March 1, acted ruthlessly to crush the demonstrations. Japanese soldiers and police fired on crowds, brutally beat demonstrators in the streets, and made mass arrests. Korean sources claim that there were as many as 7,509 killed, 15,849 wounded, and 46,303 arrested, while Japanese sources claim only 553 killed and 12,000 arrested, along with 8 killed and 158 wounded among the security forces.[23] Regardless of the numbers, the Japanese colonial government responded with great brutality, with beatings in the streets and torture in jail being common occurrences. Many of the beatings and detentions went unrecorded, skewing the official figures, and the number arrested was not higher partly because the jails were completely filled. The thirty-three signers of the Declaration of Independence and over three thousand others, including the leader of Cheondogyo, were imprisoned in Seodaemun Prison in Seoul, where many were tortured and killed.[24]

Japanese repression ended the March First Movement by the end of April, and with it ended the hope of Koreans to regain their independence by peaceful means. A decade after the end of Korea's monarchy and its existence as an independent country, its people had risen to demand their independence again, and the world had ignored them. In an era of imperialism, when the seizure of colonies and maintaining them by force was accepted international behavior, nonviolent resistance was powerless to reassert a nation's independence from imperial rule. Koreans would have to find other ways to seek their independence.

Exile and the Rise of Korean Communism

One way for Koreans to escape rule by Imperial Japan was to leave their homeland, joining Koreans who had left in previous decades. Korean emigration on a large scale had begun over half a century earlier, during the 1860s, when impoverished Koreans seeking better lives moved across the Yalu River to Manchuria and to territories in Siberia recently ceded to Russia by China. By 1910 Koreans numbered over 100,000 in China and over 60,000 in Russia. A small number emigrated to the United States during the 1900s, creating a community that numbered approximately 5,000 in 1910, mostly in Hawaii and California. After March 1919, emigration increased in all directions that international politics would allow.

The United States would be the destination for few Koreans after 1919. Congress enacted the Immigration Act of 1924, which barred immigration from Asian countries, including Japan, China, and Korea. Afterward only a small number of Koreans arrived in the United States, mostly as university or seminary students sponsored by the Presbyterian or Methodist Churches. As a result, Koreans in the United States numbered approximately 10,000 on the eve of the entry of the United States into the Second World War in 1941.

China became home to the largest population of Koreans outside of Korea. Nationalists seeking to continue the independence struggle against Imperial Japan went into exile in China after the annexation of Korea in 1910. They joined earlier economic migrants in China, and hundreds of thousands more fleeing poverty or loss of their land to Japanese interests after 1910 followed. They included the twenty-six-year-old Kim Hyong Jik, who in 1920 crossed the border into Manchuria with his eight-year-old son, the future Kim Il Sung. Japan encouraged further Korean emigration with grants of free land in conquered territories in China, where Japan sought to use them as collaborators against the Chinese. By the Second World War, approximately 1.5 million Koreans lived within the borders of modern China, most of them in Manchuria and other territories of northeastern China, with small groups in Shanghai, Tianjin, and other cities.

Russia continued to be a haven for Koreans despite the collapse of Imperial Russia and the Russian Revolution. Throughout the 1910s and 1920s, Koreans continued to settle in Vladivostok and other cities and rural areas of Siberia, unabated by the Russian Revolution in 1917 and the Russian Civil War from 1917 to 1921. Over 170,000 Koreans lived in the Soviet Union by 1937.

The movement of Koreans to the Far East regions of Imperial Russia and then the Soviet Union was a development that would profoundly affect the fate of Korea. Koreans in Russia imitated Russian revolutionaries as the empire collapsed during the First World War. A Korean section formed in the Communist Party in Irkutsk in January 1918, and a Korean Socialist Party emerged in Khabarovsk in June 1918. Years before the official formation of the Soviet Union in 1922, communism had become a significant influence on a major branch of Korean exiles. The new ideology, rivaling the religious and political ideals that Americans had brought to Korea since 1884, would alter the course of the Korean independence movement and the independent Korea that would emerge a quarter of a century later.

The Korean Provisional Government

The Korean exile communities became the new centers of the Korean independence struggle during the March First Movement. With demonstrations raging in Korea, Korean exiles in Vladivostok—a city under the control of counterrevolutionary Whites after the Russian Revolution—declared the formation of a provisional government that claimed to be the Korean government in exile. A group in Shanghai declared the formation of another provisional government in April 1919, and a similar declaration by a group in Seoul followed on April 21. As Japan crushed the March First Movement in Korea, the groups in Shanghai and Vladivostok resolved their differences and united to form the Korean Provisional Government, with its headquarters in Shanghai.

The Korean Provisional Government claimed to be the legitimate government in exile of the people of Korea, dedicated to the overthrow of Japanese rule and the reestablishment of Korean independence. It initially became the rallying point for Korean nationalists of all ideologies from around the world. In September 1919 it selected Syngman Rhee as its first president. A Christian convert educated at Seoul's leading Methodist school, since his release from prison in 1904 he had been living in the United States, where he had attempted to argue for the Korean cause before Secretary of State John Hay and President Theodore Roosevelt.[25] The first prime minister was Yi Tonghwi, who had lived in exile in Russia since 1913 and after the Russian Revolution had been one of the founders of the Korean Socialist Party in June 1918. Despite their ideological differences, they initially cooperated for the larger goal of ending Japanese rule over Korea.

Korean resistance groups that had been organizing in Manchuria during the 1910s, now affiliated with the Korean Provisional Government, attempted to take advantage of the disorder that existed in Northeast Asia after the First World War to renew the fight against Japan, but with little success. After the Chinese Empire fell in 1912 and revolution overthrew the Russian Empire in 1917, the areas around Korea became patchworks of warlord states, and Korean resistance groups used the anarchic situation to operate against Japanese forces near the Manchurian border. By 1920 the disorder also allowed them to obtain a sizable supply of weapons. The Czechoslovak Legion of Czech and Slovak prisoners of war from the army of Austria-Hungary, which had been formed into a 40,000-strong force under Russian Army command and then had become a key part of the White forces in Siberia in 1918, gave many of their weapons to the Korean forces when they withdrew east to Vladivostok and went home in the summer and fall of 1920. Korean forces lacked the ability to seriously challenge Japanese control over Korea, however, and their small fights against Japanese forces in Manchuria during the 1920s would contribute little to the independence struggle.

Their most noteworthy action was the Battle of Qingshanli in October 1920. It occurred after a Korean force raided a Japanese consulate in the city of Hunchun on the border between Korea, China, and Russia. Approximately 3,000 Koreans then fought an Imperial Japanese Army infantry brigade sent on a punitive expedition after the attack. Korean sources claim a victorious surprise attack killing as many as 1,200 Japanese soldiers and wounding up to 2,000, while Japanese Army records claim that there was only a minor action with 11 dead and 24 wounded. Regardless of what really happened, the battle did nothing to threaten Imperial Japan's grip on Korea, and the Imperial Japanese Army followed it with savage reprisals against Korean civilians living in the area. American missionaries in the area reported Japanese forces burning down nine villages near Hunchun and Qingshanli and indiscriminately killing civilians.[26] This battle and its aftermath demonstrated the futility and cost in lives of the armed resistance of the 1920s.

Diplomatic efforts to gain the support of the United States and other foreign powers were equally unsuccessful. Syngman Rhee attempted to use his years of experience in the United States to obtain recognition from the U.S. government, supported by Philip Jaisohn and other Koreans in America, but the United States had no interest in disturbing its generally cordial relations with Japan.[27] Other western powers had the same attitude, and the successors of the collapsed Chinese and Russian Empires were unwilling to risk confrontation with the power of Japan. The Korean Provisional Government found itself alone in the early 1920s, just as the kingdom of Korea had been in previous decades.

The Korean Provisional Government would be at the center of the Korean independence struggle until the end of the Second World War in 1945, but it would be a lonely and forlorn struggle. The future leaders of postwar independent Korea were there, but how they would achieve their goal was not apparent in 1919 or even two decades later. Only individuals with exceptional fortitude could have continued the fight to the end, and the Korean independence movement was fortunate to have a few. The foremost among them was Kim Ku, a leader who emerged from obscurity to become the leading national hero of modern Korea.

2

Kim Ku and the Korean
Liberation Movement

Confucian scholar in training, Tonghak rebel, Righteous Army fighter, prisoner on death row, wandering fugitive, novice Buddhist monk, Christian convert, teacher of Western ideas, terrorist, and leader of the Korean Provisional Government—Kim Ku was all of these things and more. His life encompassed practically the entirety of the experience of the Korean independence struggle. To understand Kim Ku is to understand the Korea of the late nineteenth and early twentieth centuries, from its fall under the domination of Japan to its liberation in 1945.

Becoming Kim Ku

The man known to history as Kim Ku came into the world on August 29, 1876, six months after Japan forced Korea to agree to the unequal treaty that began Korea's slide into domination and colonization. He was the only child of peasants in a rural village near the city of Haeju, sixty miles south of Pyongyang in territory that is now in North Korea. Born into one of the lowest social classes, he experienced the degrading life of a peasant in an impoverished and corrupt society. While many Korean leaders such as Syngman Rhee and Philip Jaisohn were from privileged backgrounds and were educated at the Christian missionary schools and in American universities, Kim Ku struggled down numerous paths with no formal education on the way to his eventual leadership role.

As a child, Kim aspired to learn the Chinese classics and pass the examination that would allow him to join the respected class of civil servants to the Korean monarchy, but the experience led to his estrangement from the Korea of his youth. Unwelcome at the schools for upper-class families, he began his studies at age twelve with a tutor. For a time, his father experienced paralysis, which forced his parents to sell their house to pay medical expenses and to send him away to a relative, who put him to work cutting and carrying wood. As his father recovered and the family rebuilt their lives, they were too poor to afford paper, writing brushes, and ink for his studies, and his mother had to work as a hired farm laborer and at weaving looms in order to buy them. He took the last civil service examination held in his region in 1892, before the Kabo Reforms of 1894 abolished them. There he found that bribery and influence determined who would pass the test, not talent and results. Disappointed, he abandoned his childhood aspiration and searched for a new path.[1]

The rise of the Tonghak movement attracted the young man's interest, and in January 1893 he joined the movement, drawn by its egalitarian principles and goal of ending corruption. At the age of eighteen, he exhibited the first signs of the leadership qualities that would later make him the leader of the Korean independence movement, becoming the leader of a local Tonghak group. A symbol of his new role was the first of his name changes, as he gave up his birth name of Kim Changahm and renamed himself Kim Changsu. During the Tonghak Rebellion, he joined a Tonghak army that gathered in September 1894 to seize a fortress in Haeju, held by Japanese and Korean government troops. The attack failed, and the campaign gave Kim his first experience with divisions among Korean patriots. His force existed in an uneasy standoff with a nearby Righteous Army that was an enemy of the Tonghak, and a rival Tonghak force attacked and defeated his in December.[2]

Three months in hiding after his first defeat led to a fateful encounter with the leader of the nearby Righteous Army, Ahn Taehun. Visiting Ahn in Haeju in February 1895, Kim found Ahn to be an erudite man and a respected leader who already knew of him and had been concerned for his safety. Ahn provided a house for Kim's parents and took Kim into his own home. Moreover, he introduced Kim to Ko Nungson, a well-known scholar in the region. They spoke every day for months, often joined by Ahn. Ko urged Kim to continue to struggle on behalf of Korea and taught him to embrace traditional Confucian values. Kim, still only nineteen years old, embraced Ko's advice, which became an enduring influence even after his later conversion to Christianity and acceptance of Western ideas. Ko also advised him to go to China and to establish ties that would make cooperation against Japan possible in the future. Taking Ko's advice to heart, he began a trek across northern Korea to the Yalu River and the border with China, with the goal of reaching Beijing.[3]

During his stay with Ahn Taehun, Kim also met his host's eldest son, Ahn Chunggun, who was then sixteen. Kim remembered him as exceptionally intelligent and an expert shot and hunter. Fourteen years later in the city of Harbin in Manchuria, Ahn Chunggun would assassinate the Japanese resident-general in Korea, Ito Hirobumi, who had forced King Kojong to abdicate in 1907 and completed Japan's conquest of Korea. It was the first assassination of a high-level Japanese official by a Korean, and it made Ahn Chunggun a national hero in Korea, still widely known and memorialized. The People's Republic of China has made the memory of Ahn Chunggun part of its diplomacy toward Korea, building a memorial to Ahn Chunggun in Harbin that opened in January 2014.

In China Kim went no further than a short distance into Manchuria before being drawn back to Korea. Near the border he encountered and joined a small Righteous Army of about three hundred Korean volunteers that crossed the Yalu into Korea to seize a fort and take weapons and explosives stored there. After the attack failed, he returned to his parents, who informed him that they had engaged him to the eldest granddaughter of Ko Nungson while he was away. The engagement ended after Ko learned of a previous engagement that Kim's parents had made a decade earlier, and a disappointed Kim departed for China again in late February 1896.

A pivotal event in the emergence of Kim Ku occurred during this journey to China. After three years of fruitless armed resistance against Japan and two humiliating defeats, one of them at the hands of other

Koreans, Kim finally drew first blood against the Japanese. It occurred on March 9, 1896, when he and other passengers on a ferryboat stopped overnight at an inn, after barely surviving a long ordeal hemmed in by ice on the river. Kim noticed a man who claimed to be Korean but whom he identified as Japanese and carrying a sword beneath his coat. Thinking that the man was a Japanese agent, he confronted the man, and in a brutal hand-to-hand fight took away the sword and killed him with it. According to his own account, he smeared the man's blood on his face and announced to the other passengers what he had done, terrifying them. He left a proclamation on a wall declaring, "I killed this Japanese to avenge the death of our queen," signed by Kim Changsu.[4]

Exactly what happened and who the Japanese man was may never be known conclusively, but it is clear that the reputation of Kim Ku was born that day. Kim claimed that items in the man's belongings identified him as a Japanese army first lieutenant named Tsuchida and that he may have been one of the assassins of Queen Min in October of the previous year. Japanese records identify him as a merchant from Tsushima Island who had arrived in Korea in December 1895 and had been on his way back home when he was killed.[5] Regardless of whether Kim had killed a Japanese agent or a hapless traveling merchant, on that day he committed himself irrevocably to the path that would make him famous. Half a century later, Americans dealing with Kim during the Second World War and in postwar Korea would know him as a lifelong freedom fighter who as a young man had killed one of the assassins of Queen Min.

Arrested two months later, Kim went to a prison at Inchon to await trial for murder and theft. The prison and court were Korean, the court created under the Kabo Reforms for cases involving foreigners. Kim experienced depths of despair as he waited for judgment on a crime calling for capital punishment. He came down with typhoid fever, then attempted suicide by hanging himself with his belt. During several days of questioning as he recovered, the Korean police administering the prison became sympathetic after he defiantly proclaimed that the killing had been revenge for the murder of Queen Min, not a simple murder and robbery. Nevertheless, the court sentenced him to death by hanging on October 22.[6]

A reprieve for the son of a poor peasant sentenced to death for murder unexpectedly came directly from King Kojong. Kojong was living in the Russian legation in Seoul after the murder of Queen Min, searching for ways to punish the pro-Japanese faction in the government. Given a list of criminals to be hanged, Kojong approved all of the sentences except for the one on Kim after a priest who happened to be in the room noticed and pointed out the unusual reason specified for his crime, "Revenge for the Death of the Queen." Kojong stopped the execution by sending a call to the Inchon prison on a telephone line completed only a few days earlier, without which the reprieve could not have reached the prison in time.[7]

The education of Kim Ku took a revolutionary step forward as he sat in prison. He read books brought to him by a young prison official who happened to be a Korean patriot with an appreciation for Western learning, who advised Kim to learn from the West. Kim began to learn about the ideas that he had once opposed as a youth with the Tonghak and with his mentor Ko Nungson. Inspired by his reading, he renounced his earlier rejection of Western ideas. This self-education in prison made him rethink his resistance, and he came to the conclusion that learning and spreading modern ideas and science, not armed resistance, would be the key to the future of Korea. He then made his first attempt to teach other Koreans among the illiterate thieves and murderers in the prison.[8]

Brought back from the dead and with a new perspective on Korea and the world, Kim escaped from prison a year and a half later on March 19, 1898. While Philip Jaisohn and his Western-educated Independence Club were at their peak in Seoul, Kim was a fugitive only a few miles away, with only the ragged prison clothes on his back. Begging for food along the way, he sought and found a friend from prison who had been released, who took him in and fed and clothed him. Revived and properly clothed for the first time in years, he did not go north to return home. Instead he set out on a journey through Korea that was reminiscent of the travels of Mark Twain and his fictional character Huck Finn in

America. He walked to the south on a trek through completely unfamiliar territory, the three southern provinces of Korea that would later become the western half of South Korea, a journey of over five hundred miles.[9]

Wandering through southern Korea and then returning home, Kim completed the transformation that had begun in prison. He made his way south from Seoul through Suwon and Osan, then around the mountainous southwestern province of Cholla. In the autumn he reached the Magok Temple, near the city of Kongju. There he attempted to become a Buddhist monk, and he endured the harsh treatment given to novices. Eventually the urge to learn what had become of his parents and others from his earlier life became too strong, so he left the Buddhist temple and journeyed north again in the spring of 1899. North of Seoul, he saw his parents for the first time in three years and learned that they had been imprisoned in his place after his escape, with his father not released until a year later.[10] He again left home to visit the now aged Ko Nungson, who rejected his new embrace of Western civilization. Realizing that Ko belonged to a past era, Kim returned home, only to find his father dying. His father passed away on December 9, 1900. At the end of the mourning period, Kim converted to Christianity, accepting the Western religion that he had once opposed. He was baptized in 1903.[11]

Kim married in 1904 and set about raising a family and putting into action his goal of teaching modern ideas to the Korean people, as part of the patriotic enlightenment movement spreading around Korea. He participated in public demonstrations but stayed out of the new Righteous Armies that rose after Japan declared its protectorate over Korea in 1905, instead focusing on educational and church activities.[12] Kim's ties to Korea's militant nationalists were too strong for him to stay out of trouble, however, and a series of arrests escalated during the first decade of his new life.

The first came in 1909 after Ahn Chunggun, whom Kim had met fourteen years earlier, assassinated Japan's resident-general in Korea, Ito Hirobumi. A key figure in Japan's modernization from a feudal state to an industrialized power, Ito had drafted Japan's constitution, and in 1885 he became its first prime minister, a position that he held four times.

As resident-general, Ito had established Japan's protectorate over Korea in 1905, forced the abdication of King Kojong in 1907, and secured the 1907 treaty giving Japan complete control over Korea's internal affairs. Ahn, a devout Catholic convert who in 1907 had gone into exile in Vladivostok to fight Japan, followed Ito through the train station at Harbin in Manchuria and shot him three times with a .32 caliber Browning pistol. His last words as a free man before being arrested were ironically in Russian: "*Koreya, ura!*" (Korea, hurrah!) During a wave of arrests following the shooting, Kim was arrested and jailed for more than a month but eventually released after denying any connection to the assassination.[13]

The annexation of Korea by Imperial Japan in 1910 brought Kim back into Korea's nationalist underground, this time with the New People's Association (Shinminhoe), an organization that sought to prepare for a war of independence. Its leader was Ahn Changho, a Christian convert who had been a member of the Independence Club and its main organizer in Pyongyang. Kim had briefly been engaged to Ahn's sister until the engagement broke up over Ahn having promised her to another man without their knowledge. The New People's Association planned to create an underground shadow government in Korea and establish a military academy in Manchuria to train Korean emigrants to serve as the officer cadre of a future army for a war of independence.[14] Founded in 1913, the Sinhung Military Academy produced many of the officers who fought in the Battle of Qingshanli in 1920, and some of the postwar leaders of Korea passed through it.

Kim's next arrest occurred in the following year. It happened not because of his activity with the New People's Association but rather as part of mass arrests of Korean patriots following the arrest of his friend Ahn Myonggun, a cousin of Ahn Chunggun. After his cousin's assassination of Ito Hirobumi and subsequent execution, Ahn Myonggun worked on his own schemes to assassinate a prominent pro-Japanese Korean official and to fund the military academy in Manchuria. The Japanese police arrested Ahn and his circle after a Korean informant notified them of his activities, and they then arrested 160 more individuals associated with the patriotic enlightenment movement in Hwanghae

Province, including Kim. Most were released, but Ahn received a sentence of life in prison, and Kim received a fifteen-year sentence. The Japanese authorities arrested a further 600 in Pyongan Province and sentenced 105 of them to prison terms for an alleged plot to assassinate Governor-General Terauchi Masatake, an action called the "Case of the One Hundred Five."[15]

This second term in prison, fifteen years after the first, became another transformative period in Kim's life. Physically its scars would mark him for life. Handcuffs fastened tightly to his wrists during his first several months in prison tore his flesh and left permanent marks. Regular beatings by Japanese prison guards left him with more scars and a disfigured left ear. A more profound change occurred to his identity: to symbolize his complete commitment to the cause of Korean independence, he took on a new name. In Sodaemun Prison, where the leaders of the March First Movement would be confined and tortured several years later, he took on the name Kim Ku. Meaning simply "nine," the name's plainness broke from the symbolism normally used in Korean names and signified his view of himself as an ordinary man whose identity was entirely tied to the cause of liberation. Kim Ku became the name under which he would go down in history.

Kim Ku simultaneously took on a new pen name laden with even greater significance. He called himself Paekpom, a name created from the Korean word for outcasts from society (*paekchongi*) and the word for ordinary, ignorant people (*pombu*). Like the name Kim Ku, calling himself Paekpom signified his view of himself as no better than the lowest of Korean people and completely subordinated to the liberation of all. Even further, Kim Ku's pen name signaled his aspiration that even the outcast and most ignorant among Koreans would come to possess a patriotism equal to his own and his belief that Korea would not be able to achieve complete independence until then. He was now a man of the entire Korean people, from the highest to the lowest.[16]

Kim Ku's journey could have ended in prison, but for a second time, the random intervention of a distant monarch brought him back from oblivion. His fifteen-year sentence would have seen him released from prison in 1926 at the age of fifty, middle-aged and most likely left behind by the leadership of the liberation movement. Instead, the death of Emperor Meiji of Japan in July 1912, followed by the death of Empress Shoken in April 1914, led to successive reductions in Kim Ku's prison sentence under general pardons issued by the government of Japan. His sentence first was reduced to seven years after the death of Emperor Meiji, then a third of the remaining sentence was commuted after the death of Empress Shoken. He spent the last two years of his sentence doing hard labor in Inchon Prison, where he had spent his first prison term almost two decades earlier, before being released on parole in July 1915.

Emerging from prison for the last time as Kim Ku, at the age of thirty-nine, a man who had begun his adult life as a student of the Confucian classics and then as a Tonghak rebel had undergone a transformation that mirrored that of the Korean people. A young opponent of Western thinking had become a Christian and a firm believer in the ideas of personal freedom and democracy brought by the American missionaries. Through difficult experience, much of it in prison, he had learned to focus his efforts on the education and enlightenment of the people rather than on violent revolution. Beneath the ideas that Kim Ku had embraced lay a capacity for violence, however, seen in his killing of a Japanese man nineteen years earlier. What kind of leader he would become during the next thirty years until the liberation of Korea, in the face of further hardships and death, remained to be seen.

Exodus

Kim Ku returned from Inchon Prison to his home and family, intent on resuming his teaching work, but he found himself barred from teaching by having been a political prisoner, and his friends and associates in the liberation movement in hiding or in exile overseas. For a time he managed a local farm. The nationwide wave of patriotic uprisings of March 1919 drew him irresistibly back to the liberation struggle, and on March 29, 1919, he left home for the last time and began another journey to China.

Arriving in Shanghai after riding the railroad across the Yalu and boarding a ship in the Chinese border city of Andong, Kim Ku joined a gathering of hundreds of people who had arrived from Korea, Japan, Russia, Europe, and the United States, including many whom he had known well in Korea. They made him part of the government with the title of police commissioner, responsible for the security of the Korean Provisional Government. With about twenty men, his task was to counter the actions of Japanese intelligence agents operating from the Japanese consulate in Shanghai. He worked with assistance from sympathetic French authorities in the French concession of Shanghai, who provided the Koreans with a refuge and informed them of Japanese actions against them.[17]

Shanghai was Kim Ku's world for the next thirteen years. He spent the entire period inside the city, never traveling outside of it. The cat-and-mouse game in the streets with Japanese intelligence agents and the politics of the Korean liberation movement became his work. It was an underground existence, in which Kim Ku avoided using his name in public out of concern for discovery by Japanese agents. Those agents included Koreans who for various reasons—greed, ambition, disillusionment after years of sacrifices in exile—betrayed the Provisional Government and worked as spies for Japanese intelligence. Kim Ku had to execute numerous Korean traitors and collaborators during his term as police commissioner in order to protect the security of the Provisional Government and its members.[18]

Personal tragedy continued to follow Kim Ku in Shanghai. His wife joined him during the next year, then his mother in 1922, and for the first time in a decade he and his family were able to live together. Their lives changed when his wife had a serious fall in a random accident shortly after the birth of their fifth child in 1923, then suffered from pneumonia. He brought her to a special hospital in Shanghai for pneumonia patients, where she passed away on January 1, 1924. She was buried in a public cemetery in the French concession in Shanghai. His mother, who had to take care of the children, returned to Korea in November 1925 with the youngest child, then took back the rest of them. Their departure left Kim Ku alone in Shanghai.

While living through these personal hardships, Kim Ku steadily rose in the Korean Provisional Government. In 1923, he became the interior minister. In December 1926 he became premier of the Korean Provisional Government, a position first held by Syngman Rhee from 1919 to 1925. Kim Ku would serve in this position repeatedly from 1926 to 1947, and in one capacity or another he would lead the most significant actions of the movement. The self-declared lowest of men, the Paekpom had become one of the foremost Korean leaders, over five hundred miles away in Shanghai at the age of fifty.

Kim Ku's ascent occurred after the Korean Provisional Government had already fragmented into factions, split by the division between leaders influenced by American Christians in Korea and Communists supported by the Soviet Union. The divide had been present from the beginning, with the first president, Syngman Rhee, adhering to the democratic principles learned from Americans decades earlier, whereas the prime minister, Yi Tonghwi, called for a Communist revolution in Korea.[19] Within a few years it caused the factions to part ways. Korean Communists funded by the Soviet Union met in 1923 in an attempt to start their own organization, although they failed because of disagreements and factions among the Communists themselves. They instead continued to try to turn the Provisional Government toward Communism under Soviet direction. Failing to take over the Provisional Government, they left it and the city of Shanghai, moving to Manchuria for a new strategy of building influence over Korean independence groups there. Through this rivalry between exiles in China, Korea became the first nation to be split in two by the ideological divide of the Cold War.

As leader of the Korean Provisional Government, Kim Ku faced not only the problem of disunity but also the threat of irrelevance. The Provisional Government and the Korean exile community in Shanghai amounted to fewer than a thousand souls, a small and impoverished fringe group in the international city. It was far from the sizable Korean exile communities in Manchuria and the Russian Far East, whose populations totaled over 750,000 during the 1920s. For funding to sustain itself, it relied on donations solicited from the Korean community in the United States and Hawaii, itself a struggling group of about 7,000, who had immigrated as laborers, students, and political refugees. With limited resources, little ability to organize in Korea or among the Koreans in Manchuria, and factions divided by ideology, the Provisional Government endured resignations by disappointed nationalists as well as by Communists. Kim Ku later wrote that the leadership role fell on him not because of his own merits but rather because the most able men had already left.[20]

The Korean Provisional Government had declined steeply by the time that Kim Ku took over. Syngman Rhee faced constant turmoil from the time he became the first president in September 1919 until the legislature impeached him in March 1925. Seven presidents and premiers followed in the next twenty-one months, as Rhee's successor changed the constitution from a presidential system to a premier system but died within six months, and the premiers who followed lasted only a few months or even a few days each as they failed to form cabinets. Kim Ku worked to rebuild the credibility of the Provisional Government in a first term that lasted eight months, until August 1927. He introduced a new constitution that created a group leadership system that distributed responsibilities among ministers and proved to result in fewer internal conflicts, with Kim Ku's successor lasting in office for six years.

Complete disinterest from the United States, on the other hand, was a problem that no Korean leader could overcome. During the March First Movement of 1919, Korean nationalists in the United States such as Syngman Rhee and Kim Kyusik had written appeals for U.S. assistance and recognition of the Korean Provisional Government, but the State Department filed them away without responding. At the Paris Peace Conference during the same year, Korean envoys seeking a hearing before the American commissioners in Paris were turned away. Attempts by Koreans to contact U.S. officials after the inauguration of President Warren Harding in 1921 and at the Washington Arms Conference of 1921–22 similarly ended in rejections.[21] To Washington in the 1920s and 1930s, Korea was firmly within the Japanese sphere of influence, and there was no interest in supporting opposition to the status quo.

Even within the region, the Korean Provisional Government attracted little interest from its most likely ally, China. Divided by civil war, China had nothing to gain from supporting the Korean cause against Japan. The government of China under the Nationalist Party (Kuomintang) fought a seventeen-year civil war (1911–28) to reunite the country by defeating warlords who had divided up China after the collapse of the last imperial dynasty. The Nationalist Chinese Army under Chiang Kai-shek defeated the last of the major warlords and established control over Beijing with its Northern Expedition in 1926–28, but many warlords remained outside of the Nationalist government's authority. Moreover, civil war between the Nationalists and the Communists under Mao Tse-tung broke out in 1927. The civil war continued after Japan invaded Manchuria in September 1931 and set up the puppet state of Manchukuo. Intent on defeating the Communists before confronting Japan, the Nationalist Chinese government had no use for the small Korean exile movement in Shanghai.

Ignored by the United States and China, challenged by Korean Communists influenced by the Soviet Union, and without the means to fight Japanese control over Korea, the Korean Provisional Government appeared to have little hope as the 1920s drew to a close.

From Activist to Terrorist

Kim Ku changed the terms of the struggle for Korean independence at the beginning of the 1930s. He did it by pioneering a form of warfare that would not become common until after the Second World War: terrorism.

Koreans seeking revenge against Japan had turned to assassination and bombing many years earlier. One of the first was Ahn Chunggun with his assassination of Ito Hirobumi in 1909. Another was O Song-nyun, a member of a Communist underground group, who attempted to kill Gen. Tanaka Giichi of the Imperial Japanese Army, later a prime minister of Japan, in Shanghai in 1922.[22] In 1926 Na Sokchu, a friend of Kim Ku, threw bombs at the offices of the Japanese-owned Oriental Development Company and Shokusan Ginko (Industrial Bank) in Seoul, then committed suicide.[23]

These individual actions were contemporary with attempts at guerilla warfare by Korean groups in Manchuria. The Battle of Qingshanli in October 1920 was their most noteworthy action, but it and smaller armed actions in Manchuria could not threaten Japan's control over Korea. Korean resistance groups eventually lost their sanctuary and faded away after Japan occupied Manchuria and set up the puppet state of Manchukuo in 1931.

Having found that diplomatic efforts to win the support of the United States and other foreign powers had achieved nothing and that Korean resistance groups could do little to fight Japan, Kim Ku turned to terrorism as the way to revive the spirit of the Korean independence movement and attract the attention and support of foreign powers.

Kim Ku began to create the organizational basis for a campaign of terrorism against Japan after the end of his term as premier of the Korean Provisional Government in August 1927. He founded a new political party with a military wing that he created secretly in 1931. Called the Korean Patriotic Corps (Hanin Aeguktan), it was a group of young Korean patriots willing to carry out suicidal attacks against Japanese leaders and symbolic targets. Kim Ku selected its members and led it himself, using the lessons in underground organization and covert operations that he had learned during twelve years in Shanghai.

An attempt to assassinate Emperor Hirohito in Tokyo was the first action of the Korean Patriotic Corps. A thirty-one-year-old volunteer named Yi Pongchang who had worked in Japan as a laborer carried out the attack. Kim Ku personally selected Yi for the mission for his ability to blend in among the Japanese, having learned to speak Japanese and taken on a Japanese name after being adopted by a Japanese family. After living in the heavily Japanese neighborhood of Hongkou in Shanghai and working in a Japanese-owned factory, meeting covertly with Kim Ku at night once a month, he returned to Japan in mid-December 1931 with money for living expenses and two hand grenades. On January 8, 1932, he threw his grenades at Emperor Hirohito's procession at the Sakuradamon Gate of the Imperial Palace, but he failed to injure Hirohito and only wounded one of his guards. Although he was supposed to have used one of the grenades to commit suicide, he used both of them to attack Hirohito, and he was captured.[24]

When Japan attacked Chinese forces in Shanghai from January 28 through March 3, 1932, a conflict called the Shanghai Incident in the West and the January 28 Incident in China, Kim Ku considered using his organization to support China's defense. He developed a plan for a sabotage operation, using Korean laborers working for the Japanese military to set off explosives inside airplane hangars and ammunition dumps. Before the plan could be implemented, the conflict ended in defeat for China and a peace settlement that essentially gave Japan control over Shanghai, requiring China to withdraw its army and allowing Japan to station army units in the city. Kim Ku turned his resources back to the terrorism campaign. It included unsuccessful attempts to send teams to assassinate the governor-general in Korea and prominent Japanese leaders in Manchuria, including the commander of the Kwantung Army and the president of the South Manchurian Railway Company.[25]

A successful terrorist attack occurred during the celebration of Emperor Hirohito's birthday in Hongkou Park in Shanghai on April 29, 1932. Kim Ku chose a twenty-two-year-old Korean patriot named Yun Ponggil for the task of bombing this major event, attended by all of the senior Japanese military and civilian leaders in Shanghai. Yun received bombs hidden inside a lunch box and water bottle, items that Japanese civilians had been told to bring to the celebration. The bombs were designed to be more powerful than the hand grenades used in the failed attack on Emperor Hirohito, and they did their job effectively. The bombs killed the commander of Japan's Shanghai Expeditionary Army, Gen. Shirakawa Yoshinori, and seriously wounded numerous others including Japan's minister plenipotentiary to China, Shigemitsu Mamoru, who lost his right leg; the commander of Japanese naval forces at Shanghai, Adm. Nomura Kichisaburo, who lost his right eye; and the commander of one of the three divisions of the Shanghai Expeditionary Army, Maj. Gen. Ueda Kenkichi, who lost a leg.[26]

Japanese retaliation for the bombing came quickly. Death sentences for the bombers were inevitable, and the Japanese executed Yi Pongchang in October and Yun Ponggil in December.[27] Japanese police and intelligence agents searched Shanghai to arrest Koreans suspected to be members of the Korean Provisional Government and other Korean independence groups. With the city now unsafe, Kim Ku and the Korean Provisional Government began a second exodus, this time from Shanghai into the interior of China.

Kim Ku remained in Shanghai for several weeks before beginning his flight inland. He went into hiding in the house of an American couple, Rev. George Fitch and his wife, Geraldine. George Fitch was a second-generation Presbyterian missionary in China working for the YMCA in Shanghai, living in the city's French concession. He and his wife sheltered Kim Ku in their house and allowed him to use their telephone to direct efforts to assist Korean activists and their families in escaping from Shanghai.

George Fitch afterward had a long career in mission and relief work in Asia that continued to place him in the most difficult situations of the time. In 1937, as head of the YMCA in Nanjing, he became one of the leaders of the Nanjing Safety Zone, where foreign missionaries and businessmen courageously protected thousands of Chinese civilians from Japanese atrocities during the Rape of Nanjing.[28] He returned to China in 1939 to serve with the YMCA and with the United Nations Relief and Rehabilitation Administration until 1947, after which he served in Korea and Taiwan with the YMCA until 1961.

Kim Ku attempted to protect the Korean Provisional Government and other uninvolved Koreans by issuing a public statement declaring himself fully responsible for the bombings in Tokyo and Shanghai, but it made him a wanted man without absolving the Provisional Government. The statement read:

> I, Paekpom, Kim Ku, earlier killed the Japanese army captain Tsuchida in Anak, Hwanghae Province of Korea, to avenge the death of our Queen Min. It was also I, Kim Ku, who ordered patriots Yi Pongchang and Yun Ponggil, members of the Korean Patriotic Corps, to carry out the attack on the Japanese emperor and the bombing in Shanghai's Hongkou Park. No other Korean or Korean organization was even involved in these cases.[29]

After three weeks, with Japanese intelligence agents closing in on the Fitch house, George and Geraldine Fitch used their car to drive Kim Ku out of the French concession to a train station. Kim Ku took a train to Jiaxing, an inland city in Shandong Province, where a Chinese sympathizer who had formerly been a provincial governor took him into his home.[30]

The leaders of the Provisional Government left Shanghai in May 1932 and moved their headquarters to the city of Hangzhou, one hundred miles southwest of Shanghai on the Yangtze River delta. The Provisional Government would remain there until November 1935, when it began to move further into China to escape from the reach of Japan.

While Kim Ku's bombing campaign brought Japanese retaliation that drove the Korean Provisional Government from Shanghai, it also became the catalyst that created a new alliance with the Nationalist Chinese government under Chiang Kai-shek. Chiang previously had been unwilling to provoke Japan by supporting the Korean Provisional Government in Shanghai, but Japanese aggression in the Shanghai Incident created a common interest in fighting Japan. The success of the bombing in Hongkou Park, following soon after the defeat of the Nationalist Chinese Army in Shanghai, demonstrated that the Korean liberation movement had the resolve and ability to contribute to resistance to the next Japanese invasion.

Chiang sent for Kim Ku to meet him in person, and Kim Ku left his refuge in Jiaxing and went to the Nationalist Chinese capital at Nanjing in May 1933. They met at Chiang's residence inside the Whampoa Military Academy, the elite military school that educated the leading commanders of the Nationalist Chinese Army. In a cordial one-on-one meeting, Kim Ku proposed waging an underground campaign throughout Japan, Korea, and Manchuria, supported by funding from China, to undermine an invasion by Japan. The next day Chiang responded that assassination and terrorism had their limits, since Japan could always replace assassinated generals and even an assassinated emperor. He offered to prepare Koreans for regular military operations by establishing an academy to train officers for an army that would fight a future war of independence. Kim Ku eagerly accepted, and later that year a special

Korean section opened at the branch of the Nationalist Chinese military academy in Luoyang, in Henan Province to the west of Nanjing.[31]

The Korean Provisional Government had crossed an important threshold: a foreign power had finally offered support for its struggle against Japan. The isolation of the Korean independence movement had ended, a decade and a half after the March First Movement began, and it ended because of the campaign of terrorism that Kim Ku had planned and implemented.

War with Japan and the Second Exodus

The alliance with Nationalist China that Kim Ku had created gave the Korean Provisional Government a refuge and outside financial support, but the inability of China to defeat the Japanese invasion that came in 1937 forced the Provisional Government to flee further and further inland. Lacking industrial capacity and with a poorly trained and equipped army, no navy, and a weak air force, Nationalist China could not protect its capital, its largest cities, and most of its people from invasion and occupation by the powerful Japanese army, navy, and air forces. As the Nationalist Chinese government moved to stay ahead of the advancing Japanese forces, so did the Provisional Government. This second exodus would take it from the vicinity of Shanghai in 1932 to the city of Chungking deep in China's interior in 1940.

Retreat by China in the face of Japanese aggression began even before the 1937 invasion. After the defeat at Shanghai, Chiang Kai-shek had no illusions about his ability to defeat a Japanese invasion, let alone fight a war of liberation in Korea, so he attempted to avoid war by conceding Chinese territory. The Imperial Japanese Army (IJA) seized Chinese territory around Beijing almost continuously from January 1933 to September 1936, surrounding Beijing on three sides. Chiang was willing to concede his support for the Koreans as well. Protests from Japan against Chinese military support for the Korean independence movement compelled him to close the Korean section of the military academy at Luoyang in the spring of 1934 after the graduation of its first class of sixty-two Korean cadets.

Manipulation of Korean resistance groups by Nationalist China further complicated relations within the Korean Provisional Government. The Chinese also supported a new leftist faction called the Korean National Revolutionary Party, founded in 1935 by Kim Wonbong. He was a former anarchist terrorist who in December 1919 had formed a resistance group in Manchuria and conducted a six-year terrorism campaign in Korea. Recognizing the need for more organized resistance against Japan, he joined the Nationalist Chinese Army in 1925, participating in the Northern Expedition that reunified China in 1927–28. He formed the Korean National Revolutionary Party by merging five political parties and resistance groups. For the duration of the war he would lead a movement to unify Korean resistance groups under Communist leadership. Nationalist China provided Kim Wonbong with financial support and access to its army training facilities, allowing him to form his own armed force called the Korean Volunteer Corps (Choson Uiyongdae) by 1938. Kim Ku, Kim Wonbong, and their political parties would coexist in an uneasy relationship through the end of the war in 1945.

When Japan finally launched its all-out invasion of China in July 1937, its forces rapidly defeated the Chinese armies in their path. Beijing fell on July 28, and Japanese forces in the north then swept south toward the Nationalist capital of Nanjing, 600 miles away on the Yangtze River. A Japanese amphibious invasion at the mouth of the Yangtze River captured Shanghai by the end of October and advanced west along the river toward Nanjing 170 miles away. Japanese forces converged on Nanjing on December 7 and by mid-December had conquered the city. The Nanjing Massacre or Rape of Nanjing followed, with Japanese soldiers killing an estimated 300,000 Chinese prisoners of war and civilians, raping thousands of women, and destroying a third of the city. China's main industrial center, the city of Wuhan, fell to Japanese troops advancing west from Nanjing in October 1938. Guangzhou, the only major port remaining under Chinese control, fell to the Japanese forces in October 1938, cutting China off from outside aid.

The Nationalist government refused to surrender and repeatedly relocated to stay ahead of the Japanese advance. It abandoned its capital at Nanjing just before Japanese forces surrounded the city in December 1937, moving 300 miles west to Wuhan. In October 1938 it abandoned Wuhan and moved west again, this time 450 miles to Chungking in Sichuan in the southwest of China. Geography placed Chungking inside a formidable natural fortress, separated from Japanese-held territory by the Daba Mountains, averaging 5,000 feet in height with individual peaks almost 10,000 feet high. The Japanese forces, already stretched precariously at the end of a 900-mile-long supply line from Shanghai, would never attempt to take Chungking. They instead attacked Chungking from the air with a bombing campaign that lasted five years, striking the city with 5,000 air raids that killed over 20,000 Chinese civilians. The people of Chungking endured the longest and deadliest air attacks experienced by any Allied city until the arrival of American air power stopped the attacks by the autumn of 1943.

Kim Ku and the Korean Provisional Government struggled to survive amid the turmoil of the Japanese invasion, fleeing to one place and then another in search of a new refuge. Their first reaction was to form a unity coalition of right-wing groups in August 1937. The Japanese advance soon put them in danger. Kim Ku had already left Nanjing to get away from Japanese agents sent to kill or abduct him, going into hiding in a small town near the city. When Japanese forces approached Nanjing and the Nationalist Chinese government abandoned the city in December 1937, the leaders of the Provisional Government and their families in Nanjing, about one hundred people in all, decided to move to the city of Changsha, in Hunan Province to the southwest. After waiting for compatriots in Shanghai and Hangzhou to join them, they boarded ships that took them up the Yangtze River to Wuhan, then two hundred miles south down the Xiang River to Changsha.

The one hundred who departed Nanjing ahead of the Japanese occupation and massacre were a small fraction of the Koreans who had been in Shanghai in 1932. They left behind most of those who had remained in Shanghai and Hangzhou, who found themselves in Japanese-controlled territory again. Those left behind included the widow of Ahn Chunggun. Kim Ku had sent her brother-in-law from Nanjing to Shanghai to rescue her, but he had instead rescued only his own family.[32] The idea of send-ing someone back to rescue her from Shanghai would haunt Kim Ku during the journey.[33]

In Changsha, Kim Ku and the Korean Provisional Government experi-enced a brief period of calm that ended in bloodshed and renewed flight a few months later. During this time they received generous support from the Nationalist Chinese central government and provincial government and from Koreans in the United States. Life in Changsha was also safe from Japanese police and assassins, and Kim Ku used his name openly for the first time since his arrival in China almost two decades earlier in 1919.[34] The factionalism dividing the Provisional Government appeared to be subsiding as well, as the nationalist parties in Changsha convened a conference to unite the parties in May 1938. Disaster ensued as a dis-gruntled young member of one of the parties burst into the conference room with a pistol and shot at the Provisional Government leaders inside, wounding Kim Ku and three others, one of whom died. Kim Ku spent a month recovering in a hospital, and a bullet would remain in his chest for the rest of his life. Soon afterward, the ongoing advance of the Japa-nese army compelled Kim Ku and the Provisional Government to leave Changsha. With the assistance of the governor of Hunan Province, they moved south again in July 1938, this time to Guangzhou.[35]

The move to Guanghzhou brought little relief, as the exodus resumed when Japan began a campaign to seize Guangzhou only a few months later in October 1938. With Japanese bombers striking Guangzhou, Kim Ku received permission to move to the new Nationalist Chinese capital at Chungking, and he traveled there by a long overland route that went first back to Changsha, then 400 miles southwest to Guiyang in mountain territory inhabited by the minority Miao people, and finally 240 miles north to Chungking. The remaining hundred members of the Korean Provisional Government and their families escaped Guangzhou ahead of the Japanese forces and arrived in Liu Zhou, west of Guangzhou near China's border with Vietnam. They remained there until May 1939, when after months of negotiations, Kim Ku finally succeeded in obtaining the use of six trucks from the scarce resources of the Nationalist Chinese government, whose few vehicles were urgently needed to support the army at the front. The trucks brought them to Qijiang, about 30 miles south of Chungking. Sixteen months later, in September 1940, they moved into houses in the Nationalist Chinese capital.[36]

The arrival of the Korean Provisional Government in Chungking marked the end of a long journey that had sent them across almost the entirety of southern China. For three years they had moved from one city to another in flight from the Japanese forces attempting to conquer China, along a route almost as long as that of the Long March of the Chinese Communists in 1934–35. In their new refuge in Chungking, they resumed the task of attempting to unify the Korean liberation movement and once again sought the support of the United States for their cause.

Reunification

The remnant of the Korean Provisional Government that resettled in Chungking in September 1940 faced a world that had changed dramatically since they had fled Nanjing in 1937. Japan had occupied most of China's major cities and coastline and had invaded French Indonesia to cut the supply route to China through Haiphong and Hanoi. Nazi Germany had conquered Poland in the east and France, Belgium, and the Netherlands in the west, and the United Kingdom was fighting for its life against German airpower in the Battle of Britain. The Second World War, which had begun with Japan's invasion of China, had engulfed Eastern and Western Europe and threatened to expand to the entirety of Asia as well. The United States was supporting the besieged United Kingdom and China with sales of war material but remained neutral. The future of all of the major powers and smaller nations depended on whether the United States would commit its armed forces and industrial might to the defeat of Imperial Japan and Nazi Germany.

To be an effective ally of Nationalist China, and moreover to be credible as part of the Allied cause to the distant United States, the Korean liberation movement needed unity that it had never achieved since 1919. Divided, the small number of Koreans in exile in unoccupied China could contribute little to the war against Japan, and the United

States would never provide military assistance. Without a united front, there was also no chance that they would have a voice in the discussions among the Allied powers on the future of their own country after the war. Kim Ku and Kim Wonbong, although leaders of rival factions, each hoped to achieve the unity that had long eluded the leaders of the Korean liberation movement.

They met before the Provisional Government arrived in Chungking to work out their differences and start the difficult process of unifying. With the encouragement of Chiang Kai-shek, Kim Ku visited the head-quarters of the National Revolutionary Party and the Korean Volunteer Corps in May 1939. He and Kim Wonbong quickly agreed that all rightist and leftist organizations should be unified, and they issued a joint public statement apologizing for the mistakes of years past and calling for a united nationalist movement.

Opposition to unification came from Korean exiles both in China and far away in the United States. Syngman Rhee, who had returned to the United States after stepping down as president of the Provisional Government in 1925, opposed wartime unity with the Communists, and he and other nationalists in the United States campaigned against it from afar. Kim Ku and Kim Wonbong also faced opposition from groups in their own coalitions in China that would not agree to unite with their former adversaries. A conference of seven political parties that convened in August 1939, while the Provisional Government was still in Qijiang, ended in an agreement to merge three national-ist and two Communist political parties, but it ultimately failed after Kim Wonbong and the National Revolutionary Party pulled out. The nationalist parties instead merged into a new group called the Korean Independence Party under Kim Ku. The Korean Provisional Govern-ment continued into 1940 as an organization of right-wing nationalists in the small city of Qijiang.

Change in the situation of the Korean Provisional Government began with new leadership. The premier since 1935, Yi Tongnyeong, died in March 1940. He had been one of several presidents during the year of multiple failed attempts to form a government in 1926, and he also served as the premier from 1927 until 1933. In his many years of occupying the highest position in the Provisional Government, he had been unable to bridge the divide between the factions of the Korean exile movement. In his place, the legislature elected Kim Ku as president. He would remain in the position through the end of the war. After its arrival in Chungking, the Provisional Government changed its constitution in October 1940 to abolish the collective leadership instituted by Kim Ku in 1927 and create a strong presidency with authority over all domestic and foreign affairs. The Provisional Government now had a leader committed to unifying all factions and with full authority to negotiate with the leftist parties, Nationalist China, and all other foreign powers.

Kim Ku then succeeded in bringing the leftist parties into a coalition for the war against Japan. Kim Wonbong and the National Revolutionary Party formally joined the Korean Provisional Government on December 1, 1941. The Korean National Revolutionary Party would remain integrated into the Provisional Government for the duration of the war, holding positions in the cabinet and cooperating in the government's decisions and actions. For the first time in over two decades since the nationalist and Communist factions had split in Shanghai in 1919, the Korean liberation movement had reunified.

The formation of a unified Korean army began at the same time. Korean armed resistance had continued while the political factions argued and the Korean Provisional Government retreated to Chungking, with Koreans in Manchuria and areas invaded by Japan during the 1930s fighting in guerilla bands alongside Chinese guerillas. Nationalist China wanted Korean manpower to support its struggling army, so it sponsored the formation of Korean units in the territory under its control. Kim Wonbong had formed the Korean Volunteer Corps as the military wing of his Communist faction in 1938, with support and training from Nationalist China. In March 1940 Kim Ku submitted a plan for the creation of a force that would serve as the army of the Korean Provisional Government and the nucleus of the future army of an independent Korea. The response was positive, and on September 17, 1940, a ceremony in Chungking attended by the Korean Provisional

Government, Chinese officials, and Western diplomats declared the founding of the Korean Restoration Army.

The Korean Restoration Army

The Korean Restoration Army developed into the first institution uniting all Koreans since the end of Korean independence three decades earlier. With Korea divided immediately after the Second World War, it would be the last such institution.

The commander of the Korean Restoration Army was Cho Songhwan, sixty-five years old in 1940 and a living link to the Korean military of the final years of Korean independence and the resistance fighters of the three decades in between. He had entered the military academy of the Korean monarchy in 1900 but received a death sentence for attempting to expose corruption at the academy. Released from prison three years later after having his sentence commuted to life in prison and then receiving a pardon, he became one of the founders of the underground New People's Association with Ahn Changho, then went into exile in Russia in 1907. After spending the next twelve years in resistance activities in Russia, China, and Korea, including an attempt to assassinate the prime minister of Japan in Manchuria in 1912, he joined the Korean Provisional Government in Shanghai in 1919. In August 1919 he returned to Manchuria and was one of the main commanders of the force that fought the Battle of Qingshanli. As defense minister of the Provisional Government starting in 1936, he was the main negotiator in talks with the Nationalist Chinese government on the creation of the Korean Restoration Army and became its commander. He established his headquarters in Xian, the former Chinese imperial capital, then a frontline city with Japanese forces less than eighty miles away in Tongguan.[37]

The national army gradually became a reality as its first units formed and the armed groups of the leftist parties joined it. Three units formed first, one in Xian; a second in Shuiyuan, in the southern province of Guangxi on the border with Vietnam; and a third in the Shandong Peninsula, behind Japanese lines but bypassed by Japanese forces and under Chinese control. An anarchist group that had formed in Chungking in

November 1939 and then moved to Xian joined the Korean Restoration Army in January 1941. After Kim Wonbong and the Korean National Revolutionary Party joined the Provisional Government, the Korean Volunteer Corps joined the Korean Restoration Army in July 1942, with Kim Wonbong remaining as its commander. He later became the Provisional Government's defense minister and deputy commander of the Korean Restoration Army.

The Korean Restoration Army had very limited military capability, though, having little access to manpower and other resources. Through the end of 1944, each unit of the Korean Restoration Army numbered no more than a few hundred men, totaling fewer than one thousand altogether. Cut off from Korea and from the Korean population centers in Manchuria and eastern China, the Korean Restoration Army lacked access to larger numbers of potential recruits.

The Korean people instead found themselves forced to serve Japan. The Imperial Japanese Army (IJA) drafted large numbers of Korean men, compelling them to serve the empire and army that had conquered and occupied their country. Thousands of Koreans from Korea and Manchuria served in the IJA as volunteers or under coercion starting in 1938, and in 1944 Japan began drafting Koreans on a large scale.[38] Over 200,000 Koreans served in the IJA, approximately 100,000 of them in China. Forced labor in factories and mines in Japan, Manchuria, and Korea began in 1942 in response to wartime manpower shortages and became the lot of millions of Koreans. Thousands of Korean women had to serve the IJA as "comfort women," the Japanese term for sex slaves. These men and women were among the worst victims of Japanese exploitation of the people of Korea.

Training and materiel also were lacking for the few men available to the Korean Restoration Army. To train and equip its recruits, the Korean Restoration Army relied on the Nationalist Chinese army, which during the war inducted over 4 million men but had inadequate capability to train its masses of raw manpower and very little industry to arm and equip them. Food shortages in wartime China left many soldiers malnourished and physically unfit for combat. Severe shortages of weapons, equipment, and supplies of all kinds in the ill-equipped Chinese army resulted in similar deficiencies in the Korean Restoration Army. For the Koreans to make a significant contribution to the Allied cause in the Second World War, military assistance from the United States would be necessary.

Waiting for the United States

Kim Ku and the Korean Provisional Government strived for years to persuade the United States to provide both military assistance and recognition as the legitimate government in exile of Korea. Kim Ku repeatedly contacted the U.S. embassy in Chungking and attempted to obtain the support of Nationalist China for recognition, while in the United States, Syngman Rhee as chairman of the American Commission of the Korean Provisional Government lobbied Congress and reached out to U.S. political leaders. Kim Ku also sent a letter to President Franklin Roosevelt requesting U.S. recognition in June 1941. These efforts were fruitless all the way up to the attack on Pearl Harbor on December 7, 1941.

The Korean Provisional Government acted immediately to reach out to the United States after the attack on Pearl Harbor. Two days later, it issued an official declaration of war against Japan. In the name of the people of Korea, it declared war on the Axis powers and listed conditions for Korean participation in the war. It declared the 1910 treaty of annexation and all other unequal treaties imposed on Korea by Japan to be invalid. Moreover, it called for the principles of the Atlantic Charter, issued by the United States and the United Kingdom in August 1941 and declaring the right of all people to self-determination, to be applied to Korea. In Washington, Syngman Rhee resumed his efforts to persuade U.S. leaders to pay attention to the Korean cause. He wrote to the State Department and submitted letters from the Provisional Government to the president and the secretary of state on December 9, 1941, then met with a State Department official several days later.[39]

The State Department repeatedly refused to recognize Rhee and the Korean Provisional Government from December 1941 through March 1942. After consultations with the governments of Nationalist China and the United Kingdom, the State Department's Division of Far Eastern Affairs then recommended against making any statements in support of Korean independence or recognizing any Korean group. Any statement on Korean independence would have to wait until it could be made as part of an overall statement on other colonized peoples in Asia, in particular the Indians under the British Empire, or until significant developments occurred in the Korean independence movement.[40]

Nationalist China soon emerged as an advocate of Korean independence and of raising a Korean army for the war against Japan. In early April 1942 China's foreign minister, T. V. Soong, visiting Washington to represent China on the Pacific War Council, presented a memorandum on Korea to President Franklin Roosevelt. Soong's memorandum suggested "promoting a fusion" of Korean factions, then raising, arming, and supporting a Korean irregular army of perhaps 50,000 men to operate with guerillas in northern China. They would conduct sabotage and intelligence work against Japan and eventually operate in Korea at a time to be selected by the Allied nations. As part of this strategy, the Pacific War Council could announce its intention to make Korea independent after the war and recognize the Korean Provisional Government.[41] In Chungking, the Chinese informed the U.S. ambassador that they would recognize the Korean Provisional Government.[42]

The State Department viewed the proposal to create a Korean irregular army favorably but objected to recognition of the Korean Provisional Government. The U.S. reply to China was that it had no immediate intention of recognizing the Korean Provisional Government given the lack of unity among Korean independence groups and the likelihood that Korean exile groups had little association with the Korean population at home. Nationalist China dropped its stated intention to recognize the Korean Provisional Government in early May 1942.[43] Public statements from Nationalist China in support of independence for Korea continued in 1942 and early 1943, but it did not raise the issue of recognition of the Korean Provisional Government seriously again.

Pressure on the State Department continued from Syngman Rhee, members of Congress, and a group called the Korean-American Council in 1942 and 1943. The Korean-American Council included Homer Hulbert, whom King Kojong had sent to plead with President Theodore Roosevelt on behalf of Korea in 1905, and then sent again to the Hague Peace Conference in 1907. Hulbert participated in issuing blistering statements supporting recognition of the Korean Provisional Government. They repeatedly invoked the Atlantic Charter, declaring in a letter to the secretary of state in May 1942 that

> the services of the patriots of Korea are not for sale. They are not mercenaries who can be paid for pulling the chestnuts of the United Nations out of the fire. The young Koreans are straining at the leash but Dr. Rhee will not release them. Not until the State Department, by recognizing the de facto government of the Republic of Korea, fulfills the pledge of the President of the United States and the Prime Minister of Great Britain that: "they wish to see sovereign rights and self-government restored to those who have been forcibly deprived of them."[44]

Congress also added its voice to the issue. Individual members of Congress urged the State Department to recognize the Korean Provisional Government, and Joint Resolutions calling for recognition of the Korean Provisional Government were introduced in 1942 and 1943. The Joint Resolutions died in committee, however, and pressure from Congress also did not move the Roosevelt administration or the State Department.

When assistance for the Korean Provisional Government finally arrived from the United States, it would come from a very different path. Its roots, like those of the Provisional Government, went back all the way to the first decade of the twentieth century, to the American missions that had brought the first contact between Americans and Koreans. The central figures in its story were Clarence Weems and George McCune, the experts on Korea in the newly created U.S. intelligence service.

3

Americans of Korea

Clarence Weems and George McCune

Clarence Weems and George McCune are names that spanned two generations and half a century of American contributions to Korea. Forgotten in the United States, and remembered only minimally in Korea, Clarence Weems and George McCune each appear in history first as a father among the pioneering American missionaries in Korea, then as a son who was a key figure in the opening of relations between the United States and the Korean Provisional Government.

Clarence Weems

The Weems name appeared in a prominent role in American history during the first years of American independence. Mason Locke Weems, known also as Parson Weems, was born in Maryland in 1759, the nineteenth child of David Weems, a descendant of immigrants from Scotland originally named Weemys. As a young man, he sailed on merchant ships and was studying medicine in Scotland when the American Revolution broke out. He returned to Maryland after the death of his father in 1779, then went to England in 1780 to attend a seminary. In 1784, the year after the Revolutionary War ended, he became the first American citizen ordained as a minister by the Anglican Church, which decided to exempt him from the previous requirement for all ministers to swear an oath to the king of England.

After that milestone achievement, Parson Weems preached at a church near his birthplace in Maryland, but he left the established church in 1794 for a new calling. He began a new career as an author and book-seller, writing numerous religious tracts and biographies of the Founding Fathers and traveling around the South to sell them. He wrote short and accessible lessons for the education and moral instruction of the common people of the young republic, who lacked a common history and identity and had no formal education system.

Parson Weems became a remembered literary figure for writing *The Life and Memorable Actions of Washington*, the most popular biography of George Washington during the early years of the Republic. First pub-lished in 1800, three years after the end of Washington's presidency, it went through eighteen editions during Weems's lifetime and ultimately through eighty-two known editions, the last appearing in 1927. This book introduced the story of the young George Washington chopping down a cherry tree and being unable to tell a lie to escape responsibility, which first appeared in the fifth edition in 1806. Although criticized and debunked for over two centuries, Weems's biography of Washington and its famous anecdote about the cherry tree helped to cement the first president's status as a model hero of the new nation, which was only sixteen years removed from the Revolution and governed under the Constitution for only a decade.[1]

In the generations that followed, the Weems family spread across the country, mostly to the southern states, with significant traits that survived from generation to generation. Following the example of Mason Locke Weems, the family produced many children who became well educated and served as clergymen or professors. One of them was Clarence Norwood Weems Sr., eight generations descended from a brother of Mason Locke Weems.[2] Born in the small town of Oostanaula, Georgia, in 1875, Clarence Weems was raised from the age of six in a succession of small towns in Arkansas—Waldron, Ozark, Van Buren, Altus, Conway—before earning a bachelor's degree at the University of Arkansas in 1899.[3] He became a teacher at Galloway College in Ozark, married his college sweetheart in 1902, and had two children in 1903 and 1907, David and Clarence Jr.

Like many religious young men of his generation, Clarence Weems found himself drawn toward work in the overseas missions. He had converted to the Methodist Episcopal Church, South at the age of fifteen and begun considering missionary work while in college. He became licensed as a local preacher, then formally offered himself to the church for overseas service during the summer of 1907, shortly after the birth of Clarence Jr. and at the same time as the Great Pyongyang Revival in far-off Korea.

Soon after offering himself for missionary service, Clarence Weems took a new job as principal of Smith's Grove Training School, a preparatory school for Vanderbilt University in Smith's Grove, Kentucky, and his experiences there confirmed his desire to serve overseas. He found the town split by a bitter divide between Presbyterians and Methodists, who maintained separate institutions for almost everything—banks, general stores, drugstores—except for the railroad station, post office, and school. As school principal, he found himself at the center of the feud. He received a serious beating at the hands of a Presbyterian parent whose son he had disciplined for skipping school and lying about his truancy. Presbyterian parents then withdrew their children and formed a new school for Presbyterian children only.[4] The experience reinforced his conviction to get away from the parochialism and pettiness that he found in the established churches at home and to live a purer religious life overseas.

The desire to serve in an overseas mission, focused on no country in particular, unintentionally set Clarence Weems on a path to Korea. His church had itself arrived in Korea by coincidence rather than by plan. It had been active in Shanghai and was searching northern China for mission sites in 1894 when a request to send a mission to Korea came from a Korean businessman and Korea's ministry of education. The church sent a delegation from Shanghai that arrived in Korea on October 18, 1895, eleven days after the murder of Queen Min, finding Seoul in a state of high tension. Nevertheless, the delegation was able to meet King Kojong, who although mourning the death of his wife welcomed them and asked them to send teachers to Korea. The mission opened in August 1896.[5] Clarence Weems arrived in Korea with his wife and two sons in the fall of 1909, one of thirty new American missionaries who arrived that year. It was shortly before Ahn Chunggun assassinated Ito Hirobumi in Manchuria and only a few months before Japan finally formally annexed Korea.

Clarence Weems became a leading missionary in the flourishing Christian community in northern Korea. He led Methodist missions in smaller cities that performed the same religious and educational work as the missions in Seoul and Pyongyang. In 1945 these Christian communities would be left behind and repressed by the atheist regime of North Korea.

Clarence Weems and his family went to the Methodist Episcopal Church, South mission in the city of Songdo, known today as Kaesong. Located in the center of the Korean peninsula just south of the 38th Parallel, Kaesong was in South Korea before 1950 but ended up under North Korean control at the end of the Korean War. It was only fifty miles from Kim Ku's home near Haeju, located directly to the west of Kaesong. Clarence Weems spent twenty-three years with the Methodist mission in Kaesong, from 1909 to 1932. When Weems arrived, Kim Ku was a short distance away, attempting to live in peace as a teacher and raise a family. When he left, Kim Ku was a notorious terrorist in hiding in China after the attempted assassination of Emperor Hirohito and the bombing of senior Japanese leaders in Hongkou Park.

The mission station in Kaesong had opened in 1897, soon after the opening of the first Methodist Episcopal Church, South mission in Seoul in 1896. At the end of its first year, it had conducted four baptisms and counted 46 Korean members. By September 1909 it had 2,242 full-fledged and 641 prospective Korean members, including one Korean preacher.[6] By 1930 there were two mission districts with 22 Korean preachers; 3,192 full members, more than half of them women; and 3,288 prospective members. The mission schools flourished as well, enrolling 1,473 boys and 757 girls.[7] While Kim Ku attempted to bring a program of education and enlightenment to his home region a short distance away, interrupted by prison and then ended by going into exile after the March First Movement of 1919, Weems led a mission that brought a similar message to thousands of people in the region around Kaesong.

Clarence Weems left behind a legacy in Kaesong as "a builder of churches and a builder of men." He became the presiding elder of the district and an elder of the countrywide Methodist conference in 1915. He presided over building 32 churches, 24 temporary houses of worship, and 18 parsonages. He assisted in the training of 25 Korean preachers to spread the Gospels in the new churches. His contributions to education included serving as principal of the Songdo Higher Common School, the largest Methodist school for boys in Korea, and founding two grade schools.[8] He also served on the boards of the Union Methodist Theological Seminary and Ivey Hospital, founded in Kaesong by Methodists in 1907, which continues to exist in North Korea as Kaesong Provincial Pediatric Hospital.[9]

After a brief sabbatical attending the Duke University Divinity School after the last of his four sons departed Korea to attend college in the United States, Clarence Weems returned to Korea to lead the mission in Wonsan from 1933 to 1940. Founded in 1880 as a port for trade with Japan under the terms of the unequal treaty of 1876, Wonsan was a relatively new city that was developing into a significant port and industrial center under Japanese rule. The city had already influenced Korean Christianity as the site of the Wonsan Revival of 1903–1906, which had preceded the Great Revival of 1907 in Pyongyang. The mission of the Methodist Episcopal Church, South in Wonsan had eight missionaries, fourteen Korean preachers, 1,122 full members, and 2,517 prospective members in 1930.[10] Under Weems, the Wonsan mission added ten new churches and nine new Korean preachers.[11] He served on the boards of the Methodist hospital and boys' school in Wonsan and continued on the board of Ivey Hospital.

While in Wonsan Clarence Weems was in his third decade in Korea, and his years of accomplishments had made him one of the senior leaders of the Methodist church in Korea. Upon his arrival in Wonsan in November 1933, the Methodist Church in Korea elevated him to its Central Council, and he then became a member of the Council's executive committee. He continued as chairman of the board of Songdo Higher Common School and a trustee of Union Methodist Seminary, and he became a member of the boards of Yonsei University and the Joint Commission of the Korean Methodist Church. By the end of his thirty-one years in Korea, Weems was one of the elder statesmen of the American Christian community in Korea, having spent almost half of his sixty-five years there. Korean biographers wrote of him in 1939: "The great edifices which he erected are perpetual monuments, silently and solemnly announcing his abiding work in the world. And those persons whom he trained, as disciples and brothers in His love, witness to the noble personality of this great missionary to Korean society."[12]

Life as an American missionary in Korea during this period included hardships, though, among them financial difficulties similar to those faced by most Americans during the 1930s. Methodist and Presbyterian missionaries in Korea received salaries comparable to a middle-class income in the United States, allowing them to live comfortable American lifestyles in Korea, but the Great Depression caused churches to slash salaries and wiped out the savings of many.[13] Clarence Weems found his salary cut by 35 percent during his sabbatical in North Carolina in 1932–33, and he lost approximately $10,000 in bank stocks that he had planned to use as savings for his retirement and for the education of his sons.[14]

To make up for his financial losses, Weems resorted to currency speculation after he returned to Korea for his tenure in Wonsan. Taking advantage of the artificial exchange rate fixed by Japan in Korea, he sent one of his sons to Peking with $400 in gold, which he exchanged for 4,800 Yen, which he then converted into $1,200 in Korea. The $1,200 became the nest egg for buying a house in Georgia for his retirement.[15] "I hope St. Peter does not question me too closely about the transaction," he wrote decades later.[16]

A more fundamental threat to the work of American missionaries in Korea also came during the 1930s, in the form of repressive Japanese policies that reflected the ultranationalist attitude in Japan that would soon lead to war. In 1932 the Japanese authorities in Korea began to require that all schools have their students, teachers, and administrators attend ceremonies at Shinto shrines. The State Department refused to become involved in the issue, taking the position that Japan was not violating any treaties, international agreements, or Japanese laws and that the missionaries had to work out the problem with the government of Japan themselves.[17] The Presbyterian churches saw this requirement as imposing the state religion of Imperial Japan on Christian schools, so they closed their schools in Korea in 1937–38. The Methodist churches accepted the official explanation that the ceremonies were patriotic and not religious, however, and Weems, like most Methodists, followed the church's decision and complied with the requirement for Shinto ceremonies. It bought them some time to continue their work in Korea, but that time ran out within a few years.

The looming threat of war between the United States and Japan finally brought Clarence Weems's life in Korea to an end in 1940. He returned to the United States in July 1940 for a regular furlough, expecting to return to Korea. Soon after his departure from Korea, however, the State Department advised all American citizens in the Far East to leave and return to the United States unless their presence was absolutely essential. Instead of sending Weems abroad again, the church's Board of Missions retired him from overseas missionary service, citing the state of his health and the threat of war with Japan. The board turned down his requests to return to Korea and then for an assignment to Cuba instead, and in September 1941 it finally decided to officially retire him, effective as of December 31, 1941.[18] The attack on Pearl Harbor and the outbreak of war between the United States and Japan came soon after. Weems never returned to Korea before he passed away in 1952.

The Sons of Clarence Weems

During his decades of service in Korea, Clarence Weems had two more sons and raised all four in Korea. William Rupert Weems arrived in 1911 and Benjamin Burch Weems in 1914, joining David and Clarence Jr. Each would grow to adulthood in Kaesong, attending the Songdo School for Foreign Students, and move to the United States for preparatory school and higher education. Each would return to Korea as adults. Korea made a deep impression on them, but each would follow a different path and would return to Korea in his own way.

David, the eldest, followed their father's path the closest and returned to Korea first. He left the family in Kaesong to attend preparatory school in Conway, Arkansas, graduating in 1921 from Hendrix Academy, a school affiliated with the Methodist Episcopal Church, South that their father had attended. He attended Hendrix College intending to pursue preaching as his future profession, receiving his bachelor's degree in 1925.[19] He went to Emory University for a master's degree in religious education in 1926, after which he preached in Little Rock, Arkansas, and applied for overseas missionary work. He attended Yale University for a bachelor of divinity degree between 1928 and 1930 and aimed to pursue a doctorate, but when the opportunity to do missionary work in Korea emerged in 1930, he immediately accepted it. Two years later, though, his wife Helen suffered a nervous breakdown, causing them to return to the United States in March 1933. He soon sought to return to Korea, but the church repeatedly denied his requests from 1935 to 1937, first for lack of funds, then because of his wife's health, and finally because of the deteriorating relationship between the United States and Japan. He instead became a pastor in upstate New York for the remainder of his time with the church.[20]

William followed a very different path that led to a distinguished career in aviation before bringing him back to Korea. At Georgia Tech he studied aeronautical engineering, earning a bachelor's degree and a master's degree.[21] After further graduate study at the Massachusetts Institute of Technology and part-time work in Cambridge, Massachusetts, and Brooklyn, New York (during which he met his future wife, a violinist studying at Juilliard), he became a professor in the Georgia Tech mechanical engineering program in 1937, teaching aeronautical engineering and starting a student flight training program to prepare students for military service. With the United States preparing for war, he went on leave from Georgia Tech and became an officer in the Army Air Forces in July 1941. Assigned to the Army Air Forces Engineering School at Wright-Patterson Air Force Base, he worked on early experimental guided bombs, and by the end of the war he was assistant commandant of the school and a lieutenant colonel. [22]

After the war he returned to MIT as a professor and then went to Korea to assist in developing an engineering industry. He took a leave of absence to return to Korea in 1955 to assist in rebuilding Seoul National University's engineering college after the Korean War, then moved back to Korea in 1958 to direct the Industrial Development Center of Korea, a U.S. government project to encourage the development of industry in then mostly agricultural South Korea.[23]

Benjamin, the youngest, became a noted scholar of Korea, lived most of his life there, and made it his final resting place. After graduating from Duke University in 1935, he worked as a teacher in North Carolina for three years before returning to Korea in 1939 as principal of the School for Foreign Students that he had attended as a child. He departed in 1940, in the exodus of Americans from Korea under the threat of war with Japan, but Korea remained part of his life. He married a fellow teacher from the School for Foreign Students, Ruth Kobrine, in 1942, and during the war used his Japanese and Korean language skills working for U.S. Army intelligence. He returned to Korea in 1947 to work for the U.S.-USSR Joint Commission, then went back to the Washington DC area in 1948 to head the Korea desk of Voice of America and then work as an intelligence analyst for the Air Force from 1949 to 1962. While working for the Air Force he researched and published the first Western scholarship on the Tonghak movement since 1894.[24] He returned to Korea in 1963, working at U.S. Eighth Army headquarters and then for the Peace Corps. After his wife died in 1966, he married a Korean, Shin Yoon Hee, in 1969. He later became a director of the Seoul Foreign School and taught at Hanguk University and Yonsei University. He died in Korea in 1986, and he and his first wife are buried in the Seoul Foreigners' Cemetery at Yanghwajin.[25]

Clarence Jr. would have the arguably deepest involvement with Korea of any of the four brothers, but his role would develop slowly over the course of several decades. Nicknamed "Clam" by the family, Clarence Jr. followed his older brother David by returning to Conway, Arkansas, to attend high school at Hendrix Academy, but their paths diverged from there. Unlike David and the two younger brothers, he did not start with a clear plan for his future. He was considering journalism as a profession when he started college, but his interests soon took him in a different direction.[26] He studied history at Vanderbilt University, first as an undergraduate, then in a master's degree program immediately after receiving his bachelor's degree in 1930.[27] With the country of his childhood continuing to pull at him, he delved into the history of Korea for his graduate studies. For his master's thesis, he studied the crucial problem of Korea in his lifetime, the takeover of Korea by Japan.[28]

Titled "Japan's Acquisition of Korea from the Treaty of Shimonoseki (1895) to the Annexation of Korea by Japan (1910)," Clarence's thesis was a basic history of the politics of Korea's monarchy and of the rivalry over Korea between Japan, China, and Russia. It did not go deeply into the changes and conflicts roiling Korean society during the period, mentioning the Independence Club, the Tonghak movement, and the spread of Christianity only briefly. A fuller understanding of the evolution of Korea during his lifetime would come later.

Becoming a scholar of Korea became Clarence's aspiration, but during the ongoing Great Depression, he became one of millions who found their aspirations unfulfilled. After graduating from Vanderbilt in 1933, he briefly moved to Washington for an entry-level job as a typist at a government agency.[29] Graduate studies at Harvard University followed that fall after a move to Boston. He took evening courses while working during the day as a personnel manager at a local business. Other priorities took over his life, however, and he put his studies on hold after their first year. He courted and married Jennie Dunn Ligon from Richmond, Virginia, in 1935. He returned to his studies at Harvard in 1936–37, but he stopped them again at the end of the academic year. A mundane life as a business administrator instead became his future. A son, William Sumner Weems, arrived in June 1939, adding responsibility as a father and breadwinner to his concerns. After several more years in Boston, he moved with Jennie to Shreveport, Louisiana, in 1941 to work as a personnel director at J. B. Beaird Corporation, a manufacturing company serving the oil and gas industry. Scholarship and Korea receded further and further into the past as he made a living in jobs of little interest to him.

In this way Clarence Weems spent the period when Kim Ku and the Korean Provisional Government experienced the most turbulent and difficult period in their history. Kim Ku's 1932 terrorism campaign, the alliance between Nationalist China and the Korean Provisional Government, and the long retreat of Nationalist China and the Korean Provisional Government from Imperial Japan's invasion of China in 1937 were distant events for him. Nothing that Clarence Weems did before the war indicated that he would ever return to Korea.

George McCune

While Clarence Weems led the growth of the Methodist missions in Kaesong and Wonsan, George Shannon McCune was having an equally significant impact with the Presbyterian Church in Pyongyang. McCune became a leading educational missionary, teaching and administering at Presbyterian-sponsored schools while also performing pastoral duties. From almost the beginning of his thirty-one years in Korea to their end, his role in educating Korean youth during a time when Christians were central to Korean patriotism put him at odds with the Imperial Japanese authorities.

George McCune came from a very different background than Clarence Weems, northern and Presbyterian, raised on a farm and drawn toward service overseas later in life. Born in 1873 in Allegheny, Pennsylvania, near Pittsburgh, McCune lost his father at the age of twelve and stopped school to help support his mother and sisters. He first labored on their farm outside of Allegheny, then went to Pittsburgh and worked first as an office boy and then in a brokerage and a bank. While serving as a bank clerk, he attended Duff's Business College (now the Pittsburgh campus of Everest Institute) at night, graduating in 1893. Aspiring to a higher vocation, he then attended Park College (now Park University), a Presbyterian school in western Missouri, using $250 that he had saved. At Park College he met his future wife, Helen McAfee, daughter of John A. McAfee, the founder of the college. After graduating at the age of twenty-eight in 1901, he stayed another year teaching Latin and doing graduate study, then accepted a full-time position as a professor at Coe College in Cedar Rapids, Iowa. He and Helen married in June 1904. While teaching at Coe, he studied to become a minister and was ordained in 1905.[30]

George and Helen McCune each felt the call to serve overseas in Asia soon after they married, and family connections helped to guide them toward Korea, the Presbyterian Church's most dynamic overseas mission. Helen's brother, the Rev. Dr. Cleland Boyd McAfee, was a Presbyterian minister and theologian who became Korea secretary of the Presbyterian Board of Foreign Missions in 1907, then director of the Presbyterian Board of Foreign Missions and moderator of the General Assembly of the United States Presbyterian Church.[31] At McAfee's house in Brooklyn in 1905, George met D. W. McWilliams, a railroad magnate and Presbyterian layman who as a member of the Presbyterian Board of Foreign Missions had been largely responsible for the dispatch of the first Presbyterian missionary to Korea, Dr. Horace Allen, in 1884.[32] George and Helen departed for Korea soon afterward.

They arrived in Korea at a stormy time, both literally and figuratively. On September 20, 1905, they first made landfall in Korea near Inchon in a harrowing shipwreck, after a storm drove the Japanese steamship carrying them into offshore rocks at midnight. Three days marooned on a sparsely inhabited island followed before a passing Japanese ship rescued them and delivered them to their destination.[33] It was only two weeks after the official end of the Russo-Japanese War which had sealed Japan's power over Korea and the end of Korean independence.

George McCune immediately became a leading figure in the growth of the schools that the Presbyterian Church was creating in Pyongyang and northern Korea. As a superintendent of Presbyterian schools in Pyongyang, he established numerous schools throughout northern Korea from 1905 to 1908. He then joined the administration of Union Christian College, serving as its acting president in 1908–1909 while its founder and president was on furlough.[34] He was the natural choice to lead the school, since the founder of Union Christian College had based it on Park College, the school that Helen McCune's father had founded and that George McCune had attended, which was a pioneer in allowing students from impoverished backgrounds to work for their tuition. McCune had benefited from this program while attending Park College on his meager savings from his work in Pittsburgh. By the time of George McCune's acting presidency, Union Christian College included schools for boys and girls from elementary through high school and a college.

A pivotal figure in the future of Korea attended school at Union Christian College while George McCune served as its president in 1908–1909. Kim Hyong Jik, a fourteen-year-old boy from a village near Pyongyang, attended Sungshil Middle School during those years. A Presbyterian and independence activist, Kim Hyong Jik later married the daughter of a Presbyterian minister and in 1912 had a son whom he named Kim Song Ju. As Kim Il Sung, the son would one day become the leader of Communist North Korea, with its capital at Pyongyang.

Evangelism as well as education was central to McCune's life in Korea. The Great Pyongyang Revival of 1907 began when he was one of only forty-six Presbyterian missionaries in all of Korea.[35] McCune's work in Pyongyang placed him in the middle of the wave of mass repentance and conversions that began in the city and spread throughout Korea. He took part in the fervor of the revival, and he continued to preach on the side throughout his years in Korea, as his responsibilities as an educator grew.

In 1909 McCune began one of the defining roles of his life in Korea when he became principal of the Hugh O'Neill Jr. Industrial Academy in Sonchon (then called Syenchun), a city approximately one hundred miles northwest of Pyongyang. This high school, also called the Sinsung Academy, was one of the leading institutions in the heavily Christian city of Sonchon. Sonchon's population of eight thousand was already half Christian by 1911, only a decade after the city's Presbyterian mission station opened in 1901, making it the most heavily Christian city in Korea or anywhere in Northeast Asia.[36] The assignment placed McCune at the center of one of the hotbeds of Christianity and Korean nationalism, putting him on a collision course with Japanese rule.

In Sonchon McCune became well known throughout Korea as a supporter of the Korean people in their struggle for their national identity under Japanese occupation. He and other American missionaries could not declare support for Korean resistance to Japan, as this would have resulted in criminal prosecution for sedition or expulsion from Korea. So he attempted to prevent independence activism at his school, dismissing a teacher and students who were involved.[37] His attempts to keep his school out of the Korean independence struggle failed, though, as he himself became a central figure in the mass arrests that the Japanese authorities conducted in 1911, the same arrests that put Kim Ku and other patriots in northern Korea in prison.

McCune faced false accusations that he was the leader of a plot by American missionaries and Korean Christians to assassinate the Japanese resident-general. It was part of the campaign in which the Japanese authorities arrested and imprisoned Kim Ku and other New People's Association leaders and then arrested 600 people in Pyongyang and Sonchon, leading to the Case of the One Hundred Five. Arrests began at McCune's school on October 12, 1911, and those arrested included seven teachers and numerous students, many of whom were held in prison for months and tortured. On June 28, 1912, 19 American missionaries and 122 Koreans—98 of them Christians—went on trial. The prosecutors made outlandish charges, obtained by false confessions under torture, that 19 American missionaries led by McCune had planned to assassinate the governor-general, met with Korean assassins, and obtained weapons for them, and that McCune would initiate the shooting of the governor-general by shaking hands with him as a signal.[38]

McCune and the American missionaries defended themselves and the 122 Koreans vigorously in court, but they succeeded in saving only themselves and a few Koreans from prosecution. After a series of trials in which most of the prosecution's witnesses retracted their statements as made under torture, forcing repeated retrials, the Japanese court dropped the charges against McCune and the other American missionaries but convicted 105 of the 122 Korean defendants and sentenced them to prison terms of two to ten years. They included a college president who was vice president of the Korean YMCA, a college professor, and two of McCune's teachers.[39]

Called the Conspiracy Case of 1911, this experience was a turning point for McCune. He had attempted to keep his religious and educational work out of the Korean struggle against Japan. The arrests, torture, and imprisonment of his students and colleagues affected him profoundly, however, and as he continued his educational and spiritual work, he spoke indirectly of its injustices, both in Korea and in the United States. Known for his outgoing personality and expressiveness, whether of joy, amusement, or anger, he lived up to the Korean name that he had given himself, Yun San-On, based on Shannon McCune and translated literally as "Mountain Energy," or loosely as "Volcano Ready to Explode."[40] In Korea he delivered sermons that were increasingly strident, comparing Korea to Christ on the cross and calling on people to make great sacrifices on its behalf, laced with hymns such as "Onward Christian Soldiers" and "Fight the Good Fight."[41] During a one-year furlough in the United States in 1913–14, he delivered numerous addresses on the Conspiracy Case describing the sufferings of his students and colleagues and the injustice of Imperial Japanese rule.

The Conspiracy Case of 1911 was a major crisis for the Presbyterian Church. The church faced a significant threat to its main center of worldwide mission activity, and it sought to find a course of action to protect its work in Korea. The crisis caused the church to consult with the highest level of American experts on foreign affairs, including Adm. Alfred Thayer Mahan, former secretary of state John W. Foster, former president of Columbia University and mayor of New York Seth Low, former president of Harvard University Charles Eliot, and president of Yale University Arthur Hadley.[42]

Viewing McCune as a threat to their authority in Korea, the Japanese authorities pressured the Presbyterian mission to remove him in 1915. McCune received a warning from the provincial chief of police in January, accusing him of having made an inflammatory speech in Pyongyang and threatening him with imprisonment.[43] The Foreign Affairs Department sent a demand for McCune's removal in April, requesting that the

Presbyterian mission expel McCune to "reciprocate" the favor of the Japanese authorities releasing six Koreans from the One Hundred Five. The request denounced McCune for "long cherished ill feeling against the Japanese administration," "questionable character as a Christian missionary," and being "too sensitive and careless if not thoughtless in preaching Christianity among Koreans."[44] After three months, the Foreign Affairs Department backpedaled and denied that there had been any direct demand to remove McCune, ending the crisis in July.[45]

McCune remained in Korea, but the U.S. government and Presbyterian Church mission authorities in Korea each had feared the consequences of failing to comply and had been prepared to surrender to Japan's demand. McCune already had been the central figure in the Conspiracy Case of 1911, the greatest crisis for American missionary work during the era, and for a second time his presence created a threat to the Presbyterian Church in Korea. The U.S. consul-general recommended that the mission require McCune to submit his resignation and then grant him a face-saving new assignment, starting a new mission in Manchuria. Horace Underwood agreed with the consul-general on removing McCune but viewed moving him to Manchuria as a further risk, possibly seen by Japan as an attempt to use the church to establish communications between nationalists in Korea and Korean exile groups in Manchuria.[46] Mission leaders eventually decided to allow McCune to remain in Korea with the warning that in the event of further "well-meaning but easily misinterpreted" statements, they would transfer him from Sonchon to the quieter mission in Taegu in southern Korea.[47]

From 1915 to 1919 George and Helen McCune continued to be fixtures in the Christian community of Sonchon and northern Korea. George presided over the school and preached in a rural area west of Sonchon, and he served as general superintendent of Presbyterian schools throughout northern Korea. Helen served as principal of a school for young widows in Sonchon, which later became a school for girls, and as superintendent of the women's Sunday school in one of Sonchon's churches.

The March First Movement of 1919 caught George McCune completely by surprise, as it did almost all other Americans in Korea. He had been in the United States during the second half of 1918, attending to his elderly mother as she moved to a nursing home in Pittsburgh, then touring churches to raise funds for his school. He was away from Sonchon attending meetings in Pyongyang and Seoul when the nationwide demonstrations began on March 1, 1919. The entire student body of his school and practically the entire Christian population of the city joined the demonstrations.[48]

McCune and other American missionaries avoided openly supporting the movement because they were under strict instructions from their mission organizations not to become involved. Like many missionaries, he was outraged by the brutality of police suppressing the demonstrations, but the only response available to him was to record atrocities and to release them to the Western press.[49] Staying out of the demonstrations did not protect all Americans from the Japanese authorities, though. The worst experience was that of an instructor at the Sungshil School in Pyongyang, the Rev. Eli M. Mowry, who had given shelter in his house to several of his students during the violent suppression of the demonstrations.[50] Japanese authorities arrested him on April 4 on charges of aiding student independence activists and sentenced him to six months' imprisonment and hard labor.[51]

McCune did not face criminal charges as a result of the March First Movement, but it led to prolonged official harassment. The Japanese authorities blamed American missionaries for inciting Koreans to revolt, and a wildly fanciful secret police report even singled out "Shannon McCune" as the main organizer of the movement, alleging that he was acting on instructions from President Woodrow Wilson that he received while in the United States in 1918. A prolonged campaign of harassment from Japanese police began, with the police in Sonchon frequently calling on him and questioning him at length or asking him to come to the police station to explain his movements and his sermons. In 1921 he began to receive threatening letters, some written in blood, from members of an ultranationalist organization of IJA veterans, the Japanese Ex-Soldiers Association. At this point, he feared for his life and the lives of his family.[52]

The official harassment and threats, along with concern for the health of their eldest son, George, caused George and Helen McCune to leave Korea in 1921. Their son had a heart defect requiring care not available in Korea, and this health threat was the final straw that compelled them to return to the United States. George, Helen, and their four children landed in San Francisco in March 1921 and moved to a cottage in San Jose for a period of rest, but within a few weeks George received offers to become the president of three Presbyterian colleges.[53] He accepted the position at Huron College in Huron, South Dakota, and began his work there in August.[54] He formally resigned his position as a missionary in Korea in February 1923.

By 1927 the situation that compelled George and Helen McCune to leave Korea had changed. Their son George was in better health and a nineteen-year-old college student, ready to be independent from them. When in mid-1926, the mission in Korea began to correspond with McCune about returning to Korea to serve as president of Union Christian College in Pyongyang, the McCunes considered it. The hostility of the Japanese authorities in Korea had changed as well. The governor-general, Adm. Saito Makoto, sent a letter to George McCune asking him to return to Korea in 1927.[55] In February 1927 McCune resigned from his position at Huron College to accept the offer to return to Korea as president of Union Christian College.[56]

The next decade was the peak of McCune's life in Korea. Now in his fifties and one of the elders among Presbyterian missionaries in Korea, he headed the leading institution of higher education in Pyongyang, was co-pastor in a major church in the city, and was a visiting minister in a country district west of Pyongyang. He represented the Presbyterian Church in Korea in Jerusalem itself, at the International Missionary Council in 1928. For several years during the early 1930s, his son George joined him as a colleague at Union Christian College, as an English professor. He held numerous leadership positions with the Presbyterian Church and in education in Korea, including president of the Federal Council of Churches in Korea, president of the General Board of Education of the Presbyterian Church in Korea, and organizer and first president of the Educational Association of Korea.[57]

It all came to an end suddenly in 1936, however, when he refused to compromise his religious principles in the face of increasing Japanese efforts to control and assimilate the Korean people. When the Japanese provincial governor in Pyongyang demanded that he lead his students on a visit to a Shinto shrine in Pyongyang, he refused, rejecting the official explanation that a sacrifice to the emperor of Japan was a patriotic service and not an act of worship toward an emperor officially declared to be divine. The Imperial Japanese authorities retaliated by stripping him of his teaching credentials on January 18, 1936, and placing him under virtual house arrest. Banned from the field of education that had been his mission in Korea for three decades and deprived of his liberty, he left Korea on March 21, never to return.[58]

George McCune's contributions to the defense of Korean national identity during decades of Japanese repression were well known in his time and remembered for many years afterward in Korea. In 1963 the Republic of Korea posthumously awarded him the Order of Merit for National Foundation for rendering significant service to the cause of Korean independence from 1905 to 1936, through his contributions to education and religion. Along with Homer Hulbert he has been one of the few foreigners to receive this honor.[59]

The Sons of George McCune

George Shannon McCune and Helen McAfee McCune had four children, all of them born and raised in Korea during the tumultuous period of their parents' first term from 1905 to 1921. The first were Anna Catherine and George McAfee, born in Pyongyang in 1906 and 1908; then came Helen Margaret and Shannon Boyd-Bailey, born in Sonchon in 1911 and 1913.

The lives of the sons intertwined from birth, or even before it, with the tumultuous events of their parents' first years in Korea. George McAfee, before his birth in June 1908, had been present at the Great Pyongyang Revival of 1907 in his mother's womb. Shannon was born two weeks after the early release from prison of 99 of the One Hundred Five in April 1913, after an appeal and retrial. He received his Korean name Yun An-Paek, the "Peaceful Hundredth," at the suggestion of a group of the 99 released prisoners, who were grateful to George Shannon McCune for his support of them at trial and in prison. The name would bind the newborn child to them and to the Conspiracy Case of 1911 permanently.[60]

The March First Movement of 1919 left its impression on the two young boys. Ten-year-old George McAfee and his sister, Anna, may have been the first Americans to learn of the demonstrations when Korean students informed them the day before they happened, while their parents and other American adults remained in the dark. They watched the March First Movement demonstrations in Sonchon from a hilltop pavilion near the family house, seeing Japanese police bearing rifles with fixed bayonets charging and scattering the crowd. The six-year-old Shannon, in the house and forbidden to step outside when the demonstrations began, could hear the demonstrators and joined them in shouting, "Mansei!" until told by his mother to stop.[61]

The sons as adults each would have distinguished careers as scholars, and each would also perform significant roles as civilians in government service during the Second World War. George McAfee McCune became the first scholar of Korea in the United States. His college years were nomadic, starting at Huron College in South Dakota where his father was president, transferring to Rutgers University in New Jersey in 1927 after his father returned to Korea, and ending at Occidental College in Los Angeles where he received his bachelor's degree in 1930. He then returned to Korea to teach at Union Christian College in Pyongyang from 1931 through 1933. He also bought and managed an import-export firm that he later sold to one of his father's friends, making a profit that he used to finance his graduate study. In 1934 he came back to the United States to obtain a master's degree at Occidental, then began work on a doctorate in history at the University of California at Berkeley.[62] He again returned to Korea in 1937–38 on a traveling research fellowship to study the official chronicles of the Yi Dynasty, the last ruling dynasty of Korea, which had fallen in 1910. When he received his doctorate in 1941, it was the first awarded in the United States for the study of Korea.

George McCune almost single-handedly established the study of Korea in the United States with his dissertation and other scholarship. His best-remembered prewar work, familiar to students of the Korean language, was a side project during his dissertation research. Prior to the 1930s, no system for writing the Korean language in the Latin alphabet existed, which handicapped any attempt to use the Korean language in the English-speaking world. McCune collaborated with Edwin Reischauer of Harvard University to develop a romanization system in 1938. Called the McCune-Reischauer system, it remains in use today. He began his academic career at Occidental College in 1939 as an instructor, becoming an assistant professor of history and political science after receiving his doctorate in 1941.[63] Prewar articles on his research in the Yi Dynasty chronicles and excerpts from his dissertation published after the war were among the first scholarly work on Korea published in the United States.[64]

Korea and Pyongyang in particular were deeply part of the younger George McCune's life, including his marriage. He married Evelyn Becker, also born in Pyongyang to American educational missionary parents. She had grown up on the campuses of the first two colleges in Korea, her father a science teacher and her mother a music teacher. After a period at Union Christian College in Pyongyang, in 1914 they moved to Seoul, where her father worked with Horace Underwood to found the college that is now Yonsei University in 1915. She returned to the United States for her higher education at the University of California at Berkeley, graduating in 1930, then went back to Korea to teach at the Seoul Foreign School. There she became reacquainted with George, and they married in 1933 after departing Korea for graduate study. With their shared interest in Korea and in scholarship, they worked in close partnership for the rest of their lives while raising two children.[65]

George's health problems continued, however, looming over everything that he and Evelyn did. The heart defect that had brought his childhood in Korea to a premature end at the age of twelve continued to affect him into adulthood, making him frail and incapable of any significant exertion.

Shannon McCune also remained devoted to Korea in his life and academic career. Like George McAfee, he married a daughter of American Presbyterian missionaries in Korea, Edith Blair. After graduating from the College of Wooster in Ohio in 1935, he earned a master's degree from Syracuse University and then a doctorate in geography from Clark University in Worcester, Massachusetts, in 1939. He began teaching geography at Ohio State University and remained in that academic field for the next four decades, while authoring numerous books and other works on Korea, including several on his father's career as a missionary.[66] After the war he taught at Colgate University and the University of Florida and also served as provost of the University of Massachusetts and president of the University of Vermont. He also served in numerous U.S. government and international positions, including with the Far East Program of the Economic Cooperation Administration in Indonesia in 1950–51, as UNESCO assistant director-general for education in Paris in 1961–63, and as head of the U.S. Civil Administration of the Ryukyu Islands in 1963–64.[67]

George and Shannon McCune long anticipated that war between the United States and Japan was coming, and each used travels in Asia to conduct his own personal intelligence gathering to prepare for the conflict. During George's research fellowship in Korea in 1937–38, he and Evelyn traveled from Korea to Manchuria and Beijing on the Japanese-controlled railway system, observing and taking notes about fortifications along the Manchurian railways, seaports in Korea and Japanese-occupied China, and Japanese airbases. They were in Beijing in July 1937 when Japanese forces launched their invasion there, starting the Second World War in Asia. In 1938 they expanded their travels to the Soviet Union, riding the Trans-Siberian Railroad from Vladivostok into Siberia to observe Soviet power to the north.[68] Shannon and Edith used a research trip to Korea in 1941 to collect information on economic assets in Korea. Shannon took extensive notes and photographs of factories, power plants, and railroads. He left them behind when he departed Korea, fearing that

Japanese authorities would find and confiscate them. But Edith took the risk of smuggling them onto her ship out of Korea hidden in the baby carriage of their daughter Antoinette, whose crying helped to keep the police away.[69]

Jerusalem Lost

As 1941 drew to a close, with George McAfee McCune a professor with a new doctorate at Occidental College in Los Angeles and Clarence Weems Jr. working in an office in Shreveport, Louisiana, they were two of a small group of Americans from a world that had ceased to exist. During the preceding several years, Japanese repression in Korea and growing tensions between the United States and Japan over the latter's invasion of China had almost eliminated the American missionary presence in Korea. The attack on Pearl Harbor and the start of war between the United States and Japan then rapidly brought it to an end.

The departure of George Shannon McCune from Korea in 1936 was part of the beginning of the end for the American missionary presence in Korea. McCune was one of the first to take a stand against Japan's attempt to impose Shinto ceremonies on schools in Korea, part of a campaign to assert greater authority over Koreans and assimilate them into Japan. The Methodist and Catholic Churches accepted the official explanation that the ceremonies were patriotic and not religious, but the Presbyterian Church declared that bowing to an emperor declared to be divine was against its most fundamental religious principles, violating the Second Commandment. As a result, the Presbyterian Church declared in 1938 that it would withdraw from its universities and other mission schools.

The year 1940 saw the dismantling of almost the entire American world in Korea. With war with Japan believed to be imminent and the State Department warning American citizens in the Far East to leave and return to the United States, approximately 400 Americans departed Korea during and after October 1940. The mission boards, concerned for the safety of their people, allowed only a few to remain. Benjamin Weems was one of the Americans who evacuated, and Clarence Weems Sr., on a regular furlough in the United States, found himself not allowed to return. Only 126 Americans remained in Korea by June 20, 1941, 109 of them missionaries and their family members.[70] More departed as late as November as the mission boards recalled additional missionaries.[71] By December, only a few of the most dedicated individuals remained.

One of the missionaries who remained was Horace Horton Underwood, son of Horace Grant Underwood, who had passed away in 1916 shortly after founding the college in Seoul that later became Yonsei University. The younger Underwood, fifty years old in 1940, had refused to follow the Presbyterian Church's decision in 1938 to withdraw from the university that his father had founded, remaining as its president. In October 1940 he again stood firm in Korea, refusing to follow the State Department's instructions to evacuate and staying in Seoul with his wife, Ethel, and son, Horace Grant Underwood II. He continued at the university and led a small group of caretakers of church property in Korea, in anticipation of the return of the missions to Seoul, Pyongyang, and the rest of Korea after the war.[72]

The end finally came in December 1941. It occurred symbolically in the United States, just before it occurred in Korea.

On December 5, 1941, George Shannon McCune died at the age of sixty-nine. For five years since his departure from Korea in 1936, he had taught at the Moody Bible Institute in Chicago, far from Pyongyang and Sonchon where he had lived for three decades. His passing symbolically ended the era of American Christian leadership in Korea, in which he had been a central figure for three decades.

Two days later, the attack on Pearl Harbor ended the American missionary presence in Korea, fifty-eight years after it had begun. Immediately after the start of hostilities between Japan and the United States, Japanese police in Korea warned the few remaining Americans to restrict their movements and began visiting them in their homes. Although not officially interned, the missionaries lived under constant surveillance. In early April 1942 they received notice that there would be a "voluntary" exchange of American and Japanese civilians, understood by all to be a requirement to leave. The last ninety-nine Americans in Korea, twenty-one of them Presbyterian missionaries—the last of three hundred to serve in Korea from 1884 to 1942—left Korea and gathered in the port of Kobe in Japan to board a Japanese passenger liner on June 17, 1942, for a voyage to Maputo in Portuguese East Africa (now Mozambique), where they would be exchanged for Japanese civilians who had been in the United States.[73]

Crusade in Asia

Americans had disappeared from Korea for the first time over half a century, but for many of the American missionaries of Korea and their next generation, Korea was a calling that they could not leave behind. In far-flung parts of the American war effort, they would wage a quiet crusade to regain their Jerusalem of the East.

The last missionaries began to plan their return before they had left Korean soil. On June 1, 1942, at 11:00 p.m. on an overnight train from Seoul to Pusan, the executive committee of the Presbyterian mission held a special meeting to discuss it, deciding that the chairman would call a meeting about it on board the neutral ship that would transport them from Portuguese East Africa to the United States.[74] On that ship, the Swedish passenger liner *Gripsholm*, they met daily from August 17 to August 20 in the ship's library and on the deck, beginning to plan to reestablish their missions in Korea immediately after the end of the war.[75]

Horace H. Underwood had stayed in Korea to the end along with his wife and son and was one of the twenty-one Presbyterian missionaries on the *Gripsholm*. He became the leader of the Presbyterian Church's planning to return to Korea from 1942 to 1944.[76] By 1944 he had developed a comprehensive plan. He would go to Korea first as part of a survey team of ten, among them the Rev. Eli M. Mowry, the educational missionary whom the Japanese had arrested and sentenced to hard labor for his actions during the March First Movement in 1919, a quarter of a century earlier. Evangelists, doctors, and educators would then revive the mission stations at Pyongyang, Seoul, and Taegu, followed by the reestablishment of cooperation with the universities and hospitals.[77]

While Underwood and missionaries from the older generation planned the return of the prewar missions to Korea, the younger generation of military age joined the U.S. armed services. Many returned to Asia in the uniforms of the U.S. Army or Navy. One was Horace Grant Underwood II, son of Horace H. Underwood, who immediately after returning to the United States on the *Gripsholm* joined the Navy as an officer. His three years of wartime service included participating in the Battle of Leyte Gulf, the largest naval engagement in history. He ended the war in Japan with the U.S. occupation force, as a lieutenant junior grade in a minesweeper flotilla. Another was Max Becker, George McAfee McCune's brother-in-law, who went to China as an Army Air Forces officer in 1943 as one of the founders of the U.S. operation for rescuing downed pilots in Asia, the Air Ground Aid Section.[78]

The four Weems brothers all served, some as military officers and others as civilians. William, already an officer in the Army Air Forces, continued to teach aeronautical engineering at the Army Air Forces Engineering School. David served in the army as a chaplain. Benjamin worked for the War Department as an intelligence analyst in the army's cryptography operation at Arlington Hall and then in the Pentagon, as a Japanese language expert. Clarence would also serve in the emerging field of U.S. intelligence, first as a civilian and then as a military officer. Alone among the four brothers, he joined the war effort in a role focused specifically on Korea and eventually returned to Asia in uniform.

Clarence Weems began his wartime service as a civilian working as an intelligence analyst for the army. The army's Military Intelligence Service (MIS) was a small organization with just over one thousand military officers and civilians in 1941, with its Far East Branch consisting of only eleven officers, eight civilian research analysts, and three stenographers in December 1941. Confronted with a vast array of military intelligence needs in both the European and Pacific theaters, the MIS would double in size to over two thousand by the end of 1942.[79] Recognizing its complete lack of expertise on Korea, the MIS hired Clarence Weems in February 1942 and made him its main analyst on Korean issues. The assignment brought Weems back to Washington for the first time in almost a decade, and it involved him with Korea for the first time since he had departed the country over a decade and a half earlier.

George McAfee McCune and Shannon McCune also arrived in Washington in February 1942, only two months after the death of their father. George became an intelligence analyst covering Korea for the Coordinator of Information (COI), an intelligence organization newly created in July 1941. He was recruited by Dr. John Fairbank, a colleague of Edwin Reischauer and the founder of Harvard University's China studies program in 1936, who worked for the COI and the OSS during the war.[80] Shannon became chief of the Korea-Manchuria-Formosa Unit of the Enemy Capabilities Branch in the Office of Economic Warfare (OEW), responsible for assessments of Korea and other parts of the empire of Japan outside of its home islands. The notes and photographs that he had collected in Korea in 1941 and that his wife, Edith, had smuggled out became the OEW's first information about Korea. George's wife, Evelyn, took on multiple roles as well, working first as a volunteer assistant in the Far Eastern Section of the Committee on the Protection of Cultural Treasures in War Areas—the organization that made lists of cultural monuments sent to the "Monuments Men" overseas—and also for the Army Map Service.

In these ways Clarence Weems and the George and Shannon McCune became the U.S. government's main sources of expertise on Korea during the war. For them, serving the United States in the war against Imperial Japan was not merely a wartime job to be finished so that they could go home; it was a mission to restore a home lost to the enemy. They were remnants from a world that no longer existed, with the cities of their childhoods and the churches and schools established by their fathers all lost. With the power of the United States now committed to the defeat and overthrow of Japan, they had an opportunity to use their knowledge to help Americans return to and restore the Jerusalem of the East.

Fig. 1. King Kojong in 1884.

Fig. 2. (*left*) King Kojong in a Western-style military uniform after his 1897 redesignation as emperor of Korea.

Fig. 3. (*above*) A Righteous Army group poses with an assortment of weapons and civilian and military outfits.

Fig. 4. (*above*) Sunday school class in Seoul, 1913. Photo courtesy of the Presbyterian Historical Society.

Fig. 5. (*right*) The first medical school graduating class in Korea, 1908. Photo courtesy of the Presbyterian Historical Center.

Fig. 6. Severance Medical College and Hospital, Seoul, 1922. Photo courtesy of the Presbyterian Historical Society.

Fig. 7. Sungshil Middle School, Union Christian College, Pyongyang, 1913. Kim Hyong Jik, the father of Kim Il Sung, attended this school. Photo courtesy of the Presbyterian Historical Society.

Fig. 8. Dr. J. J. Moore, a medical missionary in Pyongyang, preparing to drive to Haeju for medical work in a Ford Model T donated by a church in Colorado Springs, Colorado. Photo courtesy of the United Methodist Archives and Historical Center.

Fig. 9. Missionary with a 1913–15 Harley-Davidson, on a river ferryboat near Haeju. Photo courtesy of the United Methodist Archives and Historical Center.

Fig. 10. Kim Ku (*back row, without a hat*) as a teacher in rural Hwanghae, 1906.

Fig. 11. Prisoners from the One Hundred Five, chained together and blindfolded with wicker baskets, being led by Imperial Japanese police through Pyongyang in 1911. Photo courtesy of Antoinette McCune Bement.

Fig. 12. Korean Provisional Government leaders in Shanghai in a New Year ceremony in January 1920. Kim Ku is in the second row, far left.

Fig. 13. Officers of the Korean Restoration Army, wearing uniforms of the army of Nationalist China. Photo courtesy of the National Archives.

Fig. 14. Clarence N. Weems Sr. in the early 1930s. Photo courtesy of Peter Weems.

Fig. 15. Clarence Weems Sr. with his brothers, Roger (*left*) and Rupert (*right*), and his sons, William, David, Clarence, and Benjamin (*left to right*), at the house of the Rev. D. J. Weems in Conway, Arkansas, in 1917. Photo courtesy of Jonathan Weems.

Fig. 16. Weems family portrait, believed to be taken in 1932 in Durham, North Carolina. Seated (*left to right*): Nancy Askew Weems, Nancy Townsend Weems, and Clarence Weems Sr. Standing (*left to right*): William Weems, Clarence Weems Jr., Benjamin Weems, David Weems, and Helen Townsend Weems (wife of David). Photo courtesy of Peter Weems.

Fig. 17. Clarence Weems Jr. at the time of his military induction in 1942.
Photo courtesy of the National Archives.

Fig. 18. Rev. George Shannon McCune with his wife, Helen, and children, George, Anna, Shannon, and Catherine. Photo courtesy of the Presbyterian Historical Center.

化學 李 授教
Organic Chemistry

吉順 坡船 授教
Fertilization,
Farm Mechanics, Agr. Engineering

靜思 令 授教
Bacteriology, Plant Pathology,
Entomology

隆惠尹 師濤
Helen M. McCune,
English
Language and Literature.

國安尹 授教
Prof. G. M. McCune A. B.
English.

愼永業 授教
Physics,
Meteorology

Fig. 19. George McAfee McCune and other professors of the Sungshil School in Pyongyang, including his mother, Helen McCune, 1933. Photo courtesy of the Presbyterian Historical Center.

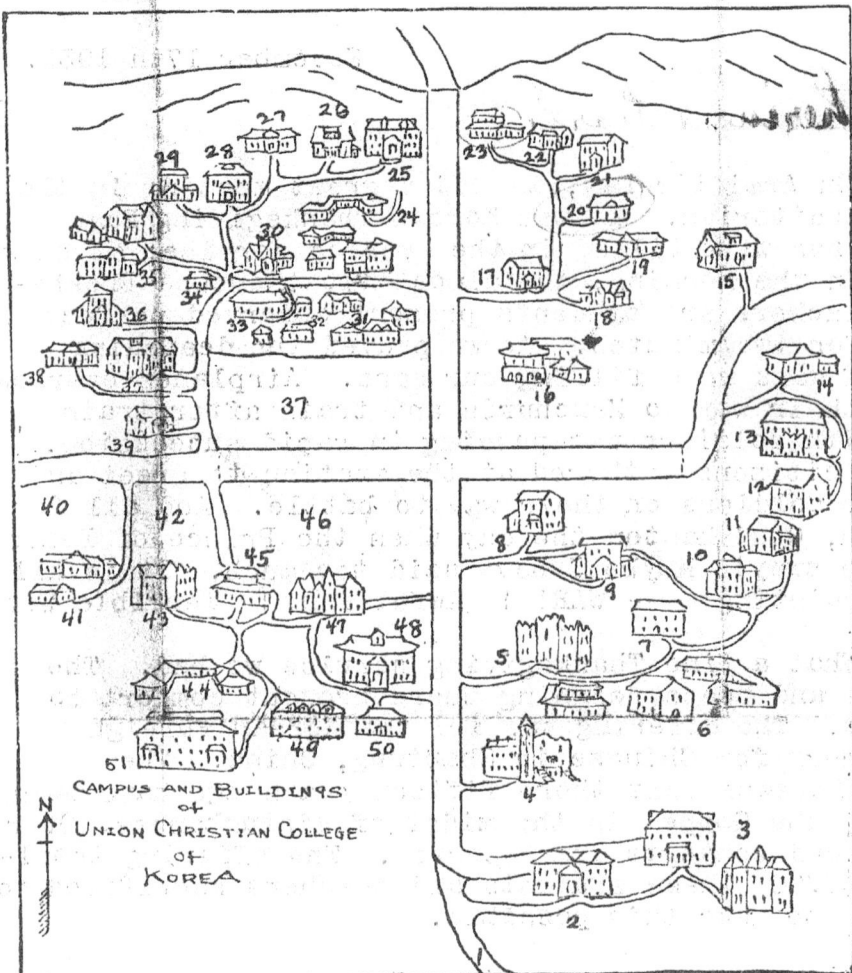

Campus and Buildings of Union Christian College of Korea

1. Entrance to Mission Compound
2. Union Christian Hospital Dispensary
3. Union Christian Hospital Buildings
4. West Gate Church
5. Presbyterian Union Theological Seminary
6. Seminary Dormitories
7. Dr. Engel's Home
8. Dr. Clark's Home
9. Dr. Erdman's Home
10. Dr. Reynolds' Home
11. Dr. Parker's Home
12. Domestic Science Building of Girls' Academy
13. Administration Building of Girls' Academy
14. Foreign Teachers' Home & Girls' Academy Dormitory
15. Y.M.C.A. Residence
16. Men's Bible Institute Buildings
17. Mr. Hamilton's Home
18. Mr. Lutz's Home
19. Dr. Swallen's Home
20. Dr. Blair's Home
21. Dr. Roberts' Home
22. Mr. Hill's Home
23. Dr. Bernheisel's Home
24. Women's Bible Institute Buildings
25. Women's Higher Bible School
26. Mr. Phillips' Home
27. Mr. Mowry's Home
28. Misses Best, Butts, Hayes Home
29. Dr. Bigger's Home
30. President McCune's Home
31. Miss Doriss' Home & Lula Wells Institute
32. Miss McCune's Home
33. Dr. Moffett's Home
34. Peng Yang Foreign School Teachers' Home
35. Peng Yang Foreign School Dormitories & Infirmary
36. Mr. Reiner's Home
37. Peng Yang Foreign School & Athletic Field
38. Dr. Baird's Home
39. Mr. McMurtrie's Home
40. Union Christian College Section of Agriculture Experiment Gardens
41. Anna Davis Industrial Shops
42. Boys' Academy Athletic Field
43. Boys' Academy Main Building
44. Boys' Academy Dormitory Quadrangle
45. Union Christian College Library
46. U.C.C. Athletic Field
47. U.C.C. Science Hall
48. U.C.C. Main Building
49. U.C.C. New Dormitory
50. U.C.C. Old Dormitory
51. U.C.C. Auditorium-Gymnasium

Fig. 20. (*left*) Map of the Presbyterian Mission and the campus of Union Christian College in Pyongyang in the 1930s, including West Gate Church, the Presbyterian Theological Seminary and the missionary residents on the right, and the college and boys and girls schools on the left. Drawn by Evelyn McCune. Courtesy of Helen McCune.

Fig. 21. (*above*) Outdoor ceremony on the athletic field of Union Christian College, with American football goalposts in the background. Photo courtesy of Antoinette McCune Bement.

Fig. 22. McCune family reunion with friends from Korea in the summer of 1941. The Rev. George S. McCune is at the center left, Shannon and Edith McCune are second and third from the left, and George M. McCune and his daughter Helen are on the right. Photo courtesy of Helen McCune.

PART 2

Crusade in Asia

4

The OSS and the Korean Provisional Government

Clarence Weems and George McCune joined an emerging U.S. intelligence service that would soon diverge from half a century of U.S. policy toward Korea. While the State Department had for decades rejected contact with the Korea Provisional Government and refused to recognize it, concerned with the diplomatic and international law issues that recognition would create, U.S. intelligence viewed the Korean Provisional Government as a potentially valuable ally in the war against Japan. Its interest in the Koreans began at the very top with its leader, William "Wild Bill" Donovan.

Origins: William Donovan and Korea

An American intelligence service came into existence only after the attack on Pearl Harbor. At the beginning of the Second World War, a wide variety of organizations including the Army, Navy, State Department, and the Federal Bureau of Investigation were responsible for various intelligence roles. In July 1941 President Franklin Roosevelt appointed Col. William Donovan to head the office of Coordinator of Information (COI), with the task of coordinating U.S. intelligence operations and creating a central organization for intelligence.[1] On June 13, 1942, a presidential order established the Office of Strategic Services (OSS), headed by Donovan, as an organization for the collection and analysis of strategic information for the Joint Chiefs of Staff and for conducting special operations not assigned to other agencies. Considered the predecessor of the Central Intelligence Agency of the postwar era, the OSS was an entirely new agency that needed to recruit thousands of personnel with expertise on foreign countries in order to fulfill its analysis and operations missions.

Donovan brought a unique appreciation of Asia and Korea to his role as leader of the COI and then the OSS. Donovan's interest in Asia began as early as 1905, the year of his graduation from Columbia University, which coincided with the Russo-Japanese War that sealed Japan's conquest of Korea. In that year he won the George William Curtis Medal for Public Speaking with an address entitled "The Awakening of Japan."[2] Fourteen years later in the summer of 1919, after distinguished service as a Medal of Honor–winning officer commanding an infantry battalion during the First World War, his interest in Asia drew him into a tour of Northeast Asia. It began as a second honeymoon for his wife, Ruth, to repair their relationship after his absence during the war, but it became a personal fact-finding mission surveying the political problems of the region. He and Ruth toured Japan, Korea, and China together in June and July 1919. They were treated as visiting VIPs in each country, and they met with the U.S. ambassadors in Tokyo and Beijing. From Beijing he went by himself through Manchuria and across the Russian Far East on the Trans-Siberian Railroad, all the way to Omsk, to meet the leader of the White forces fighting the Bolsheviks in the Russian Civil War.

The journey made Donovan the only senior leader of the U.S. government during the Second World War to have seen Korea with his own eyes before the war. The Donovans landed in Korea at Pusan on June 25, and the next morning they took a train to Seoul, where they toured the city and met the U.S. consul-general to discuss affairs in Korea.[3] They arrived three months after the March First Movement, with the demonstrations ended but Japanese soldiers and police still patrolling the streets. Donovan learned a great deal of the history and situation of Korea during his day in Seoul, based on the diary that he kept during the journey. On June 26 he recorded the story of the Three Kingdoms of Korea and the country's unification in 668 AD, the succession of the ruling dynasties, and the contest between Chinese, Russian, and Japanese influence that led to the annexation of Korea. The next day, after his train crossed the Yalu and he had left Japanese-ruled territory—releasing him from any concerns about Japanese police inspecting his baggage and papers—he recorded observations about Japanese repression in Korea that he had refrained from writing while in Seoul. Based on his own observations and those of American businessmen whom he met on the train, he described an atmosphere of military occupation with Japanese soldiers and police widespread, Japanese control of the economy, and the Japanese language being forced on Koreans.[4]

Two decades later when the Second World War began, Donovan had a well-informed appreciation of the strategic position of Korea between Japan, China, and the Soviet Union, and he knew about the potential for Korean resistance to Japan as no one else in the U.S. government did. Immediately after the attack on Pearl Harbor on December 7, 1941, Donovan set in motion a program to create a wartime alliance with the Korean exile resistance movement that he knew existed in China. By January 1942 Donovan was organizing a mission to China to contact the Korean Provisional Government, which the U.S. government had previously avoided in China and in Washington.

Arrangements for military training for Koreans began at the same time. Donovan obtained Lt. Col. Morris DePass, a protégé of Army Chief of Staff Gen. George C. Marshall, for the COI from the army's infantry school at Fort Benning. Donovan put DePass in charge of preparing the training cadre and program for a training school specifically for Koreans, using a group of Americans with experience in Asia.[5]

For the mission to China, Donovan recruited Dr. Esson Gale, a scholar with personal ties to the earliest Christian missionaries in Korea and many years of experience in Asia. Dr. Gale was a nephew of a Presbyterian missionary from Canada, the Rev. James S. Gale, who had arrived in Korea in 1888 and served there for forty years.[6] His wife had been born in Seoul to American parents who had arrived in Korea in 1885, her father serving as a personal physician to King Kojong.[7] Esson Gale had been a professor at the University of California at Berkeley, Northwestern

University, and the University of Michigan. From 1908 to the 1930s he had served with the U.S. Consular Service in Peking and Shanghai, then with the government of Nationalist China as a revenue administrator.[8]

Donovan sent Gale to China in February 1942 to contact the Korean Provisional Government in Chungking and negotiate terms for working together to organize an intelligence network and sabotage campaign throughout Northeast Asia. Donovan took the plan directly to President Franklin Roosevelt, stating that he was sending Gale "to negotiate for us the possibility of using the Koreans to operate against the Japanese in Japan proper and in Korea and certain occupied areas on the Continent, including Manchuria." He asserted that the Koreans had potentially unique value to the Allied cause because their presence throughout important centers of the empire of Japan in Korea, China, and Japan itself made them able to operate where Caucasians or Chinese could not.[9]

The COI came up with an ambitious plan for operations with the Koreans. DePass had drafted a plan for Korean sabotage operations against Japan dated January 27, 1942, with the code name "Olivia." It called for a sabotage campaign against military installations and economic infrastructure in areas occupied by Japan and also actions against high-ranking enemy commanders, comparable to Kim Ku's attack on the commanders of the Japanese forces in Shanghai in April 1932. The COI mission would set up a base in the vicinity of Chungking and work in close cooperation with Nationalist China, with operations in China and Korea and as far south as Thailand, Vietnam, and the Dutch East Indies (now Indonesia) contemplated. Seven U.S. Army officers would fly to Chungking to set up a training school, field operations, and an administrative and supply organization. Field operations would eventually have sections for Korea, North China, the Yangtze River, Formosa, Indochina, Thailand, the Philippine Islands, and the Dutch East Indies, each headed by an English-speaking foreign civilian familiar with the language, customs, geography, and people of the area.[10]

The U.S. government knew very little about the Korean Provisional Government, however, so Donovan and Gale had to plan the mission with almost no reliable information about its actual situation. In Washington the COI had reached out to Syngman Rhee and other Korean leaders in exile to learn more, but COI staff were at first too unfamiliar with their Korean interlocutors to understand with whom they were dealing. One senior COI staff member reported a meeting that he had in mid-February 1942 with "Dr. Sigmund Rhee," whom he identified as "provisional President of Korea."[11] Information provided by Korean sources was often inaccurate and wildly inflated. Donovan could not say anything with certainty about the Korean resistance movement in his report to Roosevelt, stating that there was a "so-called Korean provisional government army in China" reported by Korean sources, with "questionable" claims of having 35,000 men, with 9,250 claimed to be in the Chungking area – wildly inflated numbers that were an order of magnitude greater than reality.[12]

The Gale mission to Chungking, handicapped from the beginning by lack of information, ended up failing in the face of opposition from the State Department. The U.S. ambassador, Clarence Gauss, was a professional Foreign Service officer with thirty years of experience who had served in diplomatic posts in China for twenty-two years before becoming ambassador in 1941. Throughout his wartime term he had a bitterly confrontational relationship with the U.S. military commander in the region, Gen. Joseph Stilwell, and the interagency battle extended to the COI as well. When Gale arrived by air in Chungking on March 8, 1942, Gauss viewed the mission as interfering with a politically sensitive issue, contradicting the State Department's foreign policy decision not to recognize the Korean Provisional Government. Gale's conduct of the mission created further antagonism, as he bypassed Gauss and approached the government of Nationalist China and the British embassy independently, following Donovan's orders. Relations between Gale and Gauss became so poor that Donovan had to recall Gale in June 1942, setting aside the plan to work with the Korean independence movement.

The only significant achievement of the Gale mission was recruiting the first full-time officer in China for the emerging U.S. intelligence service. Gale found a young American professor who had studied and taught at universities in China since the early 1930s, Clyde Sargent. He had experienced the Japanese invasion since 1937 and had evacuated with his university from the coastal city of Tsinan to Chengdu, deep in the interior of China. Sargent became the representative in China of the COI, then of the OSS after its creation later in 1942, working from the U.S. embassy in Chungking under the cover of being a special assistant to the U.S. ambassador. He would be the OSS's most experienced officer in China through the end of the war.

McCune and Weems in Washington

Clarence Weems, George McCune, and Shannon McCune all arrived at around the time that Gale departed for Asia in February 1942, and their arrival changed the state of ignorance about the Koreans that had existed at the beginning of the year. Almost immediately, their familiarity with Korea since childhood and knowledge of the country and its struggle against Imperial Japan created a new understanding of the Korean independence movement in U.S. intelligence.

George McCune at the COI led the effort. Within days of arriving in Washington, he reached out to the Korean expatriate community and Americans supporting the Korean cause, starting with the Korean Liberty Conference in Washington in late February, where he was the sole U.S. government observer.[13] He immediately saw that the Korean cause was poorly understood in official Washington, with little interest in it outside of the COI and false information about it rampant. Years of State Department disinterest in the Korean Provisional Government meant that almost no reports on it from the U.S. embassy in China existed, and Korean groups in the United States gave information that was often contradictory and self-serving.[14] In modern American intelligence parlance, U.S. knowledge of the Koreans was mostly "rumint," rumor intelligence. In early March, after discussions with his brother Shannon and Weems, George McCune stepped forward and offered to prepare a thorough study of the Korean independence movement, which he believed to be urgently needed to help formulate a coherent U.S. policy toward Korea and to make possible wartime cooperation between the United States and the Koreans.[15]

McCune completed his study in late April and presented it in two reports, one on the history and current state of the Korean independence movement and the other on the potential for Korean assistance in the war against Japan. They were the first U.S. assessment of the Korean independence movement, and they remained the primary reference on it through 1945, influencing the approach of U.S. intelligence toward the Koreans to the end of the war.[16]

McCune delved into the history of the March First Movement, the violent Japanese reaction, and the emergence of Korean exile groups, identifying two general approaches to Korean resistance: the largely nonviolent approach of the Provisional Government in Shanghai, which sought the support of foreign powers, and underground armed resistance by Korean guerillas.[17] He described the initial cooperation of the two sides, with the Provisional Government combining Syngman Rhee with his diplomatic approach as president with Yi Tonghwi of the armed resistance groups as prime minister, and the split that soon developed between them, mirrored in the emergence of separate organizations of supporters in the United States. The report traced the failure of the attempt to reunify the factions of the Provisional Government in 1924, the growth of Communist militant organizations during the 1920s and early 1930s, and the eventual support of Nationalist China for both the Korean Provisional Government and the rival Communist-led Korean Volunteer Corps.[18]

McCune concluded that Koreans had the potential to contribute significantly to the Allied cause against Japan. He pointed out Korea's population of 22 million, strategic location, and resources that were vital to the Japanese war effort, and moreover the presence of 2 million Koreans outside of Korea, in China and in Japan itself. In Korea, Koreans could engage in espionage, sabotage, and eventually open revolt against the Japanese. In China, Koreans were already fighting the Imperial Japanese Army with the Chinese Army and in their own exile army. Koreans living in the United States already were serving as translators and regular soldiers in the U.S. armed forces and voluntarily assisting U.S. counterespionage work.[19]

McCune recognized the difficulty of reconciling the divisions between rival Korean groups and the problem of selecting a group with which to deal, but he assessed the problem as possible to overcome. He observed that only two factions remained, the Korean Provisional Government and the Korean Volunteer Corps, and that the Korean Communists were nationalists who would set aside their ideology in order to fight more effectively against Japan.[20] He did not know that the reconciliation of the Korean Provisional Government with the political wing of the Korean Volunteer Corps had already happened in December 1941 because of the efforts of Kim Ku, since it had escaped notice by U.S. diplomats in Chungking.[21]

Addressing an even more significant issue that would continue to the end of the war and beyond, McCune attempted to reconcile the Korean Provisional Government's desire for official recognition by the United States with U.S. policy that refused to grant it. McCune acknowledged that recognition would affect the postwar settlement of the status of Korea, which the U.S. government was not ready to decide upon yet. He suggested that the United States deal with a group that did not claim the status of a government. To make wartime cooperation possible, he recommended a declaration of the freedom of Korea as essential moral support, as well as a program of material aid.[22]

Less than six months after the attack on Pearl Harbor, while the Gale mission to China was trying and failing to establish a connection with the Korean Provisional Government, George McCune laid out the state of the Korean liberation movement and the conditions necessary to bring it effectively into the Allied cause. Putting his recommendations into effect would be a long and difficult task, however, and years would pass before U.S. intelligence succeeded in reaching the Korean Provisional Government and making a wartime U.S.-Korean alliance a reality.[23]

The Long Path to Alliance

Whether the COI and its successor, the OSS, succeeded in reaching out to the Korean Provision Government was of little consequence in 1942, as the war situation made the small Korean independence movement in China irrelevant to the course of the war. U.S. and Allied forces in Asia spent the first six months of 1942 in retreat, with large numbers surrendering after being trapped by the Japanese advance. Hong Kong and Singapore soon fell, U.S. forces in the Philippines surrendered in April, and Japanese forces overran Burma and reached the border of India in May. The U.S. Navy inflicted a crushing defeat on the Imperial Japanese Navy in the Battle of Midway in early June 1942, but the first Allied offensive at Guadalcanal required a long back and forth campaign from August 1942 to February 1943. A massive military buildup and two more years of costly naval and amphibious operations across over three thousand miles of the South Pacific would be necessary to bring U.S. forces within striking distance of Japan and the core of its empire. Before then, any clandestine actions in Korea, China, or Japan would be too distant to have a significant impact on the war, and they would be suicidal for anyone involved in them.

In China, which came under the China-Burma-India (CBI) theater command led by Gen. Joseph Stilwell, the United States had little military power available. In early 1942 the only American military formation in China was the American Volunteer Group, known as the "Flying Tigers," fewer than one hundred American mercenary pilots and American-made P-40 fighter aircraft under the command of Gen. Claire Chennault. The U.S. Army Air Forces created a China Air Task Force under Chennault's command in July 1942, which began with only fifty-one P-40 fighters and seven B-25 medium bombers, then in March 1943 upgraded it to the Fourteenth Air Force. With the broad mission of protecting the air supply route from India to China over the Himalayas, defending Chinese cities from Japanese air raids, and providing air support to Chinese ground forces, it operated from a main air base at Kunming near the China-Burma border and a string of smaller bases, protected only by the poorly equipped army of Nationalist China. No U.S. ground forces were available in China.

The failure of the Gale mission meant that the COI had no established role in the CBI theater in early 1942, and more than two years of negotiations with the U.S. military commands and Nationalist China would be necessary before it and the OSS secured a role in China. General Stilwell accepted a COI presence in the CBI theater in April 1942, but he required its commander to be his personal choice, who turned out to be Capt. Carl Eifler, an Army Reserve officer who had served under him in Hawaii. Eifler spent the rest of 1942 setting up OSS operations in Burma. A year passed before the United States and China reached an agreement on intelligence cooperation in April 1943, called the Sino-American Special Technical Cooperative Agreement (SACO). Prolonged negotiations were necessary before the OSS secured a role for itself in China by agreeing with General Chennault to establish a joint intelligence operation supporting his Fourteenth Air Force in April 1944.[24]

While the OSS worked to establish its wartime role in Asia, it turned away repeated requests for military support from the Korean Provisional Government's representatives. Led by Syngman Rhee, they made repeated appeals for training and equipment in 1942 and 1943. In September 1943 Rhee sent to the Office of Lend-Lease Administration a detailed request for arms, equipment, and supplies to equip a force of one thousand Koreans in China, specifying everything from small arms and explosives to uniforms, medical supplies, and vitamin tablets, as well as funds to support a training program.[25] The OSS considered these requests but did not approve them, finding that the situation was not right.[26] The War Department directed the Korean Provisional Government to contact the government of Nationalist China with requests for assistance.[27] Rejected by agencies of the U.S. government, Rhee contacted the White House directly, but the White House sent the request back down the chain of command.[28]

The OSS could make only minimal gestures toward working with the Korean Provisional Government in 1942 and 1943. At the beginning of November 1942, Donovan and OSS leadership considered the Korea project again and decided to defer it until later.[29] Instead, they arranged to train twelve Koreans from the Korean Restoration Army and then return them to Chungking. The sole purpose was to make a gesture to maintain the goodwill of the Korean Provisional Government and

Syngman Rhee, as all parties in China considered the token effort to be "a complete waste of time and effort."[30]

Even preparing a small number of U.S. military personnel for a future role working with the Koreans proved to be difficult. In early 1943 the OSS recruited eight Americans of Korean ancestry and had them inducted into the army as enlisted men, for future service as intelligence personnel in Asia. When Donovan attempted to enroll them in the Combat Intelligence course at the army's Military Intelligence Training Center at Camp Ritchie, Maryland, the commandant declared that it would be impossible because of the demands of other theaters of war.[31]

The only noteworthy Allied work with the Koreans through the end of 1943 was a contingent from the Korean Restoration Army sent to Burma to serve with the British Army. The British, who lacked sufficient numbers of personnel able to speak Japanese for military intelligence work, such as prisoner interrogation and deciphering intercepted radio messages, issued a request for Japanese speakers that the Korean Provisional Government agreed to fill. Koreans from the Korean Restoration Army served with the British Army in Burma from September 1943 until the end of the Burma campaign in July 1945, rendering significant assistance to the British campaign to reconquer its former colony in Burma from Imperial Japan.

While Donovan's idea of an alliance between the OSS and the Korean Provisional Government went on hold for a year, then another, the McCune brothers and Clarence Weems went their separate ways.

George McCune was the only one to remain in Washington. Because of his frail health with heart problems, the OSS considered him fit only for light duty involving no physical activity.[32] He later took his brother Shannon's place as chief of the Korean-Manchuria-Formosa Unit in the OEW, then became the Korea desk officer for the State Department's Far Eastern Division in May 1944. Although Korea was almost nonexistent as a priority at the State Department, McCune often worked night and day on problems related to Korea. His efforts included preparing the State Department's briefing on Korea for President Roosevelt before the Yalta Conference in February 1945. In it he urged the State Department and Roosevelt to keep Korea undivided after the war, despite the discussions of joint trusteeship over Korea with the Soviet Union that were occurring by 1945.[33]

Shannon McCune departed Washington in August 1943 for an overseas assignment with the Foreign Economic Administration, a wartime agency created for overseas economic actions. He spent the rest of the war in Asia, India, Ceylon, and China. For his work in China, he received the Presidential Medal of Freedom in 1946.

Clarence Weems joined the army as an intelligence officer during the summer of 1942. It set him on a path to return to Asia, but more than a year would pass as he made his way through the stateside training system and bureaucracy of the vast U.S. military of the Second World War. Weems received a commission as an officer in the Army Air Corps in July 1942 and began active duty as a first lieutenant in September.[34] Officer training school in Miami Beach occupied him from September through November 1942, then the army's Intelligence School in Harrisburg, Pennsylvania, from November 1942 through January 1943.[35] The army then assigned him to the San Francisco Port of Embarkation at Fort Mason, the main shipping and logistics hub for U.S. military operations in the Pacific, to await further assignment. He moved to San Francisco with his wife, Jennie, in January 1943.

With his background in Korea, Weems attracted the attention of the OSS, and he officially joined the OSS on March 8, 1943. The OSS recruited him as its first Korea expert for deployment overseas, but months of bureaucratic infighting were necessary before he finally departed for Asia. The commanding officer of the OSS office in San Francisco refused to release him, and for the entire spring and summer of 1943, OSS headquarters in Washington DC and the San Francisco office debated what to do with him.[36] His situation finally appeared resolved in August, when OSS headquarters issued Captain Weems with orders to transfer to the Research and Analysis (R&A) Group of its Far East Division in Washington to work there for three months in preparation for deployment to Asia. Two weeks later, though, it rescinded the order after continued opposition from the San Francisco office, declaring that Weems would stay in San Francisco until his final transfer to the Far East.[37]

Weems finally received orders to depart for Asia on October 1, 1943, over a year and a half after he had first volunteered for service with Army intelligence as a civilian and almost seven months after he joined the OSS. He flew out of San Francisco on October 13, 1943, bound for New Delhi.

Weems joined R&A intelligence analysts at the OSS station in New Delhi who were supporting operations by OSS Detachment 101 in India, Burma, and Thailand. Detachment 101, the first OSS organization overseas, was the product of the April 1942 agreement between the COI and General Stilwell. Carl Eifler spent 1942 building it up from scratch.[38] In 1943, with only a few hundred Americans, it began operations to gather intelligence, harass the Japanese through guerilla warfare and sabotage, and rescue downed Allied airmen. It relied on recruiting and supporting resistance fighters from the Kachin peoples of northern Burma, who numbered several thousand by the end of 1943.

In China the OSS began setting up operations in April 1944 after the agreement with General Chennault to establish a joint intelligence operation to support the Fourteenth Air Force in China. Weems became part of a cadre of OSS personnel sent to supplement the existing intelligence organization of the Fourteenth Air Force, which with limited resources had already created effective operations to gather targeting intelligence for U.S. bombers, provide early warning of Japanese aerial attacks, and rescue downed Allied airmen. One of its leading intelligence officers was Capt. John Birch, remembered after the war for his name being appropriated by a far-right organization but renowned among the U.S. forces in China as a brilliant intelligence officer.

John Birch was an extraordinary figure of the American wartime presence in China, brought into the war by an improbable coincidence, who became perhaps the most successful American intelligence officer of the Second World War. Born in India into a family of American missionaries, he grew up in Georgia and attended Mercer College in Macon, then a Baptist seminary in Texas. Immediately after graduating in 1940, he went to China as a missionary. After the attack on Pearl Harbor, when the Japanese rounded up Americans in China for internment and repatriation, Birch fled inland to stay in China and continue his ministry alone. In April 1942 he entered the war after the Doolittle Raid on Tokyo, when the B-25 bomber of Col. Jimmy Doolittle happened to crash land near him in Jiangxi Province while seeking to land in friendly Chinese territory. Birch helped to take Doolittle and his aircrew to General Chennault, and Doolittle and Chennault were so impressed by the young Mandarin-speaking preacher that Chennault recruited him to serve as an intelligence officer. After his commissioning on July 4, 1942, he spent the war organizing intelligence networks of Chinese civilians, often living in disguise deep in enemy-controlled territory for months at a time.[39]

A newly created OSS Detachment 202 took over the mission and all intelligence personnel in China. Detachment 202 was responsible for a vast theater of operations stretching from Manchuria and Korea in the north to Indochina in the south, encompassing the entirety of China, Korea, and Vietnam. It had fewer than two hundred Americans, operating from a headquarters at the main Fourteenth Air Force base at Kunming and a station in Chungking. This small organization had a formidable array of missions, including gathering targeting intelligence for the Fourteenth Air Force, organizing and training Chinese resistance groups, and counterintelligence against Japanese espionage. It also supported the Chinese Communists under Mao Tse-tung and Vietnamese Communists under Ho Chi Minh as allies in the immediate struggle against Japan.

The changed strategic position of the United States and the Allied powers in 1944 revived Donovan's idea of working with the Korean independence movement. In the two years since the Battle of Midway, the U.S. Navy had established superiority at sea, and U.S. forces had advanced toward Japan in a series of amphibious operations. Japan's home islands came within range of B-29 Superfortress bombers with the capture of the island of Saipan in June and July 1944, and U.S. forces then landed in the Philippines in October 1944, destroying most of the remaining Imperial Japanese Navy in the Battle of the Philippine Sea and the Battle of Leyte Gulf. With an invasion of Japan becoming a possibility, two years after the failure of the Esson Gale mission to Chungking, the OSS again looked to the Koreans for their unique ability to operate deep within Japan and its empire.[40]

In 1944 two separate OSS operations working with Koreans emerged. The first, Project NAPKO, aimed to insert a small number of highly trained Korean agents, under U.S. command, into Korea by sea. The second, Project Eagle, would be a joint operation by the OSS and the Korean Restoration Army in China, the alliance between the United States and the Korean Provisional Government that Donovan had sought since December 1941.

Project NAPKO

Project NAPKO, short for Naval Penetration of Korea, was among the most highly secret and compartmentalized OSS operations. Commanded by now Col. Carl Eifler, the original commander of OSS Detachment 101 in Burma, it involved a specially created OSS organization with the intentionally generic name Field Experimental Unit (FEU). The mission of the FEU was to infiltrate Korean agents into Korea and into Japan itself from the Pacific using submarines. The Korean agents would initially engage in espionage and organizing underground Korean resistance groups, then guide the resistance in sabotage operations and armed rebellion. They were entirely under U.S. command, not affiliated with any Korean organization.[41]

In January 1944, while on temporary duty in Washington, Eifler started to search the OSS for personnel suitable for the operation.[42] By mid-June he had six officers and five enlisted men.[43] In late July 1944 he went to Hawaii to recruit Koreans from the Korean immigrant community in the territory, which numbered approximately seven thousand during the 1940s. The OSS continued to search for volunteers among the Korean communities of Hawaii, California, New York, and Chicago into 1945. Additional volunteers came from Koreans being held as prisoners of war at Camp McCoy, Wisconsin, after surrendering while serving in the

Imperial Japanese Army. The recruitment of these Korean volunteers involved a deception in which the camp commander recorded them as escaped prisoners of war in his records and to the Red Cross, to obscure their betrayal of Japan and involvement with the OSS.[44]

Eifler and the FEU also sought to recruit sons of American missionaries in Korea for their language skills and familiarity with the country. The FEU requested Benjamin Weems and Richard Underwood, the youngest sons of the Weems and Underwood families, in the spring of 1945. Benjamin Weems, already serving as a Japanese language expert for Army intelligence, had vital expertise in both the Japanese and Korean languages, but the OSS could not persuade Army intelligence to release him. Richard Underwood, not yet eighteen years old, had been among the last Americans in Korea along with his father, Horace Horton Underwood, and brother Horace Grant Underwood II, and like them he had been repatriated to the United States in 1942. He brought native-level ability to speak Korean and experience navigating the western coast of Korea, where he and his brothers had sailed during their childhoods.[45] The army inducted him as a private immediately after his eighteenth birthday in June 1945, for immediate assignment to the OSS and the FEU.[46]

The FEU had a comprehensive plan for infiltration of Korea by March 1945. It aimed to build an organization that would operate under American command to collect intelligence and "eventually, if directed, embody the support of twenty-three million people for an active revolutionary movement."

The FEU made its plan based on its own assessment of the potential for underground resistance activity in Korea. Its assessment used interviews of more than one hundred Korean residents of the United States; returned American missionaries, government officials, and businessmen; Korean prisoners of war; and eighteen Koreans recruited into the FEU. The FEU concluded that there was little reliable indication of the existence of an actively operating underground in Korea and that U.S. forces could not rely on making contact with any organized resistance group to provide them with intelligence. U.S. forces would have to obtain intelligence by introducing agents into Korea, prior to any U.S. military operations in the country. Korean agents would be necessary to operate in Korea, and they would have to be able to build networks of family and personal friends, developing known, trustworthy personal contacts into an espionage system and underground movement that could assist U.S. military operations during an invasion.[47]

Northern Korea and its large population of Korean Christians were the main hope of the FEU. Noting the leading role of Christians in the March First Movement of 1919, the FEU's assessment considered them to be the strongest source of support for a resistance movement against Imperial Japan, and what is now North Korea with its large Christian population to be the best area for OSS agents to operate. "The most distinct group that could be relied upon to act wholeheartedly and patriotically in an anti-Japanese resistance movement would be the Christian element in Northern Korea," stated the report. The decades of work by missionaries in Pyongyang and other areas of northern Korea now would become an instrument in the war against Imperial Japan.[48]

The FEU planned an operation in two distinct phases. In the initial phase, OSS-trained teams of Korean agents would land in Korea and establish clandestine networks, operating under deep cover. There would be ten groups of one to five members each, compartmentalized so that no group would know of the existence of any other. They would be equipped with clothing of Korean manufacture, glasses from Korea or Japan, radio sets, and money, with no other equipment to be carried. Agents would contact people already known to them, and as soon as possible, establish radio contact in code with listening stations to be established in northern China and the Philippines. The teams would radio out information of interest, and they also would establish contact points where Koreans could be withdrawn for training and eventual reinsertion into Korea, for evacuating scientists and other people with information of value, and for smuggling downed American pilots out of Korea.[49]

The OSS teams would then prepare Korea for a guerilla war against Japan. They would identify rural areas with strong opposition to Japanese rule, eliminate persons who were not anti-Japanese, and recruit and train Koreans for resistance, with the goal of establishing control over whole rural areas and islands of Korea. American officers would then move in to act as liaison between the Korean OSS teams and the U.S. military and to guide and run the underground organization for the OSS. On the orders of the high command, the underground organization would conduct sabotage or bring in weapons and ammunition for resistance groups, with a full-scale revolution against Imperial Japanese rule as the ultimate aim.

Two teams were trained and ready for action by March 1945, one to operate in the Seoul area, the other in northern Korea. Each had networks of relatives and associates identified as ready to be organized into underground resistance organizations. They were hidden products of the fifty-eight years of the American Christian presence in Korea, discovered by Colonel Eifler and his team during almost a year of effort to recruit Koreans capable of working underground as agents in Korea.

The team preparing to operate in the Seoul area would be able to use an existing network of relatives, friends, and business associates that its leader had built before the war. The team of five had a leader born in Korea but raised and educated in the United States, who attended grammar school and high school in Nebraska and earned a degree from the University of Michigan. Between 1927 and 1941, he had built a successful business in Seoul with branches in Korea, Manchuria, and Japan, each managed by a relative or trusted friend who was a Korean patriot.[50] He had expanded his business and selected its managers hoping that one day it could serve as the basis for an underground organization in a struggle against Japanese rule, and when the FEU found him, he eagerly volunteered himself and his organization. He enlisted in the army in January 1945, at the age of fifty, specifically for assignment to the FEU.

The other team members were thirty-nine to forty-nine years of age, all from regions currently in North Korea, three of them longtime residents of the United States and the fourth a former prisoner of war. One was born in Pyongyang and educated at an American mission school, immigrating to the United States in 1915. The OSS had originally recruited him in December 1942, then released him in February 1943 after his group of Korean Americans was denied placement in the army's Military

Intelligence Training Center. The OSS recruited him again to join the FEU in January 1945. Another, also from Pyongyang, had immigrated to the United States in 1922, attending Northwestern University on a scholarship. He enlisted in the army in August 1943, so determined to serve in the war against Japan that after the army initially rejected him because he already was married with a child, he made himself eligible by divorcing his wife with an understanding that they would remarry after the war. He became a staff sergeant in the Military Intelligence Service, then was recruited by the FEU in September 1944. The third U.S. resident entered the United States in 1925 and attended Huron College while George McCune was its president, enlisting in January 1945 to join the FEU. The former prisoner of war was from Changdo, a mountainous area south of Wonsan, and had traveled around Korea as a salesman. Drafted into the Imperial Japanese Army and captured on Saipan in June 1944, he had the most current knowledge of conditions in Korea and was eager to fight against Japan.[51]

The team for northern Korea was preparing to operate from Pyongyang to Wonsan, across the entire width of the Korean peninsula, with three men very different from each other. In Pyongyang, the team leader was from a branch of the Korean royal family, with properties and business interests throughout Korea. His older brother had an import/export business between Korea and Japan with employees all over Korea, which gave the team an already existing network to support agent movements and operations. His early education had been in Japanese military schools, and in 1937 he had moved to the United States, where he studied at George Peabody College, Vanderbilt University, Boston University, and Harvard University. Working as a researcher at the New York Public Library when the war began, in March 1942 he joined Army intelligence as a translator in New York, then in August 1942 went to work for the Office of War Information, first in New York and then in San Francisco in March 1943, writing scripts and announcing for radio broadcasts to Korea and Japan. Age thirty-five in 1945, he had experience with the Japanese military system, command of both the Korean and Japanese languages, and complete confidence in his ability to operate clandestinely in Korea.

The second member of the team had a very different background and set of skills. From North Pyongan, a mountainous region in the far northwest of Korea on the Yalu River, he had come to the United States as a twenty-five-year-old student in 1927 to study engineering. From 1928 to 1938 he earned bachelor's and master's degrees in science at the University of Southern California and also studied geology at the Colorado School of Mines. For most of the war he worked as a metallurgical chemist at an aircraft manufacturer, and for a time he also worked as a mining prospector, giving him considerable experience with surveying and mapping and living in the wilderness. He spoke Korean, Japanese, and Mandarin Chinese fluently and also English well. His knowledge and experience made him well suited to rough outdoor living and intelligence collection on industrial and military targets.

The third team member lacked the exceptional skills of the other two but was considered a willing and dependable complement to them. His family in Wonsan had sent him to the United States for his education in 1917, at the age of fifteen. He studied at various high schools and colleges until 1927, when he went to work to send money back to Korea to support his family, eventually starting a successful small produce business in Los Angeles. He organized several anti-Japanese movements in the United States, including a boycott of Japanese shipping and the Japanese consulate in Los Angeles in 1937. The oldest of the three at forty-three, he was a mature and hardworking individual who was equally eager to join the fight against Japan.[52]

Four more teams were in the process of organizing in March 1945. In the province of Pyongan, near Pyongyang, a team of four would land on the west coast to organize in the rural districts. South of Seoul on the west coast, in the Seosan district, a team of three to four would land to organize in the city and rural districts. In Kim Ku's home province of Hwanghae, near the former home and mission center of the Weems family in Kaesong, two natives of the province and one or two additional team members would penetrate and organize. There also would be a landing at the far southwestern extremity of Korea near the port of Mokpo, a crucial transportation hub between Japan, Korea, and China, in a strongly anti-Japanese area with several mountainous islands rarely visited by the Japanese.[53] A native of the area, captured on Saipan in June 1944 after being drafted into a Japanese labor battalion, would lead the team.[54]

Delivery of the Korean OSS teams to the landing sites, on shores still patrolled by Japanese aircraft and warships, would be by submarine. The NAPKO plan called for the use of Navy fleet submarines either to release agents near the shore, with the agents swimming ashore using a small nylon boat that had already been developed, or to deliver a special boat for covert landings that was under development. The new boat, with minimal radar signature and a hundred-mile range, would be released out of radar range and land under cover of darkness.[55]

The boats, code-named GIMIK, were ready by May 1945, and the OSS took delivery of the first two on June 10, 1945. They were semisubmersibles, not capable of submerging, but with their decks awash to minimize their visual and radar signature.[56] Each boat had a plywood hull approximately eighteen feet in length and a steel cabin amidships, with a forward-facing pilot station enclosed by a plexiglass canopy and a compartment that could hold two agents facing rearward, packed tightly together. The only structures above the water, the air intake and exhaust stack for the engine and an air shaft for the pilot and passengers, were wrapped in steel wool to break up their radar signature.[57] There were plans to build as many as twenty-two GIMIK boats for the full-scale NAPKO mission.[58]

During the summer of 1945, the staff of Project NAPKO used the GIMIK boats to train the boat pilots and Korean agents at the OSS training facility on Catalina Island. There were two training camps already established on Catalina Island in April 1945, and two additional camps opened in May and June, with six more planned.[59] Sixteen Korean recruits arrived in the first group of trainees, four for each of the four camps, with none knowing of the existence of the other camps.[60] Army and Navy teams taught them about estimating distances, testing water depths, looking for fortifications, and using American radios. In each camp, two learned to parachute and two trained to be infiltrated by boat. The boat pilots, Navy Ensigns George McCullough and Robert Mullen, had a separate base on Catalina Island.[61]

Training runs occurred once a week, with each boat taking two Korean recruits from Catalina Island to the mainland. Runs occurred at night without running lights to simulate conditions in a real operation. The OSS did not register the boats with the Coast Guard and the Army Air Corps, which were patrolling the coast, and U.S. patrol ships or aircraft could have identified the boats as enemy vessels and sunk them. Piloting the boats was difficult with the pilot's head barely above the water and the steel passenger compartments causing the magnetic compasses on board to deviate from true north, requiring correction almost daily.[62] With the boats running at only about six knots, each twenty-mile voyage from Catalina Island to the mainland took three and a half hours. Most of the Koreans would get seasick after hours spent crammed into the tiny, constantly pitching boats, so they would get a day of rest after each training run.

The training runs were all successful, establishing that the GIMIK boats were suitable and the boat pilots and first teams of Korean agents were ready for their landing operations. The boats penetrated the harbor defenses of Newport Beach and Los Angeles undetected by radar or patrol boats, and they successfully landed agents at Newport Beach and San Clemente. No Korean agents were seen or caught while landing or moving inland.[63]

To prepare for espionage and underground operations in Korea's cities, Korean agents went on training missions in cities in southern California. These exercises sent teams with their radio equipment to move around a city, find suitable locations for sending transmissions, and then transmit to an airplane overhead or to a distant station in the state of Washington. Involving groups of Asian men moving around American cities, likely to be seen as Japanese spies, these exercises were far more difficult than actually operating in Korea, where a group of Koreans would blend in. One team that set up its equipment on the roof of the Biltmore Hotel in Los Angeles was caught by the hotel's head of security, who had served with Colonel Eifler in the Los Angeles Police

Department before the war and was cooperating with Project NAPKO. Another team on an exercise in San Diego set up its radio site in Balboa Park only a short distance from a U.S. Army communications center and found themselves detained at pistol point by an Army officer who probably thought that he was stopping Japanese spies.[64]

The Korean agents and GIMIK boats of Project NAPKO were deployed to the western Pacific for action after the capture of Okinawa in April–June 1945.[65] The OSS shipped the GIMIK boats from Long Beach to Okinawa and their crews from San Francisco to Okinawa by sea, while the Koreans flew to Okinawa for final training.[66] After the completion of further planning and training in Okinawa, the FEU set the departure date of the first mission to Korea for August 26, 1945.

Project Eagle: The Korean-American Alliance

Project Eagle emerged gradually in late 1944 to early 1945, with the OSS and the Korean Provisional Government cautiously joining their forces for a combined operation. It was completely separate from Project NAPKO and differed fundamentally in being a U.S.-Korean operation. Project NAPKO was a strictly U.S. operation using Korean personnel, and Project Eagle was an alliance between the OSS and the Koreans in exile in China, under the joint command of the OSS and the Korean Restoration Army. While the cryptically named Project NAPKO operated in the shadowy world of a covert operation, hidden from foreign eyes and compartmentalized from other Americans and even within itself, Project Eagle brought the OSS and the Koreans into overt cooperation.

Donovan's vision in the earliest days after the attack on Pearl Harbor finally came to fruition with Project Eagle. Three years earlier, in January 1942, he had dispatched the Esson Gale mission to Chungking, to establish an alliance with the Korean Provisional Government that he believed could strike at the heart of Japanese power in Korea and in Japan itself. In 1945 the plans for a U.S.-Korean alliance, long set aside, finally became a reality.

Even more significantly, Project Eagle was the real starting point of the relationship between the United States and Korea. For six decades since the two nations formally opened a diplomatic relationship in 1882, Koreans had sought the support of the United States in their struggle for independence, first as a kingdom, then as a nonviolent revolutionary movement, and finally as a government in exile. For six decades the United States had stood aside. Project Eagle became the first time in history that Americans and Koreans cooperated toward a shared goal, under the authority of the governments of the United States and Korea. The modern relationship between the United States and Korea began with it.

Project Eagle began at the initiative of the Korean Provisional Government, which reached out to the OSS in Chungking with a plan for a combined U.S.-Korean operation in Korea. In October 1944 Gen. Yi Pomsok of the Korean Restoration Army approached the OSS station in Chungking with a proposal for a combined operation. The mission would be for the United States to train a select group of Koreans and send them to Korea, with the dual objectives of collecting intelligence and maintaining regular contact with the Korean underground, organizing it into a revolutionary force to aid future Allied military operations. Korean agents would penetrate Japan as well as Korea through Korean communities living in Japan as migrant or forced laborers.[67]

The OSS began to take a close look at the Korean Restoration Army and its potential after receiving General Yi's proposal, and the officer sent for the task was Capt. Clarence Weems. The OSS had recruited him a year and a half earlier for his knowledge of Korea, and as the chief intelligence analyst in China for Korean affairs he was finally in the right place at the right time. Weems went to inspect the Korean Restoration Army's Second Detachment near Xian, commanded by General Yi. His report in January 1945 was favorable, judging that the Korean Restoration Army men that he observed possessed individual capabilities, spirit, and solidarity that made them suitable for OSS training and operations. He concluded, "This writer's continuous investigation of the Korean Movement and of Korean organizations during the past three years permits confidence that the time is appropriate and that the Second Group under General Li [Yi Pomsok] is made-to-order for the OSS's needs in a Korean Intelligence Plan."[68]

Capt. John Birch was another OSS officer sent to establish the relationship with the Korean Restoration Army. Birch, who had years of experience recruiting and training Chinese to operate deep behind Imperial Japanese lines for General Chennault's air force, visited the Third Detachment of the Korean Restoration Army in January 1945. Birch worked out details of a program for OSS training of troops in infiltration of enemy territory and radio communications. By mid-February the terms of OSS–Korean Restoration Army operations were established.[69]

OSS headquarters in Washington began a search for an officer capable of leading the operation almost immediately after receiving Yi Pomsok's proposal. On October 17, 1944, the OSS Director's Office issued a request for an Army captain to serve as the commanding officer of an operation that would recruit and train Koreans to operate behind enemy lines. He would have demonstrated ability to assume responsibility and leadership and to command Koreans and speak fluent Japanese, Korean, Chinese, and English. Moreover, he would have to be a native Korean, prominent in Korea and known to and commanding respect from Koreans, but with higher education in the United States and familiarity with American methods and procedures.[70] It was a demanding request that the OSS would search for someone to fill for the rest of 1944.

The Korean Restoration Army took on added significance at the beginning of 1945 as the OSS became aware of the potential for mass desertion by Korean conscripts in the Japanese armed forces. With the IJA using large drafts of Koreans to replace its losses starting in 1944, Korean deserters began to appear in large numbers in China as the year progressed. The risk of desertion by 100,000 Korean draftees in China became a significant weak link for the IJA, and it became an opportunity for the Korean Restoration Army as well. The Korean Restoration Army had been cut off from Korea and the Korean populations of Manchuria and eastern China since its foundation, but now a new hope had emerged. By drafting Koreans, putting them through military training, and sending them to the front line in China, Japan was delivering exactly what the Korean Restoration Army had needed for years.

A pivotal development was the arrival of a group of approximately fifty men who had made a break from their posts soon after their arrival at the front line during the summer, surrendered to Chinese guerillas, and then joined the Korean Restoration Army's Third Detachment. They included Kim Woo Chun, who had been a university student in Pyongyang before being drafted. After several months of training, these men became second lieutenants in the Korean Restoration Army in October 1944. A dozen stayed at the front line, including Kim Woo Chun, while thirty-seven went to Chungking to serve as cadres for the Korean Provisional Government.[71]

A ceremony in Chungking announced this development to the OSS on January 31, 1945. On that day, the Korean Provisional Government presented the thirty-seven recently commissioned officers at an event attended by foreign embassy staffs and news services. The thirty-seven officers publicly declared their dedication to serving the independence movement and pledged their allegiance to the Korean Provisional Government. Kim Ku remembered the ceremony as an event filled with emotion for him and his compatriots, who after years in exile were finally seeing a sudden influx of young men to reinforce their movement.[72]

Clarence Weems attended the ceremony for the OSS, and he immediately recognized the significance of what he saw. At the ceremony he made a statement to Kim Ku in Korean that made such an impression that one of Kim's aides years later remembered it and recorded it in his memoirs: "*Songsaengnim, hobagi nongkulchae tuk torojyossumnida*" (Teacher, a pumpkin has fallen to the ground from the branches with the vines still attached to it).[73] Using a common Korean expression about good fortune learned during his childhood in Kaesong, at the same time when Kim Ku worked as a teacher and independence activist a short distance away in Haeju, he acknowledged to Kim Ku that a remarkable event had occurred, an unexpected windfall for the Korean cause.

Weems immediately sought to bring the arrival of the Korean deserters to the attention of his superiors in the OSS. On February 3 he invited Lt. Col. Willis Bird, with the OSS's China headquarters in Kunming, to "a very informal luncheon at the Sino-Korean Cultural Relations restaurant for an interesting group of Korean arrivals and a few of the leaders of the Korean community here."[74] This cryptic reference in an unclassified letter appears to have started the OSS toward learning about approximately one hundred thousand Korean conscripts in the Imperial Japanese Army in China and their potential to help the Allied cause. By the end of March, the Koreans in the IJA in China had become known throughout the OSS, and OSS headquarters in China was studying the scale of the use of Korean conscripts in the IJA and the potential of encouraging desertions and using the men against Japan.[75]

Weems, Birch and Capt. Clyde Sargent, the latter now with the OSS Secret Intelligence (SI) branch, would develop the plan for the combined OSS-Korean operation that General Yi Pomsok had proposed. It was ready by February 24, 1945. Titled the "Eagle Project for SI Penetration of Korea," and also called the Korea Intelligence Plan, it called for the OSS to train, equip and support a force of Korean agents drawn from the Second Detachment of the Korean Restoration Army under Yi Pomsok and from newly arrived deserters from the Imperial Japanese Army.[76]

Approval of Project Eagle from higher levels of command in the OSS and the U.S. military in China came quickly. The operations committee of the OSS China theater headquarters in Kunming approved it on February 28, 1945.[77] General Chennault, who was in command over OSS operations in China because the OSS was serving as the intelligence organization of his Fourteenth Air Force, received the plan from OSS China theater headquarters on March 3, 1945, and approved it immediately.[78]

So at the beginning of March 1945, a plan for the long-awaited military alliance between the United States and the Korean Provisional Government was finally in place. It was three years after William Donovan had dispatched his first mission to the Korean Provisional Government and Clarence Weems had joined the army intelligence service as its first Korea expert, and almost exactly two years to the day that Weems had joined the OSS. Making the planned military alliance a reality would be a complicated task for both the Koreans and the Americans involved in it, however, and they would struggle to overcome many obstacles during the ensuing six months until the end of the war.

5

Project Eagle

Making the Project Eagle plan into a reality would be a difficult task for both the Koreans and the Americans. The operation itself presented a daunting challenge, which the OSS and the Korean Restoration Army had to solve with limited resources. Further complicating the combined effort was a lack of trust, with each side having to learn to work with the other for the first time in history. Most of all, the political and strategic situation that was completely outside of the ability of the OSS or the Korean Provisional Government to influence hung over the operation at all times. Despite these difficulties, the OSS and Korean Restoration Army officers entrusted with Project Eagle fulfilled the plan and created a unique organization of the Second World War era, a repository of American experience in Korea from 1882 to 1942.

The Eagle Plan

The plan was to create a force of forty-five Korean agents and infiltrate them into Korea during the summer and fall of 1945. They would enter Korea in several ways: overland from China, using courier networks through territory controlled by Japan that Korean resistance groups had established years earlier; by sea from the coast of China; and by air, dropped by parachute from U.S. Fourteenth Air Force aircraft.

Much like Project NAPKO, Project Eagle aimed to gather intelligence and then to expand its actions to sabotage and possibly a Korean revolution. Project Eagle's agents would report on industrial production, war supplies, target data, invasion beaches, land communications, and public morale and its reflection of the potential for Korean underground and revolutionary activity. After making contact with Korean underground groups and assessing the situation, they would expand their operations from intelligence collection to sabotage or outright revolution. The agents would move to five areas of strategic importance to Japan, from the Yalu River in the north to Pusan in the south, to collect and report intelligence.[1] The five areas were the northwestern border area with China; the northeastern border area with China and the Soviet Union; north-central Korea, from Pyongyang and the port of Nampo in the west to the ports of Wonsan and Hungnam on the east coast; south-central Korea, around Seoul and Inchon; and the southern coast from Pusan in the east to Mokpo in the west.[2] Each area would have six agents and an area station with a radio operator and code man.[3]

Eagle agents would operate under the direction of the OSS SI field office in Tu-Ch'iao, near Xian, which was the Chinese-controlled territory closest to Korea and the location of most of Eagle's Korean personnel. The agents in the field and headquarters would communicate using radios and a courier network established in occupied China and Korea by Korean nationalists.[4]

The timetable set the ambitious goal of having the force of Korean agents trained and ready to deploy within three months. It would start with 120 men of the Korean Restoration Army, of which the best 60 would be trained, with 45 to go to Korea. Of the 120 men, 80 would be from the Second Detachment of the Korean Restoration Army, based in Xian and under the command of Gen. Yi Pomsok. The other 40 would be from the Imperial Japanese Army deserters who had become Korean Restoration Army officers and gone to Chungking. They were considered to be the best men available among the Korean exiles in China, called "the university students" by both the Korean Provisional Government and the OSS because they had been well educated in Korea before being drafted. The OSS staff of Project Eagle would start with a training cadre of seven officers and seven enlisted men, then expand to ten officers and twelve enlisted men during active operations in Korea.[5]

The Eagle and the Iron Horse

On the U.S. side, Project Eagle became the responsibility of Capt. Clyde Sargent. He had planned Project Eagle, led it from its first day to its last, and would become the sole caretaker of its memory after it was over. He deserves to be considered synonymous with Project Eagle.

Sargent had roots in the United States that were almost as old as those of the Weems family and also a long personal history in China. In the 1800s one of his ancestors founded the town of Sargentville, Maine, on the east coast of Penobscot Bay, where some of the Sargents live today. His father, R. Harvey Sargent, a topographer with the U.S. Geological Survey, had journeyed 1,800 miles across the interior of China with a scientific expedition in 1903 and 1904, as part of a distinguished career mapping China, Alaska, and South America.[6] During the 1930s Clyde Sargent studied Chinese language and civilization at the College of Chinese Studies in Beijing and worked on a doctorate in Chinese studies at Columbia University. Although not especially religious, he accepted an educational missionary position at Cheeloo University, a school founded jointly by Presbyterians and Baptists in the city of Jinan (then called Tsinan) on the Shandong Peninsula on the east coast of China. He taught there for six years, becoming chairman of the foreign languages department.

Working as a scholar in China brought Sargent into the war. With Jinan one of the early targets of the Japanese invasion in 1937, Cheeloo University evacuated and relocated to a campus in Chengdu, almost 1,000 miles to the west. Chengdu, along with Chungking, was a center of the Nationalist Chinese stronghold in Sichuan where the government of Chiang Kai-shek held out against the Japanese invasion from 1938 to 1945. Sargent witnessed Chengdu devastated by Japanese air raids, including the largest one on July 27, 1941, in which 108 bombers left behind widespread destruction and hundreds of corpses in the streets.[7]

When old China hand Esson Gale arrived in Chungking in early 1942 to contact the Korean Provisional Government, he recruited Sargent in May 1942 to serve as the new intelligence service's representative in China.

Sargent became a pioneer for the OSS in China, performing leading roles in many areas over the course of the war. He began as the chief intelligence analyst for the OSS's Research and Analysis branch, then became the principal field representative for counterespionage in September 1943. In April 1944 he switched to intelligence collection with the SI branch and also ceased to be a civilian, receiving a commission as a captain in the army.

On the Korean side, implementing Project Eagle was in the hands of Gen. Yi Pomsok. Yi's life had been defined from childhood by the struggle for independence from Japan, like that of Kim Ku, but a generation younger and from the opposite end of Korean society. Born into a branch of Korea's royal family in 1900, his father an official of the Korean monarchy during its final years, Yi spent his childhood watching Japan conquer Korea and reduce its people and culture to second-class status in their own country. At the age of only fifteen, he left his family to journey to China and join Koreans in exile attempting to organize an armed resistance movement. In 1916 he entered a military academy in Manchuria that was training young Koreans for a liberation army. He was the top cadet at the academy, and by his graduation in 1919 he had received the nom de guerre "Chulgi" (Iron Horse) in recognition of his toughness and leadership skills.

The nineteen-year-old Yi Pomsok briefly considered joining the Korean Provisional Government but instead stayed on the course of armed action against Japan. During the March First Movement of 1919, he went to Shanghai for the first meetings of the Korean Provisional Government, and he was urged to join its military branch. He became disappointed by the Korean Provisional Government's arguing and infighting, however, and he left it and would not work with it again for over a decade. No doubt with a teenager's desire for action, he returned to the Korean forces in exile in Manchuria. He participated in the attack on the consulate in the border city of Hunchun that lured Japanese forces into the Battle of Qingshanli, then commanded a unit in the battle in October 1920.

In 1922, as increasing Japanese control over Manchuria made resistance there impossible, Yi and a few remaining followers sought refuge in the Soviet Union. It was during a period of internationalism in the early Soviet Union before the rise of Joseph Stalin and his policy of "socialism in one country," when foreign Communists and revolutionaries were welcome. Yi claimed to have been an officer in a Red Army cavalry unit. He left in 1925, after the Soviet Union signed a treaty with Imperial Japan normalizing relations for the first time since the Russian Revolution. He returned to Manchuria, where he soon became engulfed in the Chinese Civil War.

Yi experienced great personal losses during this period. In the Soviet Union he married a Russian woman, but he had to leave her behind during his escape to Manchuria in 1925. He later learned that she had committed suicide. He remarried later that year, to a Korean woman born in Russia named Maria Kim, but Japanese police arrested her. Tortured in detention, she died soon after being released.

Back in China, caught in the civil war between the Nationalists, Communists, and warlords, Yi served one side and then another in order to stay alive and continue his fight against Japan. He led a small Korean armed group that allied with one faction and then another, fighting on the Communist side against the Nationalists in one battle, then fighting on the Nationalist side. In 1928 Yi joined the Nationalist army during its Northern Expedition that reunified China, appointed as a major.

Yi served as a highly regarded officer in the Nationalist army during the 1930s before becoming a founder of the Korean Restoration Army. The Nationalist army made him one of its leading officers for work with foreign militaries, including military advisers from Europe. He traveled to Germany and the Soviet Union in 1931–32 as part of Nationalist military delegations sent to study German and Soviet military methods. Soviet authorities briefly detained him, remembering his earlier time in the Soviet Union in 1922–25. In the aftermath of Kim Ku's successful terrorist attack in Shanghai in 1932, he served as the leader of the short-lived

Korean section created in 1933 at the Nationalist military academy in Luoyang. He then worked with military advisers from Germany and Italy who arrived in China in 1933 to build up China's army and air force. Promoted to major general in 1936, he spent several years fighting the Japanese invasion of China, including in the Chinese victory at the Battle of Taierzhuang in 1938. He rejoined the Korean liberation movement permanently when he became one of the leaders of the Korean Restoration Army at its formation in 1940.

By 1945 Yi Pomsok had spent thirty years in exile in the struggle against Japan. His years at war or preparing for war against Japan may have been the most of any officer in any of the Allied armies during the Second World War, and he had seen much of Asia and Europe and witnessed the rise of Communism and Fascism. Americans knew little about his long history, but everyone in the OSS who worked with him was struck by the commanding presence that his experiences had given him. With his bearing and an array of foreign symbols of authority that he brought with him at all times—a swagger stick, an American Smith & Wesson revolver, and a German Shepherd—Yi was well suited to motivate and lead men in exile preparing for a dangerous mission.[8]

Clyde Sargent and Yi Pomsok began their work together in late March 1945 with a meeting in Xian, Yi's headquarters since 1940. Sargent was only thirty-five years of age and an Army captain with over a decade of experience in China but new to the Korean cause. He now served as a diplomat to Kim Ku and senior leaders of the Korean Provisional Government whose struggle against Japan had begun before he was born. He first met Yi and other leaders of the Korean Restoration Army and Korean Provisional Government for several days in Xian, then flew with Yi and others to Chungking on March 31. There he moved further up the Korean chain of command with a dinner meeting on April 1 with Gen. Li Chong Chon, commander in chief of the Korean Restoration Army, and two of Kim Ku's closest advisers.[9]

A meeting with Kim Ku himself finally occurred at the headquarters of the Korean Provisional Government on April 3. Expressions of satisfaction with the new cooperation between Koreans and Americans dominated the meeting, with Kim Ku declaring his appreciation of American interest and his intention to cooperate fully, as well as his complete confidence in Yi Pomsok and the developing relationship with Sargent and the OSS. Concern over the future of Korea in the postwar world intruded as well, though. Referring to Gen. Douglas MacArthur's return to the Philippines as a liberator accompanied by the president of the Philippines and other high Philippine officials, Kim Ku stated that the Korean Provisional Government accompanying an Allied invasion of Korea would influence the people of Korea, causing them to revolt against Japan and support American operations. It was an unsubtle attempt to raise the issue of the future status of the Korean Provisional Government, a question that Sargent had no ability to decide.[10]

Sargent emerged surprised and impressed by the man known to the OSS as a killer and a terrorist in previous decades. He reported, "In spite of his 70 years, which he showed completely in both appearance and manner, he bore himself with dignity and composure tempered by modesty and gentleness that seemed incompatible with the patriotic assassin and terrorist of 25 years ago."[11] It was the beginning of a process of discovery for Sargent in which he would get to know the Korean Provisional Government and the Korean Restoration Army as no other American had.

While Sargent and Yi established their partnership in Project Eagle, Clarence Weems took on a different role. He continued to be the leading OSS expert on Korea, with primary responsibility for OSS relations with the Korean Restoration Army. He stayed away from Project Eagle in Xian, however, working primarily with the Third Detachment in Anhui under Gen. Kim Hak Kyu. The OSS kept Weems away from Project Eagle because of opposition to him from Yi Pomsok and other leaders of the Korean Restoration Army, who expressed doubts about their ability to work with Weems during Sargent's April 1 meetings with them in Chungking. Yi Pomsok particularly opposed working with Weems, claiming that there had been a great deal of misunderstanding between them on Weems's role.[12] What likely happened was that Weems, overly excited by developments, overstated his role and made promises that he lacked the power to fulfill while inspecting Yi's Second Detachment in late 1944. The consequence was that Weems would not be involved in commanding operations in Project Eagle; instead, he would remain an intelligence analyst and head the OSS training center for the Third Detachment in Anhui.[13]

Creation of the Eagle Force

Sargent and Yi met again to commence Project Eagle back in Xian, where the OSS was creating a base complex for the many operations that it was planning against Japanese forces in China. An Army officer with the OSS China headquarters in Kunming, Maj. Gustav Krause, arrived in the Xian area with forty-six OSS personnel on April 10, setting up a headquarters in an abandoned Seventh Day Adventist mission a mile outside of the city and starting to build a set of bases around it. They would support operations by multiple branches of the OSS, including Secret Intelligence, Morale Operations, and Counterintelligence, with Project Eagle only one of many operations based there. Major Krause was in command of the base complex in Xian but had no operational control over Eagle, which was directly subordinate to the chief of OSS Strategic Intelligence in Kunming.[14]

The Project Eagle base at Tu-Ch'iao was twelve miles southeast of Xian, a few miles away from a massive earthen pyramid that was located over the tomb of the first emperor of China, Qin Shi Huang, who had unified China in 221 BC and died in 210 BC. The tomb of the first emperor would be discovered by local farmers in 1974, over two thousand years after it had been constructed and buried, then forgotten. The Terracotta Army that has become one of the most renowned artifacts of any civilization in the world was one of the archaeological treasures that lay buried and waiting to be rediscovered only a few miles away from the base, where the Koreans and Americans of Project Eagle worked together to create their own army during the summer of 1945.

The "base" was a makeshift compound outside of a rural village, built around an abandoned Buddhist temple. The small temple, three smaller buildings, and two mud and thatch huts were the only structures.

There, Yi Pomsok's Second Detachment had sent 160 men for Project Eagle to make into the force of agents to be sent deep into Japanese-controlled territory.

Sargent arrived at the Project Eagle base on May 11, and what he saw confirmed earlier favorable impressions of the Korean Restoration Army but also exposed the hopelessly inadequate support that they had received from China for years. Sargent found the discipline and morale of the men to be high and Yi Pomsok to be "a sincere patriot, a conscientious commander, and a straight-shooter." The troops were not adequately clothed and fed, though, let alone ready to train hard for a difficult mission. Never having received proper clothing from the Chinese army supply system, many lacked uniforms, and instead of boots or shoes they wore sandals made of grass.[15] Their food supply was sufficient for only two meals a day, consisting of nothing but rice and a soup made from boiled water and soy sauce—completely inadequate for the demands of the training program ahead of them.[16]

Sargent first had to address the basic nutrition and living conditions of the men. Immediately drawing on the U.S. military supply system, he obtained new uniforms and shoes, and put the men on a diet of three meals a day, including meat, vegetables, and eggs, and weekly vitamin tablets. To have adequate barracks, training facilities, and office space, he rented five abandoned small buildings a quarter of a mile away and a house in the nearby village, and he supervised an urgent renovation and construction program to prepare each building in the Project Eagle base. Constructing the base was a slow process that continued well into July.[17]

Lack of OSS personnel was a further problem throughout the summer. The presence of the OSS in China was so meager that of the fourteen Americans required under the Project Eagle plan, only Sargent was available in China in March 1945. New recruits to the OSS who were in training in the United States would have to fill the other positions. The hope was that they would arrive in China by the end of April.[18] They were slow to arrive, and at the end of May, Sargent had only himself and four other Americans—a first lieutenant to lead the training program; an intelligence specialist and a photographer, both junior enlisted men; and a civilian communications expert to set up the unit's communications equipment and train agents in the use of radios and codes.[19] In June two officers and an enlisted man arrived, but an officer and an enlisted man left for new assignments elsewhere.[20] For two months, this small group of no more than half a dozen Americans labored to build the base camp and start the training program.

Being at the end of a long supply line deep in the interior of China, the Project Eagle team also had to contend with lack of the support that U.S. military personnel were accustomed to having. In their isolated camp miles away from the center of the Xian base complex, they had only one truck assigned to them for the transportation needs of the entire Eagle force. Major Krause helped by lending them a jeep from the small motor pool of the Xian base complex. The team did not even have a cook assigned to it. At first they had borrowed an Army cook from the Xian base complex, but they soon lost him, forcing them to take turns spending time away from their primary duties to cook their own meals. They lived with this burden at a time when each man was already doing the work of several to make up for the personnel shortage.[21]

Compounding the problems of Project Eagle was a lack of basic language skills, A situation comparable to the Tower of Babel existed, with Korean, English, Japanese, and Chinese all necessary in the training program and the day-to-day functioning of the base, but few of the Americans and Koreans were able to speak more than one language or communicate with each other. At the end of May, there were no Americans who spoke Korean, and only twenty of the Koreans spoke any English. Sargent knew Mandarin and used it to speak with Yi Pomsok, who spoke all of the necessary languages except for English, which he was working on learning as his fifth language. One American private first class spoke Japanese and could communicate with Japanese-speaking Koreans. A fifth language spoken in the base was Russian, as Yi Pomsok had trained his German Shepherd to respond only to commands in Russian, which he had learned during his three years in exile in the Soviet Union.[22]

In the face of these difficulties, the Project Eagle training program began on May 21. Sargent set an ambitious schedule in which a first class would finish by mid-June and a second one by mid-July, each receiving a three-week crash course in knowledge and skills that they would need to operate in Korea. Of the 160 men assigned to the program by the Korean Restoration Army, 50 would be in the first training class and 50 would be in the second. The rest were 20 Korean Restoration Army officers assigned to the Project Eagle command staff and 40 extra men to be used as support personnel at the base.[23]

The Project Eagle training course compressed into three weeks a range of knowledge and tradecraft that should have occupied months of instruction and exercises. In eighteen days of instruction, the program ran through a long series of subjects in rapid succession: preparing intelligence reports, economic reporting, political reporting, psychological reporting, bombing damage reporting, topographic and beach reporting, coast watching and ship reporting, morale operations, airfield information, map reading and sketching; the Japanese order of battle, Japanese police and intelligence agencies, entry into Korea, cover stories, developing informants, interviewing procedures, recruiting and handling agents, organization, underground and resistance groups, intelligence communications, police methods and security, and airdrops. Radio instruction occupied two hours each day, to teach the essential skills of radio communications without which agents would be cut off from the outside world.[24] Project NAPKO had months to train its agents and well-prepared training facilities in California. Project Eagle had to rush its agents through three weeks of training followed by a week of field exercises in facilities still under construction.

Weapons training, primarily for personnel assigned to base security, also began in June. Reflecting the secondary priority of the China Theater, the weapons issued to Project Eagle were mostly superseded models no longer used in front-line service by the U.S. armed services. Instead of the M1 Garand semiautomatic rifle that was the standard U.S. infantry weapon, they had the M1903 Springfield bolt action rifle, obsolete and phased out years earlier, and the M1941 Johnson semiautomatic rifle, used by the Marine Corps early in the war and replaced by the M1 Garand.

For sidearms, they had .38 caliber and .45 caliber revolvers normally issued to noncombat personnel, instead of the standard-issue M1911A1 semiautomatic pistol. The Thompson submachine gun was available in small numbers, along with one Browning .30 caliber machine gun.[25]

In addition to training the men from the Korean Restoration Army, the Eagle team went to work on problems unique to the upcoming operation in Korea. One such problem of fundamental importance was codes for the Korean language. A code system would be essential for secure communications between the OSS in China and agents in Korea, but no code system suited to the Korean alphabet existed when Project Eagle began. Work on a code system appears to have occurred simultaneously at the beginning of June in both the Eagle base in Xian and OSS headquarters in China in Kunming. Project Eagle's civilian communications expert, William Scudder Georgia, already busy with radio training for the agents, worked on the problem, at the same time that Lt. Kim Woo Chun, the Imperial Japanese Army deserter turned Korean Restoration Army officer, worked on it in Kunming at the instruction of Clarence Weems.[26] A code system based on numerical substitution was ready by June 6, 1945. Compatible with the one time pad that the OSS used for encryption, this code system became the basis for communications by Project Eagle agents.[27]

Another key problem was transportation and communications between Xian and Korea. The distance from Xian to the nearest field point near Seoul was approximately 850 nautical miles (over 1,000 miles), and almost 1,100 nautical miles (over 1,250 miles) separated Xian from the furthest field point in northeastern Korea. These distances were beyond the ranges of both C-47 transport aircraft and the field radios issued to Eagle. Eagle's civilian communications expert worked out by early July that establishing a sub-base in territory controlled by Chinese guerillas in the Shandong Peninsula, far behind the Japanese front line, would reduce the distances to within the ranges of both the aircraft and radios—600 miles from Xian to the Shandong peninsula, with a final jump of 260 miles to the closest field point around Seoul or 500 miles to northeastern Korea. The sub-base would be less than 100 miles from where Clyde Sargent had once taught at Cheeloo University in Tsinan, the capital of Shandong Province.[28]

The Project Eagle team also came up with a plan for psychological operations in Korea. The Morale Operations branch representative with Eagle began to consider the problem in early July.[29] He soon had devised a plan called Boa, a far-reaching propaganda plan to foster support of Korean revolutionary activities, undermine Koreans collaborating with Japan, and affect the morale of Japanese residents of Korea, integrated with Morale Operations throughout the China Theater. It would rely on Yi Pomsok's Second Detachment of the Korean Restoration Army and its knowledge of Korea. The unit had a Propaganda Committee that would plan, write, and carry out morale operations for Project Eagle.[30]

As the Koreans and Americans of Project Eagle worked to prepare for their mission despite the shortages and language barriers, Clyde Sargent gained more insight into how years of adversity had shaped the men of the Korean Restoration Army under his command. They had been born and raised under Japanese rule, second-class subjects in their own country. Most of them had been separated from home for years, many as draftees in the Imperial Japanese Army, others after leaving Korea to live in the exile community in China. Whether forced to serve Japan or free but impoverished in exile, they then became pawns of Nationalist China in its long war against Japan. They had many reasons to be disillusioned and cynical, but Sargent found them eager to prepare for the mission. "I continue to be impressed by the caliber of our men, and they uniformly impress all visitors, which is a tribute to General [Yi]'s leadership of them," he wrote. "Discipline and morale are excellent, which is amazing in view of the way they have been pushed around in the past."[31]

The ability of the Koreans and the Americans to work together despite the differences between them and the language barrier further struck Sargent. He reported at the end of May that "a gratifying esprit de corps between Americans and Koreans is developing and should elevate the spirit of endeavor by Korean personnel of this Project. . . . This is possible largely because of the excellent esprit de corps General [Yi]has developed among his men, and because of his own personal qualities and energetic cooperation." He concluded, "I am convinced that the potentialities of this project are unlimited—except by the length of 'the duration' and by reinforcements of Korean personnel."[32]

Sargent was optimistic about the progress made by Eagle after the first training class was completed on June 25. The physical condition of the men was slow to improve, and Sargent observed, "It is unfortunate that the Physical Condition of the Students is not up to par but it is expected that after they have been on their present diet for a while, they will show a marked improvement. Prior to entering upon the Eagle Project, the diet of these men was extremely meager and the wonder is that they are not complete physical wrecks." Nevertheless, he found that their eagerness and ability to learn the skills required for Project Eagle made up for their physical limitations. "The Students are willing, cooperative and intelligent," he wrote. "Their motivation is of the highest and it is believed that they will be of invaluable assistance to the over-all Allied effort."[33]

By early July Sargent and the OSS training staff believed that Project Eagle would be able to meet its goal of having teams of agents ready to deploy to Korea within three months. A training conference on July 7 concluded that teams would be ready for operations by August 8 and that they would depart for Korea no later than August 15. There would be six teams of four, each consisting of three agents and a radio operator.[34]

As the OSS personnel originally planned for Project Eagle began to arrive in July, they gave Project Eagle a new character as a large contingent of Korean Americans arrived with them, making up half of the OSS staff by the beginning of August. Two were Army officers, among the few Korean Americans commissioned as officers during the war.[35] The first was 2nd Lt. Woon Sung Chung, an officer already serving in Chungking with the 308th Bombardment Group, a unit of B-24 Liberator bombers of the Fourteenth Air Force.[36] He arrived on July 7. Capt. Ryong Chyun Hahm arrived on July 29.

Hahm was a product of the American Protestant churches and universities of Korea, and before the war he had been both a Methodist minister and an activist for Korean independence. Born and educated in Korea, he studied at Korea University and Union College of Theology in Seoul.[37] He had worked as a criminal defense lawyer in Seoul between 1925 and 1929, then as a Methodist minister in Kaesong from 1929 to 1931, while Clarence Weems Sr. led the Methodist mission there. He emigrated to the United States for graduate religious studies at Vanderbilt and Yale and stayed, marrying an American from a town in Arkansas only thirty miles from Clarence Weems Sr.'s hometown of Conway.[38] For several years he had been an organizer of a group in the United States that supported Korean resistance against Japan.[39] A fluent speaker of Korean, Japanese, and Chinese, after the United States entered the war against Japan he taught East Asian languages at Harvard University, the U.S. Navy School of Military Government, and the Naval Reserve Midshipmen's School, then worked as a translator for the Office of Naval Intelligence in New York.[40]

The OSS identified Hahm as an ideal leader for its operation in Korea and almost made him the commanding officer of Project Eagle instead of Clyde Sargent. The OSS recruited him in October 1944 at the start of its search for an officer to lead Project Eagle. It first had him inducted into the army as an enlisted man in December 1944, then had him commissioned as a captain in February 1945. U.S. citizenship was necessary for his commissioning, so he became naturalized on January 2, 1945. The SI branch planned to make him the leader of Project Eagle, finding him uniquely matched to its needs, with extensive personal connections to leaders of the Korean Provisional Government and a history of activism against Japan.[41] He did not deploy from the United States to China until late June, however, and with Sargent already established as the commanding officer, Hahm became the intelligence officer.

An even more direct connection to the American Protestant churches of Korea also arrived in late July 1945. Horace Horton Underwood, son of the founder of Yonsei University in Seoul, came aboard as an intelligence analyst.[42] Already involved in planning the return of the Presbyterian Church to Korea for the Presbyterian Board for Foreign Mission in New York, in June 1945 he joined the OSS to deploy to China as a civilian expert on Korea.[43] Age fifty-four in 1945, he had joined the

OSS with his son, Richard, and within a few weeks the OSS rushed him to China to join Project Eagle while Richard joined Project NAPKO.[44] Project Eagle now included the head of the foremost American missionary family in Korea, who had stayed in Korea to the end in 1942 and was already leading the Presbyterian Church's campaign to return to Korea.

In August the character of the Eagle force changed further with the arrival of a large number of Korean American enlisted men. Nine Army privates arrived on August 1, all language specialists, and a corporal from OSS counterintelligence arrived on August 21.[45] They finally gave Project Eagle a substantial number of Americans who could communicate with Koreans and speak the other necessary languages. All nine of the arrivals on August 1 were fluent in English, Korean, and Japanese, and all knew Mandarin Chinese from childhood except for one whom the OSS sent to a Chinese language program at Yale University at its own expense.[46]

These twelve men represented a significant part of the first generation of Koreans who immigrated to the United States before 1941 and served in the Second World War. Eight were at least forty years old and only Army privates, the lowest ranking of enlisted men, recruited and inducted into the OSS in January and February 1945 specifically to serve as interpreters with Project Eagle. Despite their low military ranks, most were college graduates, and several had graduate-level educations. Even the youngest, the corporal, had three years of postgraduate study of biology before he enlisted. Before the war they had mostly worked in menial jobs despite their educations, finding few opportunities during the Great Depression and in an era when Asian Americans faced discrimination that excluded them from many occupations.[47] Wartime service in the U.S. Army was a new beginning for them, as it was for Japanese Americans who served during the war in the Japanese American 442nd Infantry Regiment or as interpreters. Several became U.S. citizens after their induction into the army, after over a decade of living as aliens.

Through the efforts of Clyde Sargent, Yi Pomsok, and the OSS training staff of Project Eagle, the Eagle force met its goal. By August 4 thirty-eight men had completed the training program and were considered ready for action. More were in training to add to their numbers, with ten men in

Xian waiting to start and eleven more newly arrived from Chungking.[48] Preparing this force in only three months in the face of adversity was an accomplishment that gave Project Eagle the opportunity to make a contribution to the defeat of Japan and the liberation of Korea.

In preparation for unleashing Project Eagle and other operations in China, OSS China Theater headquarters established new regional commands on August 1, 1945. OSS Southern Command covered China south of the Yangtze River and French Indochina. OSS Central Command included all of China north of the Yangtze River. A new OSS North Eastern Command, headquartered at Xian, would be responsible for Korea and the mainland of Japan.[49] The stage was set for OSS operations throughout Asia that would support the invasion of Japan and bring the war in the Pacific to an end.

Disunity among Allies

While Clyde Sargent, Yi Pomsok and their men labored in their remote base camp, events beyond their control conspired against them. From its beginning, Project Eagle faced problems created by the relationship between the United States and the Korean Provisional Government, by the Korean Provisional Government's relationship to Nationalist China, and by conflicts between the Allied powers. Division within the OSS and U.S. forces in the Pacific Theater also affected it, as other organizations competed for resources and authority. These issues threw complications at Project Eagle throughout its existence, and ultimately they would become Project Eagle's downfall.

Within the OSS, Project Eagle and Project NAPKO were preparing to conduct identical operations in Korea, differing only in their command authorities and their methods for deploying agents to Korea. Between them they split the limited pool of Koreans available to the OSS, with Project NAPKO having had first pick of those in the United States, and Project Eagle having the Korean Restoration Army. Project NAPKO secured the best men for the task, older men in their thirties and forties with the experience to operate in Japanese-occupied territory and who had family and social networks with which to work. Project Eagle had young men in their twenties, selected from ordinary enlisted men in the Korean Restoration Army, few of whom had confidence in their ability to operate in occupied Korea or the social stature to have useful networks.[50]

In addition to dividing the personnel and other assets available to the OSS, Project Eagle and Project NAPKO proceeded separately, loosely coordinated without sharing information or cooperating in their planning. OSS headquarters in Washington did not share the Project NAPKO plan with its China command until April 27, 1945, two months after the approval of the two projects, and the China command raised objections to the division of effort until mid-May.[51] Col. Richard Heppner, commander of OSS Detachment 202 in China, argued that Project NAPKO was a duplication of effort that could be better accomplished from China through Project Eagle's contacts with the Korean Provisional Government. Donovan responded that the OSS had to use every opportunity to penetrate such an important and difficult target as Korea and that it should take full advantage of Carl Eifler's genius as an operator.[52] Despite further objections from Heppner, based on the logistical burden of Project NAPKO, Donovan ordered that both projects should proceed, coordinated through the OSS China Theater command, subject to the approval of the commanding general in the China Theater, Albert Wedemeyer.[53] The Joint Chiefs of Staff and General Wedemeyer reaffirmed this order in August.[54]

The Korean side of the combined operation had its rivalries and internal divisions as well. Clyde Sargent observed them starting with his first meetings with the Korean Provisional Government on April 3. Kim Ku and Yi Pomsok dominated the relationship with the OSS, and the Korean Restoration Army's other main commander, Kim Hak Kyu of the Third Detachment in Anhui, resented his secondary role and insisted on including operations from his base in Anhui in Project Eagle. Sargent also found that the Korean Communists in Kim Ku's wartime coalition had not approved of Project Eagle and that they wanted an audience with General Wedemeyer to discuss it separately from the rest of the Korean Provisional Government.[55]

The relationship between the OSS and the Korean Provisional

Government was further complicated by the ambiguity of the U.S. attitude toward the Korean independence movement. The wartime relationship with the OSS came with no U.S. government official endorsement or declaration on Korean independence. With little reason to trust the newly established relationship with the OSS, the Korean Provisional Government withheld much of its own limited personnel and assets.

The asset whose emergence had contributed to the creation of Project Eagle—Korean deserters from the Imperial Japanese Army—was withheld from the beginning. The thirty-seven newly commissioned officers whom Clarence Weems had seen in Chungking on January 31, 1945 were at the top of the agenda when Sargent initiated Project Eagle at the beginning of April 1945. Sargent inspected them in the Korean settlement near Chungking and made securing their participation a high priority, recording that he was "greatly impressed. . . . Every member of the group appeared to be intelligent, alert, and keen. As a military group, it was the most intelligent group that I have seen, and the caliber I think would compare favorably with any group of young American officers." Most of them were college graduates, and several spoke passable English.[56] Despite Sargent's repeated requests, the entire spring and summer passed without them arriving to join Project Eagle. The Korean Provisional Government was unwilling to commit its best men to the combined operation, not trusting how the United States would use them.

Kim Ku and Yi Pomsok tried to persuade higher U.S. authorities to increase the independence and role of the Korean Restoration Army. Kim Ku and his foreign minister visited General Wedemeyer on April 17 to propose a plan for increased U.S.-Korean military cooperation and ask for additional U.S. military equipment and training.[57] The plan called for a U.S. amphibious landing in Korea to cut off Japanese forces in China from Japan, supported by an expanded Korean Restoration Army under U.S. command that would collect intelligence, sabotage enemy military installations, interrogate prisoners of war, win over Korean officers and enlisted men serving in the Imperial Japanese Army, and spread propaganda against Japan.[58] It was a proposal with no chance of being accepted, given the lack of any plan for a landing in Korea in U.S.

plans for the invasion of Japan. Yi Pomsok bypassed Sargent to make demands directly to Sargent's superior, the head of the OSS's SI branch in China, Col. Paul Helliwell. When Helliwell visited the Project Eagle camp in mid-June, Yi Pomsok submitted a list of requests that included direct access to OSS headquarters in China.[59] Like Kim Ku's proposal for a larger combined military operation, Yi Pomsok's requests had no chance of being accepted.

The late arrival of the United States in supporting the Korean Provisional Government further complicated relations by compelling the OSS to deal with preexisting relationships that the Koreans had with Nationalist China and the British Empire. With Nationalist China having worked with the Korean Provisional Government since 1932, Chiang Kai-shek's intelligence chief, Maj. Gen. Tai Li, viewed it and other Korean exile groups as Chinese assets and was determined to maintain Chinese control over them. The British had used Koreans as intelligence personnel in its army in Burma for almost two years since September 1943, and they were similarly interested in maintaining their claim over Koreans in China. Throughout its existence Project Eagle would have to contend with Chinese and British schemes aimed at undermining cooperation between the Koreans and the Americans.

Allegations of a plot by Chinese intelligence to assassinate Yi Pomsok hung over Project Eagle at its beginning. On April 5, during the initial meetings between Clyde Sargent and the Korean Provisional Government, Yi told Sargent of the discovery by Korean intelligence of a plot by Tai Li to provoke a Korean living in Hong Kong to assassinate him. Chinese intelligence had informed the young man that Yi Pomsok had ordered his father's death several years earlier, which actually had been at the hands of Chinese intelligence, and assisted his travel to Chungking to kill Yi Pomsok in retaliation. If successful, the assassination would have disrupted the start of OSS-Korean cooperation while allowing Tai Li to deny any involvement. Whether this alleged plot actually existed appears to have been unconfirmed, but the existence of the allegation indicates that considerable tension existed between the Korean Provisional Government and its previous Nationalist Chinese patron.[60]

Tai Li definitely did make other attempts to subvert the OSS-Korean chain of command. Using connections that dated back many years, Tai Li conducted talks with Yi Pomsok and other Korean leaders to influence them behind the scenes.[61] As a further inducement making up for earlier Nationalist Chinese neglect of the Korean Restoration Army, he created a new military training center for Koreans in Chengdu, as an alternative to OSS support and Project Eagle.[62] At least one OSS officer, Maj. Quentin Roosevelt, believed that Yi was working for both.[63] Project Eagle had to contend with this atmosphere of rumor and intrigue.

A British and Chinese attempt to storm through the front gate of the Project Eagle compound followed. On the morning of May 26, a British Army colonel with the British military mission in Chungking visited the compound, accompanied by a Nationalist Chinese general. With a "rude and obnoxious" attitude, the British colonel "stamped through the compound" demanding to interrogate Koreans who had recently arrived after deserting from the Japanese Army, but Korean officers refused his demands.[64] Clyde Sargent ordered the British and Chinese officers to leave, and his superiors backed his decision.[65] OSS China Theater Command instructed the British not to approach OSS compounds without authorization from Wedemeyer's headquarters and ordered Sargent not to admit any Allied personnel to any compound except with orders from China Theater headquarters.[66]

This intrusion was one of numerous British and Chinese attempts to penetrate U.S. intelligence operations and installations in China. They included British offers in June to transfer Korean personnel under their control to the OSS, in order to infiltrate Project Eagle.[67] Tai Li attempted in late July to send an officer on an official visit with gifts to the Project Eagle compound to collect information.[68] These attempts continued throughout the summer of 1945.

All of this intrigue was over the 100,000 young Koreans in the war in China, most of them in the Imperial Japanese Army, but with increasing numbers wandering as deserters across the vast no-man's land deep in the interior of China. They were a valuable source of manpower for each of the major powers in the pursuit of its war aims against Japan, and there was a race to find and recruit them as groups appeared all along the front. At one point in mid-July, Project Eagle learned of a group of fifty-three Korean deserters in Hunan Province, more than six hundred miles away from Xian, along with two other possible groups in Hunan. Sargent requested that a nearby oss officer investigate these reported groups and made arrangements to transport them by air to Xian for screening and possible recruitment into Project Eagle.[69] Efforts by oss and Korean Restoration Army officers to locate and recruit them went on through the end of July and brought in eighty-three men.[70] Men like them were the prize in the game between U.S., Chinese, and British intelligence, and at stake for them was whether they would have the opportunity to fight for their own cause with the Korean Restoration Army and Project Eagle or for the interests of the British Empire or Nationalist China.

Alliance Confirmed: The Donovan Visit to Project Eagle

After an entire summer of preparation and training and of inter-Allied disputes, Project Eagle received validation of its significance when oss director William Donovan traveled to China to observe demonstrations of Project Eagle in Xian and endorse the mission just before it began its operations in Korea. It was one of three visits to China by Donovan during the war. The first in December 1943 and the second in January 1945 had been to work out the oss role in Asia with the government of Nationalist China and with U.S. Army, Navy, and State Department leaders in China. Donovan visited China in August 1945 for a tour of the many operations that the oss had established since January. His inspection of Project Eagle signaled his approval of the U.S.-Korean combined operation that he had sought since the first days after the attack on Pearl Harbor, whose origins stretched back to his observations during his travels through Japan, Korea, and China on his way to Siberia in June 1919.

Donovan arrived in Xian on August 7, after several days of meetings with Chiang Kai-shek and oss leaders in Chungking. Kim Ku and other leaders of the Korean Provisional Government also flew from Chungking to Xian for the occasion in a Fourteenth Air Force transport plane. It would be the first and only meeting between Donovan and Kim, who each by his actions had unknowingly influenced the other from the opposite side of the Pacific Ocean, for a quarter of a century since the March First Movement of 1919.

Their meeting began with a conference at the headquarters of the Korean Restoration Army's Second Detachment. They sat on opposite sides of a stage, with the Stars and Stripes at the left front behind Donovan and his officers, and the *taegukgi* flag of Korea at the right front behind Kim Ku, Yi Pomsok, Li Chong Chon, and other Korean Provisional Government officials. It was the first time in history that senior leaders of the United States and Korea had met officially under their respective flags. At the end Donovan rose and declared the beginning of cooperation between the United States and the Korean Provisional Government for secret operations against their common enemy, and Donovan and Kim Ku exited side by side with cameras recording the moment.

After Donovan departed Xian, a day of tactical demonstrations by Project Eagle agents followed, showcasing the training that they had received. At the Project Eagle base, Kim Ku and other Korean Provisional Government leaders observed tests of marksmanship, use of explosives, descending and climbing cliffs, river crossings, and other skills. The next day they returned to Xian, satisfied with the progress of Project Eagle and the readiness of their men for their upcoming covert mission in Korea.

Precisely what William Donovan and Kim Ku each thought about the other during their meeting will never be known, since neither recorded his thoughts for posterity, but their actions afterward showed that each came away from the experience with a new understanding of the significance of the U.S.-Korean combined action that they had set in motion. In the weeks that followed, while back in Washington dealing with issues worldwide created by the end of the war, Donovan made Korea and the Korean Provisional Government a higher priority than at any other time since he dispatched the Esson Gale mission to China in early 1942. Kim Ku and the Korean Provisional Government immediately set aside their earlier caution in dealing with Project Eagle and the OSS and now offered their complete cooperation, free of the limitations that they had imposed since the beginning.

Kim Ku and Korean Restoration Army commanders moved rapidly after the Donovan visit to deepen their relationship with the OSS and concentrate their resources and efforts in Project Eagle. On August 10 Kim Ku and a delegation that included Li Chong Chon returned to the base complex at Xian to offer their unqualified support for Project Eagle. Project Eagle would now receive first priority in the selection of personnel from all available Koreans in China, including the thirty-seven officers who had been withheld in Chungking since January. Moreover, they now offered complete access to all intelligence possessed by the Korean Provisional Government from its intelligence network across northern China, Manchuria, and Korea, delivering intelligence reports that they had withheld all year. They also gave a guarantee of noninterference by opposition elements within the Korean Provisional Government. With these new terms, cooperation between the OSS and the Korean Restoration Army was ready to reach a higher level.[71]

Yi Pomsok and Li Chong Chon had a further meeting with Clyde Sargent later that day at 9:00 p.m. in which they talked for two hours to expand the terms for cooperation. Li offered the complete subordination of the Korean Restoration Army to the U.S. military, with all Korean personnel suitable for intelligence operations to be sent to Project Eagle and all others to be centralized in China, the Philippines or Okinawa to be trained under American officers to fight as guerillas in support of an American amphibious landing in Korea. Li, as commander in chief, would personally accompany the OSS team sent to recruit and screen Korean personnel for Project Eagle, to ensure the cooperation of the entire Korean Restoration Army.[72]

For Yi Pomsok and Clyde Sargent, the discussions on August 10 were a continuation of conversations that they had had throughout the summer about Project Eagle and its place in the long-term future relationship of Korea and the United States. Yi Pomsok had for thirty years lived in exile in a hopeless armed struggle against Japan, searching for an ally first in the Soviet Union and then in Nationalist China, and Project Eagle now offered the hope that Korea and the United States would become partners in Asia. It harkened back to the hopes of King Kojong when he signed the first treaty between Korea and the United States in 1882. Neither Yi nor Sargent had been part of the earlier experience of Koreans and Americans together in the churches, schools, and universities of the American missions in Korea, but they were now the leaders of a new stage in the history of the two nations together.

Yi had repeatedly expressed to Sargent the importance of Project Eagle to Korea and to the U.S. role in postwar Asia. "It is true that the plan for our cooperation is for the present," Yi wrote in one instance. "However, it has been my personal belief from the first that although our cooperation is born of present necessity, out of our cooperation will grow American-Korean international cooperation. I am confident that the Koreans will make a great contribution with Americans in the general attack on Japan, and with Korean support the efforts of the United States on the Asiatic Continent will be long effective in world history." Sargent had to emphasize to Yi that the mission of Project Eagle was intelligence as part of the current war, not influencing postwar Korea.[73] Nevertheless, both men were aware of the historic nature of the mission that they were commanding, and after the hard work of the summer and the approval of their higher leadership, the future appeared promising for the fledgling relationship. Within a few days Project Eagle agents would begin their deployment to Korea overland, by sea, and by air, bringing Koreans into the war against Imperial Japan and beginning the liberation of Korea.

6

Lost Crusade

The End of Project Eagle

The fate of Project Eagle, and with it the entire emerging U.S.-Korea relationship, changed when the atomic bombs dropped on Japan. They struck Hiroshima on August 6 and Nagasaki on August 9, and on August 15 Japan announced its surrender, ending the war in Asia. The Allied invasion of Japan now became unnecessary, and so was Project Eagle's operation in Korea in support of the invasion. The liberation of Korea now was imminent and expected to be bloodless, without any need for Koreans to participate in a military campaign. Suddenly Project Eagle and cooperation between the OSS and the Korean Provisional Government lost their original purpose.

A new menace appeared at the same time from the Soviet Union. On August 9 the Soviet Union declared war on Japan and launched an invasion of Manchuria with a vast force of more than 1.5 million men and 5,500 tanks, which rapidly swept through the weak forces of the Imperial Japanese Army that remained in Manchuria. The Red Army crossed the China-Korea border within two days and at the same time landed naval infantry on Korea's east coast. On August 24 the Red Army reached Pyongyang. Soviet occupation of northern Korea occurred with the agreement of the United States, which had offered the 38th Parallel as an arbitrary boundary between postwar U.S. and Soviet occupation zones almost without thought, based on a cursory look at a National Geographic map by two colonels in the Pentagon.[1]

The Soviet forces included a thirty-three-year old major in the Red Army named Kim Il Sung. He had left Korea with his parents in 1920 as an eight-year-old, and in 1945 he returned as an officer in the army of the Soviet Union. He would become the leader of the Communist regime that the Soviet Union installed in Pyongyang and northern Korea. The division of Korea with a Communist regime ruling the north, which has defined much of the modern history of Korea, had begun.

The End of the War in Asia

The atomic bombings and the surrender of Japan caused the OSS to move rapidly to secure U.S. and Nationalist Chinese interests in territory from which the Japanese forces were withdrawing. Far from ending OSS operations in China, the Soviet advance into Manchuria and Korea compelled the OSS to move faster. On August 10 Colonel Heppner quickly informed Director Donovan and General Wedemeyer's headquarters that there would be immediate operations in Japanese-occupied China and Korea.[2] They would include parachuting commando teams into key Chinese cities to secure U.S. and Nationalist Chinese interests and raid Japanese headquarters for intelligence, airlifting teams into Manchuria to be on the ground ahead of the Soviet forces, and flying teams to strategic locations in Korea before Soviet occupation.[3]

By August 15 the OSS had organized nine operations whose missions were to locate and evacuate Allied prisoners of war and interned civilians and to conduct intelligence operations, from Manchuria and Korea in the north to Vietnam and Laos in the south. Each operation used a bird code name: Cardinal, to Mukden; Flamingo, to Harbin; Magpie, to Beijing; Duck, to Weihsien; Sparrow, to Shanghai; Pigeon, to Hainan Island; Quail, to Hanoi; Raven, to Vientiane; and Eagle, to Seoul.

Most of these missions were successful, liberating thousands of prisoners of war and civilians and making significant intelligence contacts. At Weihsien, on the Shandong Peninsula, seven OSS agents with Operation Duck parachuted from a B-24 bomber and liberated over 1,400 civilians from an internment camp. Operation Cardinal parachuted five OSS agents and a Chinese interpreter into the POW camp at Mukden and rescued 1,600 POWs, just ahead of the arrival of Soviet forces. Operation Magpie rescued 624 POWs; Operation Pigeon, over 400. Operation Quail became the most famous of the missions, as it landed at the Hanoi airport and observed the Vietnamese Communists' seizure of Hanoi, its men witnessing the start of the thirty years of wars in Vietnam fought first by France to maintain its colonial empire in Indochina, then by the United States to preserve a non-Communist South Vietnam. These missions became part of the postwar lore of the OSS, their stories retold as some of the agency's greatest successes.

Operation Eagle became the most troubled of the missions from its outset. Unlike the other operations that used teams of Americans assembled specifically for the mission, Operation Eagle derived from Project Eagle and therefore included the Korean Restoration Army. The OSS leadership knew that the Korean Provisional Government and its army would be significant to postwar Korea, but how the OSS and the U.S. government would relate to them after the war was unclear. The OSS was far ahead of the rest of the U.S. government in its relationship with the Korean Provisional Government, and the international politics of postwar Korea were unclear in Washington, Chungking, and Xian.

For the Korean Provisional Government, the end of the war was a tragedy. It prematurely ended their years of effort to participate in fighting the war alongside the Allies and secure a voice in the postwar handling of Korea. Kim Ku remembered the end of the war as "disastrous news," meaning that "all of our preparations of the past several years to fight in the War came to nothing. . . . What worried me the most was that we would be able to exercise little clout in future international negotiations deciding the fate of our country, given that we contributed little to the victory in this War." He recalled that "our Restoration Army was in a dejected mood at the War's end, whereas the American trainers and soldiers were leaping all over in so much joy."[4] Kim Woo Chun, the young lieutenant with the Third Detachment in Anhui, remembered the end of the war similarly. In his autobiography half a century later, he recalled sadness at not being able to fight for their own cause and concern about Korea's future.[5]

While the leaders of the Korean Provisional Government and the Korean Restoration Army were disappointed by the loss of their opportunity to join the war, many if not most of the common soldiers who would have carried out operations in Korea must have been relieved by the cancellation of their mission. An indication of their attitudes comes from an assessment by an OSS psychologist concluded in early August, which found fear of the mission to be widespread. The assessment rejected eleven of the forty men that it reviewed, with most of the eleven and half a dozen others found to be so afraid of operating in Japanese-controlled territory that they should not be deployed to Korea.[6] Those men would have been thankful to have avoided the mission and survived the war, and many of the others must have felt the same.

Disappointment over the missed opportunity and relief at avoiding the mission and surviving were only initial reactions to the end of the war, however, and the leaders of the Korean Provisional Government understood that they needed to look ahead to postwar Korea and in particular at preventing Communists installed by the Soviet Union from taking over the country. Disputes with Korean Communist factions dated back to the earliest years after the founding of the Korean Provisional Government in 1919, and the wartime government had been a coalition with Communists assembled by Kim Ku after years of argument and negotiation. The advance of Soviet forces into Korea in August 1945, far ahead of the arrival of any U.S. forces, made a Communist takeover likely.

Yi Pomsok knew the threat better than anyone in the Korean Provisional Government and probably better than anyone in the United States, and he tried to persuade U.S. leaders to take immediate action. Two decades earlier Yi had seen the Soviet Union firsthand when he sought refuge there and lived in the country for three years. For twenty years since then Yi had experienced conflict with Chinese and Korean Communists as an officer in the Nationalist Chinese Army and then as a general of the Korean Restoration Army. Immediately after the announcement of the surrender of Japan, he urged the OSS and the U.S. military command in the China Theater to work with the Korean Provisional Government to enter Korea as soon as possible. He foresaw an upcoming conflict between the Soviet Union and the United States in Asia and the need to act immediately to protect U.S. interests in the region and the independence of Korea. Establishing a presence in Korea as soon as possible would be necessary to prevent the advancing Soviet forces and the Korean Communists from seizing control.[7]

Operation Eagle went to Korea with these issues of crucial importance to Korea and entire postwar world hanging over it. They brought intractable political problems into an already complicated military mission that would prove to be the most difficult of the nine postwar rescue missions of the OSS in Asia.

Operation Eagle

Planning for Operation Eagle began immediately after the dropping of the atomic bombs on Hiroshima and Nagasaki and the start of the Soviet invasion of Manchuria. On August 10 Project Eagle received orders from OSS China Theater headquarters to prepare to deploy teams of agents with radios to Korea within two weeks, with Sargent held personally responsible for carrying out the order. The orders revealed little about their purpose, referring only vaguely to "recent war developments" making the operation necessary.[8] On August 14 headquarters revealed the purposes of the operation. The primary mission would be to contact Allied prisoners of war and give them aid and comfort until relieved. The secondary mission would be intelligence collection, followed by planning for a postwar intelligence network in Korea and the organization of an OSS headquarters where reinforcements could be sent.[9]

Operation Eagle faced the same daunting problem of distance and aircraft range that Project Eagle had attempted to resolve. Operation Eagle had to fly over 1,000 miles to reach Seoul from Xian, more than twice the flight distance of most of the operations. Operation Cardinal covered a similar distance in its flight to Mukden, but it parachuted from a B-24 Liberator bomber, one of the longest-ranged aircraft in the U.S. inventory, equipped with extra fuel tanks to give it the range to make the round-trip. For the flight to Seoul, Operation Eagle received only a C-47 transport aircraft with no special equipment, with a maximum range of

1,600 miles, which was not enough to fly to Seoul and return. Project Eagle had planned to create a base at a forward airstrip in the Shandong Peninsula to refuel C-47s on their way to Korea, but it had not yet done so. Operation Eagle would have to improvise and hope that somehow it would be able to obtain extra fuel along the way—a risk that could leave the mission stranded and result in death or captivity for its team.

The situation that the mission would face on the ground in Seoul was equally formidable. Operation Eagle would land a small group of men armed only with their personal weapons, on territory that had been part of the Japanese Empire for thirty-five years, before any U.S. attempt to land in Japan itself. The other OSS operations were venturing into occupied territories in China and Southeast Asia where the Japanese forces were in retreat. Previous landings on territory of the Japanese Empire had been the amphibious operations on Okinawa and Iwo Jima that resulted in long, costly battles. Whether Operation Eagle would be met by Japanese forces willing to cooperate, or by a force eager to destroy a small U.S. incursion into their territory before their country's formal surrender, would not be known until the mission arrived in Seoul.

A nearly complete lack of intelligence about the prisoner of war camps in Korea was a further problem for Operation Eagle. Aerial reconnaissance of Korea was limited, and little human intelligence was available. Operation Eagle received information that as many as seven POW camps existed in Korea, but their locations and the numbers and nationalities of the people held in them were unknown. Even this minimal information turned out to have been grossly incorrect after the war, when U.S. forces found that there were only three camps, located near Seoul, Inchon, and Hungnam. Operation Eagle would have to locate and learn about the camps from scratch after landing in Korea, and it would be possible only with Japanese cooperation.

As if Operation Eagle were not already difficult enough, it became even more complicated when the commander changed just before it departed. On August 14 Colonel Heppner relieved Sargent of command over the mission, stating that Director Donovan was displeased with Eagle's lack of action and had sent a direct order to replace him. Donovan had a habit of shaking up commands after visiting OSS stations, spontaneously deciding to promote or demote officers after briefly meeting them in the field, and Sargent's command over Project Eagle and Operation Eagle became one of them. Heppner put his deputy, Lt. Col. Willis Bird, in command instead. The change had been coming since the first orders for Operation Eagle, as Heppner had sent Bird to Xian to plan and lead the mission to Korea on August 11 without officially relieving Sargent.[10] Sargent remained with Operation Eagle only to support the mission under Bird's command.[11] With Operation Eagle about to send Koreans and Americans from Project Eagle on a risky mission to Korea, the commander of the mission would be an officer with little familiarity with Yi Pomsok or anyone in Project Eagle and no knowledge of Korea.

Bird was an especially questionable choice to command Operation Eagle. Before the war he had worked for Sears, Roebuck's mail order business in Chicago, and during the war he was an Army ordnance officer, originally transferred to the OSS in February 1944 to serve as a supply officer in China—hardly experience relevant to commanding a politically complicated intelligence operation.[12] Bird's most significant independent action before Operation Eagle had been clandestine OSS negotiations with the Chinese Communists in December 1944, in which he had offered them generous OSS support including weapons and training. The offer had not been authorized by the OSS or the State Department, and it caused a diplomatic firestorm between the United States and Nationalist China and between General Wedemeyer and the U.S. ambassador in China, over the apparent attempt to bypass both the State Department and the government of Nationalist China and directly support the Chinese Communists.[13] Bird's failure to follow his orders and the controversy that it caused should have been a warning of his unsuitability to command Operation Eagle.[14]

The OSS China Theater command considered the Korean Provisional Government and Yi Pomsok in particular to be of fundamental importance to the operation, and Bird should have understood it. On the day when he replaced Sargent with Bird, Colonel Heppner sent Bird a priority message explaining the OSS relationship with the Korean Provisional

Government and its significance to the postwar world. It stated that the Korean Provisional Government was certain to become an important part of the postwar government of an independent Korea, with its strategic location next to Manchuria and Russia, so good relations with it were essential. Bird was to give maximum consideration to Yi Pomsok and treat him as a partner rather than a subordinate. Sargent, Captain Ryong Chyun Hahm, and other Project Eagle personnel with their knowledge and experience of Korea also would be essential and would have to be used as much as possible. Heppner emphasized the necessity of the "utmost tact" in working with Koreans as the first Americans to enter Korea, as "our actions will have much bearing on whether the United States, Russia, or Britain have [the] dominating role in that area and much bearing on our post war establishment there."[15]

The final plan for Operation Eagle that emerged from five days of frantic activity, a change in command, and the announcement of the surrender of Japan was a daring gamble. An initial plan on August 12 followed the original Project Eagle concept of operations, calling for air-dropping three small teams of four men each by parachute into the Seoul area, with a contingency plan for a sudden end to the war instead having a C-47 with as many men as it could carry fly to Seoul and attempt to land at an airfield.[16] After the announcement of the surrender of Japan on August 15, the C-47 landing became the plan. With enough range for only a one-way trip from Xian to Seoul, the mission would take a chance that the Japanese would be willing and able to provide aviation fuel for the return flight. The crew of the C-47 consisted of volunteers who were willing to accept the mission's risks. Once on the ground, Operation Eagle would attempt to get information from the Japanese military command about the POW camps and gain access to them.[17]

Twenty men boarded the initial flight to Seoul with Operation Eagle. There were ten from the OSS: Bird, commanding the mission; Maj. Oswald Stewart, Bird's deputy; and eight from Project Eagle—Sargent, Capt. Ryong Chyun Hahm, Lt. Woon Sung Chung, Capt. Albert Evans, Lt. Evan Koger, Navy Photographic Specialist 1st Class Frank Hobbs, Pvt. Sang Pok Surh, and Project Eagle's civilian communications expert,

William Scudder Georgia. Yi Pomsok went with three of his officers from the Korean Restoration Army. The C-47 crew of six men completed the Operation Eagle team.[18]

For Yi Pomsok, the flight to Seoul must have been a long awaited moment, but one filled with mixed feelings. He had left Korea thirty years earlier as a fifteen-year-old, and now he was finally returning for the first time. He was doing it in an American military airplane, with the most powerful armed force in the world, in a mission that was an early indication of the interest of the OSS and the United States in countering Soviet influence in Korea. He would have been acutely aware that he was participating in a hastily organized and risky operation under the command of an unfamiliar officer with little experience in Asia, however, with Sargent, his trusted co-commander, demoted to little more than a handler for him and his officers. The status of the Korean Restoration Army would have been a significant concern as well. As Colonel Heppner had emphasized in his orders to Bird, arriving as an independent Korean force and not merely as subordinates to the United States would have been essential in the Korean Restoration Army's first foray into Korea. Photographs of Yi and his officers during Operation Eagle show that they wore their own uniforms instead of the U.S. uniforms issued to them for Project Eagle, to demonstrate that they were going as representatives of the Korean Restoration Army and the Korean Provisional Government.[19]

Bird appeared to be unconcerned with political nuances despite Colonel Heppner's orders, however. In his last message to Heppner before the start of the mission, he bragged about his personal influence over the Koreans and showed little thought about the political situation. "Most KPG realize that I was almost first to give them concrete foothold with U.S. when they were having trouble," he wrote on August 15, apparently referring to the contact with the Korean Provisional Government that Clarence Weems had made for him in February 1945. He made the unlikely claim that his presence made the Koreans willing to participate in the operation, stating, "That is reason appeal to General [Yi] for action received prompt acceptance." He concluded, "Should

Russians beat us it will be a nice ride and we are there to look after PW's [prisoners of war] officially. . . . Everything now depends on plane and peace. Should Korean Japs not be aware of events it was nice to know you all. Regards."[20]

Operation Eagle assembled at the Xian airfield and took off at 4:00 a.m. on August 16 for what was to be a six-hour flight to Seoul. At the halfway point, though, the C-47's radioman picked up radio broadcasts indicating that Japanese aircraft were still attacking U.S. ships, fighting was continuing in Manchuria, riots were occurring in Korea, and that the Emperor of Japan had broadcast an appeal to keep Americans out of Japanese homeland waters until word of the cease-fire could be given to all commands of the Imperial Japanese Army. Bird decided to abort the mission and return to base rather than risk continuing all the way to Seoul.[21]

Back in Xian, Bird prepared for a second attempt to fly to Seoul. First, another airplane had to be found because the mission's C-47 damaged one of its wing tips beyond repair while taxiing on the ground, delaying the operation by another day to August 18. Bird also requested that this time China Theater headquarters broadcast by radio to the Imperial Japanese forces in Korea that the mission was coming and why, but this request was denied. He also changed the team with the addition of two more members. One was Captain Teel from the Air Ground Aid Section, the organization in China responsible for the rescue of downed pilots, which George McCune's brother-in-law Max Becker had helped to create in 1943. He was an appropriate addition to a team flying into hostile territory to find and aid prisoners of war. The other was less appropriate, a civilian war correspondent named Henry Lieberman from the Office of War Information (OWI).

The OWI was a large and influential wartime U.S. government agency, largely forgotten after the war, that operated in China as part of its worldwide role of providing information to civilians in the United States and abroad. In the United States, it created radio programs and collaborated with Hollywood in producing films about the war. To reach foreign audiences, it founded an official broadcasting service, Voice of America. In Europe and Asia, OWI conducted psychological warfare and propaganda operations, with a significant presence in China. During preparations for Operation Eagle, OWI demanded that the OSS take a war correspondent on its mission to Korea, claiming authorization from the Pentagon. The OSS China Theater did not object to the demand, but it laid down that the war correspondent could not go on the first flight, which was fully loaded.²² Bird made room for the OWI war correspondent on the flight without first clearing the move with theater command. It was an attempt by Bird to make himself famous with a press release about his daring mission into enemy territory, and a few days later it would put him and Operation Eagle into serious trouble.

The second attempt took off at 5:30 a.m. on August 18. This time the team took the initiative to announce its arrival to the Imperial Japanese forces, with radio transmissions announcing the purpose of the mission and its intent to land at a military airfield in Seoul and requesting landing instructions. Captain Hahm made the announcements in Japanese, beginning at 9:15 a.m. with the flight approximately four hundred miles from Korea and repeating every fifteen minutes, with the destination becoming forty miles closer each time. He repeated the message nine times, and the flight closed to less than one hundred miles from Seoul with no response. With only half an hour of flight time to Seoul remaining, contact finally occurred at 11:40 a.m., and it came not on the radio but in the form of a Japanese fighter, approaching the C-47 from head on. After what must have been a tense wait to see what would happen, with the fighter easily able to shoot the unarmed and unarmored C-47 out of the sky, the fighter swerved out of the C-47's path, and there was a radio transmission from the fighter in Japanese. Its pilot stated that the mission was expected from its radio broadcasts, and the Japanese forces would guarantee a safe landing. The C-47 descended to land at an airfield near Seoul that later became Kimpo Airport.

The airfield was filled with Japanese military aircraft, and the Operation Eagle team found themselves surrounded by Japanese troops. There to meet them was the commander of the Japanese forces in Korea, Lt. Gen. Yoshio Kotsuki, with his chief of staff, Maj. Gen. Junichiro Ihara, their presence showing that the Japanese expected that the plane would be carrying a mission of great importance. Bird exited the C-47 and approached Kotsuki, speaking with him through Captain Hahm, attempting to explain that they had flown to Korea to aid Allied prisoners of war and make a survey to help prepare for their future evacuation when the Allied occupation force arrived. Kotsuki and Ihara expressed amazement at the mission, stating that they had received no advance notice until the radio transmissions from the flight a few hours earlier, and they had expected that the mission would be the advance party of an occupation force and sent to negotiate surrender terms. Kotsuki then had the Operation Eagle team escorted under guard from their airplane to a hangar, where his discussion with Bird continued.

The discussion in the hangar was completely unproductive, as the Japanese were unprepared and had nothing to say about the POW camps. Kotsuki told Bird that they should not have come and that for them to stay would be dangerous, because he could not guarantee them safety from his troops. He told Bird that they should leave immediately and that he could not give him any information about the POWs in Korea except that he should convey to General Wedemeyer that they were safe and in good hands and were being properly taken care of. Bird attempted to discuss the situation further, but Kotsuki ordered that Bird and the Operation Eagle team be escorted under guard to a more remote part of the airfield, away from the airfield's operations.

Kotsuki then continued the discussion with Bird, but only about the terms of Operation Eagle's withdrawal. Bird pointed out that they could not leave even if they wanted because they had no gasoline for a return flight to China, and he suggested that they could be held in custody until Kotsuki received instructions from his government that would permit visiting the POW camps. Kotsuki responded that his forces would provide gasoline but that he would not request any instructions from his government. When Bird informed him that the C-47 needed 100 octane gasoline, it created another problem, as he received the response that there was none available at the airfield because Japanese aircraft used lower octane fuel. After some discussion, Kotsuki's officers informed Bird that 100 octane gasoline would be brought in the following day and he and his team would be permitted to remain overnight. A staff officer, Col. Hisao Shibuda, told Bird that he and his men would receive billets for the night and an evening meal.[23]

With the discussions concluded and the status of Operation Eagle decided, Bird asked Colonel Shibuda to have a radio transmission sent to General Wedemeyer's headquarters informing them of the mission's arrival in Korea and the Japanese demand that it leave. Bird received permission to send only a message censored by the Japanese command, with the transmission to be monitored and stopped immediately if any part of it changed from the censored script. The message ended up delivering Bird's report with comical-sounding praise of Japanese cooperativeness. "Arrived safely with friendly and helpful attitude from Japanese command. They state all prisoners of war and civilians are safe and no need to be concerned. Due to fact that there are as yet no instructions from their government our presence embarrassing and they suggest we return China and come back later. We will stay night and return tomorrow with gasoline they have been kind enough to provide." It concluded briefly, "Would like to return on mission when formal peace signed." Due to difficulty establishing radio contact with Xian over a thousand miles away, the message did not transmit until 3:00 a.m.[24]

Colonel Heppner in Kunming and Director Donovan in Washington were eagerly awaiting news. When Heppner received Bird's message from the station in Xian, he immediately forwarded it by radio to Donovan in Washington. Heppner had Xian relay a response to Bird that gave him some freedom of action but urged him to remain in Seoul. "Use your own judgment. However if possible stay until we can get guidance from higher authority. Keep in frequent touch with us and give full details regarding prisoners and camp."[25]

In the evening, the Japanese brought the twenty-two Americans and Koreans to their quarters for the night. They received five rooms in a house on the airbase, where they were to stay under armed guard. Colonel Shibuda rejoined them later with an aide, Maj. Hideo Uyeda, and they took Bird aside to one of the rooms for a conference. Bird claimed in his official after-action report that it lasted for three hours, with him repeatedly explaining the mission and requesting permission to visit the POW camps, which Shibuda refused politely but firmly. Shibuda ended the conference with a request to join the senior members of the party in their quarters for dinner, as he wanted to meet them and carry on the discussion. Bird stated in his report, "This was done and after a late dinner the mission retired at approximately 2300 on the 18th of August."[26]

What Bird did not state in his report was how friendly Colonel Shibuda and Major Uyeda turned out to be, and the conduct of the men under his command during their dinner with the Japanese officers. Shibuda and Uyeda livened up the dinner by having enlisted men bring in bottles of Kirin beer and large amounts of sake. Presumably after several rounds of drinks, Major Uyeda asked for the name of the U.S. Air Force song, and in response there was a chorus of "Off We Go into the Wild Blue Yonder" led by the flight commander, Capt. John Wagoner. Uyeda smiled, beating time on the table with his fingers, and responded by singing the Japanese Air Force song.[27] As a spontaneous moment of friendliness between enemies at the end of a long and terrible war, it was understandable, but not reporting it would end up becoming yet another in a series of mistakes during the mission by Bird.

In the morning, there was a long wait in their quarters for the promised gasoline to arrive that stretched into the afternoon, and a tense standoff with the Japanese forces resulted. Bird's own account described a comedy of errors as he repeated his demands of the previous day to one Japanese officer after another of steadily decreasing rank. First, Lieutenant General Kotsuki stopped by, but excused himself and left after Bird again asked him about visiting the POW camps. Colonel Shibuda returned later in the morning and left after Bird demanded that he take to the top of both the military and civilian chains of command the request to stay in custody in Seoul and visit the camps. A major approached an hour later and conveyed Shibuda's response that the Japanese governor and commanding general both were aware of the mission and refused to receive it. Bird then demanded that the major send back a request for an official letter on the position of the Japanese authorities to convey to General Wedemeyer, as well as information on the POWs held in Korea.

When no response came, Bird demanded to see Colonel Shibuda, who returned and told Bird that a letter would be forthcoming, but that after the gasoline arrived he would have to leave by noon. The letter arrived carried by a junior officer, who repeated the demand that Bird would have to get his men ready to depart immediately. Bird again complained upon seeing that the letter was only an unsigned receipt for a letter that he had delivered on arrival.

The Japanese response to Bird's complaint to their final messenger was to bring up two tanks, which swung their turrets toward the rooms of the mission's quarters, along with infantry who set up mortars and machine guns in plain sight. This show of force finally made Bird give up. He and the twenty-one men under his command moved from their quarters to the C-47 at 12:15 p.m., under the guns of the Japanese tanks and infantry.

At the C-47, they found that the promised gasoline had not arrived yet, and another wait ensued, this time with everyone in and around the C-47 on the airstrip. Colonel Shibuda showed up later with his entire staff, asking Bird not to make further demands and telling him that the gasoline was still en route and that it would be only five hundred gallons, not eight hundred gallons as Bird had requested, as that was all of the 100 octane gasoline that they could find. The gasoline eventually arrived, and the plane took off at 3:30 p.m.

Without enough fuel to reach Xian, Bird decided— "hastily," in his own words—to attempt a landing at the Japanese airfield at Weihsien, on the Shandong Peninsula approximately half of the way to Xian. Operation Duck had already parachuted into the area two days earlier to liberate the civilian internment camp at Weihsien, but the airfield had not been an objective of its seven-man team. Attempting a landing there was yet another risk for Operation Eagle, as the airfield was still under Japanese control as far as the mission knew, and there was no assurance that more gasoline would be available there. The C-47 arrived at Weihsien and landed at 6:05 p.m. The airfield appeared deserted, but soon after the plane landed the Operation Eagle team found themselves surrounded by apparently friendly Chinese, who warned them that two hundred Japanese troops were near the airfield and might be hostile.

The security of the Operation Eagle team on the ground at Weihsien ended up being guaranteed by a local Chinese military commander who had collaborated with the Japanese forces for years. Now, after the announcement of Japan's surrender, he declared himself to be the Nationalist Chinese government's commander in the area, and he also claimed to be a friend of Yi Pomsok from before the war. The former puppet general, Li Wenli, offered to provide guards for the C-47 at the airfield and accommodations for the group as guests in his house. He also agreed to send a message to Operation Duck at the internment camp and to provide transportation the following day to link up with Operation Duck.[28]

The flight from Seoul to Weihsien found OSS headquarters in China in a different frame of mind on August 20 than only one day earlier. Colonel Heppner had received a request from China Theater for Operation Eagle to remain in the field and concentrate on POW work, shortly after he had sent his message to Bird on August 19.[29] He was now preparing to reinforce the mission by deploying to Seoul the team originally organized for Operation Flamingo, the POW rescue mission to Harbin, which had been cancelled after Soviet forces occupied the city first.[30] Under the pressure of events, Heppner also may have been displeased by the way that he had received news of the flight from Seoul to Weihsien, which came not directly from Bird but as a surprise in an interagency open meeting. The commander of the Air Ground Aid Section, one of whose officers was with Operation Eagle, had reported learning of the flight from OSS officers in Kunming, which embarrassed Heppner and other OSS senior leaders.[31] The news came from a report that Operation Duck sent by radio after receiving the message relayed by Li Wenli, which Duck had not addressed to Heppner.[32]

Heppner's response was completely different from a day earlier when he had given Bird latitude to stay in Korea or leave. He immediately radioed Bird to instruct him that the theater command wanted him "to stay where you are and not, repeat not, to come out."[33] After radioing Major Krause to prepare to send gasoline to either Weihsien or Seoul, he sent Bird the follow-up message: "Return, repeat return, to Korea

immediately, repeat immediately, and stay there, repeat stay there."
Bird was to return to Seoul immediately if he had sufficient gasoline
in Weihsien, and if not, gasoline would be flown to him immediately.
"Get in even if it involves internment" was Heppner's order, which he
explained was essential to head off the Russians, who "may soon be all
over Korea . . . unless the OSS got there and stayed."[34]

At the same time, information was spreading about the upcoming U.S.
military presence in Korea that would make Operation Eagle irrelevant.
On August 20 Col. William Davis, Heppner's operations officer, sent Bird
and Heppner the information that the U.S. Army's XXIV Corps had been
designated to land in Korea and accept the Japanese surrender in the
American occupation zone in Korea south of the 38th Parallel.[35] If Bird
received this message in Weihsien, it may have reinforced his thoughts
that the mission to Korea was an unnecessary risk.

Instead of following Heppner's orders, Bird did the opposite. Two
days later on August 22, he boarded the refueled C-47 with the aircrew
and only two others, his deputy and the OWI war correspondent. He
left the rest of the mission behind in Weihsien, including Yi Pomsok
and his officers and all of the Americans from Project Eagle, thirteen
men in total. Bird flew all the way to Chungking, over 1,100 miles away,
to meet OSS China Theater leaders in person to plead that they call off
returning to Seoul before the final conclusion of a peace with Japan. Bird
also met General Wedemeyer in the afternoon to make the same plea.[36]

The initial reception to Bird's unexpected appearance in Chungking
and his reports on Operation Eagle appears to have been favorable.
Colonel Davis sent a report to Heppner that described Bird's meetings
with him and Wedemeyer and stated, "Bird had no alternative but
to leave and in my opinion whole party was lucky to get away safely.
Remember Korea is not the same thing as occupied China. Bird should
not repeat not attempt return to Korea until peace is actually signed or
until MacArthur has taken forceful action to direct Japanese protection
of this mission." Davis further commented on Heppner's orders on
August 20: "Under present circumstances believe your orders for Bird
to return were given before you knew completely facts and were not

in agreement [with] your previous instructions for him to use his own judgment." Davis recommended that Bird remain in Chungking until the situation was clarified, then return to Weihsien to pick up the party left behind there and go back to Seoul.[37]

Bird's afternoon meeting with General Wedemeyer coincided with an event that he had set in motion, however, and it brought disaster to himself and Operation Eagle. The OWI war correspondent, brought back from Weihsien by Bird, finished and submitted to OWI a news story that provided a detailed and colorful narrative of Operation Eagle's arrival and experiences on the ground in Korea on August 18–19. The story reported names and operational details of Operation Eagle, without authorization from the OSS, and the security violation that it represented would have been a serious problem in itself. Far worse, it described the beer, sake, and singing with Japanese officers which Bird had left out of his accounts of the situation in Seoul.[38] The worldwide OWI news radio broadcast aired the story early the next morning, and Wedemeyer heard it and became infuriated. The story created the impression of fraternization with the enemy, and it contradicted Bird's reports of the hostility of the Japanese forces that had received Operation Eagle. Wedemeyer also learned that in order to take along the war correspondent, Bird had not loaded his airplane with food and medical supplies for rescued POWs, which increased his fury even further.[39]

General Wedemeyer's outrage brought about the rapid demise of Bird's command over Operation Eagle. Wedemeyer immediately ordered that all POW rescue efforts "be reconstituted and completely divorced from the Eagle project."[40] His chief of staff recommended sending Bird back to the United States to face disciplinary action.[41] Colonel Davis advised Heppner to replace Bird immediately as commander of Operation Eagle. Heppner did so and also instructed Davis to "take whatever steps you deem necessary to keep Bird out of contact with all persons outside OSS and theater headquarters."[42] Heppner informed Director Donovan of what had happened and urged him to "take whatever steps may be necessary to protect the organization."[43] The next day Donovan replied, "Make sure that action [against Bird will be] taken for violation of your orders. If necessary, send Bird home at once or, in your discretion, prefer charges."[44]

Bird's credibility with the OSS in China was finished, although neither Wedemeyer nor Heppner wanted him to face a court-martial.[45] Heppner reported to Donovan on August 26, "General Wedemeyer does not desire any harsh action taken against Bird. It is his feeling that he was guilty of bad judgment only, and that his actions exhibited great courage and ability. After a suitable time it is our plan to send him home and we want it clear that he is being sent home without any stigma attaching to him because of the Korea mission."[46] Bird remained in Xian into September, connected with Project Eagle on paper but with no real duties or responsibilities.

Left in Weihsien without a commander, Operation Eagle remained in limbo for almost a week. Heppner immediately chose a new commander, Maj. Robert Wampler, a veteran of OSS Detachment 101 in Burma. He was far away in Kunming, however, and multiple stages of military transport flights taking several days would be necessary for him to join the remaining Eagle mission.[47] He would not arrive in Xian until August 27.[48] Meanwhile, in Weihsien, Clyde Sargent was now the mission's senior American officer, and he and Yi Pomsok were in charge again. How they occupied themselves while waiting in Weihsien is not apparent from the record, but on August 24 Sargent radioed a four-sentence intelligence report with "scraps [of] info" from Korea that included the demobilization of Koreans in the Imperial Japanese Army and a general amnesty for political prisoners. He concluded with the sardonically brief report, "Good crops expected this year."[49] The thirteen men in Weihsien returned to Xian on August 28, minus the civilian communications specialist and Navy photographic specialist, who remained in Weihsien to support Operation Duck.[50]

While Willis Bird faced the consequences of his mistakes in Chungking, John Birch was killed on August 25, 1945, on his way to the Shandong Peninsula in support of Operation Eagle. The OSS had sent him to survey airfields in the Shandong Peninsula for use as relay points for Operation Eagle and other POW rescue missions. On August 20 Birch set out from Anhui with three Americans, seven Chinese, and two Koreans on a 300-mile overland journey to the Shandong Peninsula. Their first task there would have been to establish contact with another Nationalist Chinese general who had collaborated with Japan but was ready to change sides, Hao Pengju. Hao was also collaborating with the Chinese Communists, who had seeded his staff with agents, and the Chinese Communists knew about Birch's mission and moved to intercept him. At the city of Xuzhou (called Suchow then), Chinese Communist forces repeatedly stopped Birch and his party, who were moving on foot because of damage to the railways in the area. A confrontation resulted, and the Chinese Communist forces killed Birch, shooting him and then mutilating his body with bayonets. They also shot and wounded Birch's deputy, Lt. Dong Qinsheng, and detained the Americans, Chinese, and Koreans with the mission.[51]

The name and death of John Birch became well known only long after the war, when an organization of anti-Communist conspiracy theorists created the John Birch Society in 1958. It had no connection other than its name to John Birch, who had no history of supporting any of its political views. Nevertheless, he became inextricably connected to the John Birch Society, which considered him a martyr of the Cold War as its first American casualty. His real actions in China during the Second World War, including his involvement with the Korean Restoration Army, were almost completely forgotten.[52] Also forgotten was the role of Operation Eagle in the death of John Birch, which made him in a way the first American casualty of the postwar conflict for Korea.

General Wedemeyer and Colonel Heppner called off any further missions to Korea two days after the Operation Eagle team returned to Xian. The initial orders to Major Wampler and Operation Eagle had been to reorganize in Xian and prepare for another mission, but the order to cancel came on August 30. Any attempt to find POW camps in Korea was unnecessary, since U.S. forces were planning to occupy Korea soon.[53]

In this ignominious way, the first U.S. military action in Korea in the twentieth century ended. Operation Eagle had accomplished nothing, and it had discredited Project Eagle, the first cooperation between the

United States and Koreans.[54] Even worse, it was the first in a series of disappointments that would discredit the United States to Yi Pomsok and other Korean leaders. The chaotic organization of the operation, the risky flight to Korea, Bird's clumsy handling of talks with the Japanese that showed no understanding of how a military chain of command operated, Bird's abandonment of his team, days spent purposelessly stuck deep inside enemy-controlled territory—these experiences would have made an impression on Yi Pomsok and others who had placed great hopes on an alliance with the United States. There would be more such experiences in the months to come.

The End of Project Eagle

After the failure of Operation Eagle, Project Eagle soon ended as well. The end had been set in motion several days earlier, at the same time as the controversy over Lieutenant Colonel Bird's self-serving news radio story, but with a rational strategic purpose behind it. With the official surrender of Japan imminent and preparations for the surrender ceremony under way, the Joint Chiefs of Staff on August 24 directed the commander of U.S. Pacific Fleet, Adm. Chester Nimitz, to call off Project NAPKO. The order also went to General Wedemeyer in China and General MacArthur in the Philippines for their information.[55] Two days later General Wedemeyer ordered all preparations for both Project NAPKO and Project Eagle in his area of responsibility to cease.[56] On August 29, on the day after Operation Eagle returned from Weihsien to Xian, OSS China Theater headquarters issued an order to liquidate Project Eagle.[57]

It was a rapid end to a project that had commenced with great hope in April and received the OSS director's personal approval only three weeks earlier, and it occurred at a bad time for U.S. preparations for the postwar world in Asia. The expertise on Korea accumulated in Project Eagle and its connections to the Korean liberation movement should have made key contributions to the U.S. liberation and administration of Korea after the defeat of Japan. Instead, Project Eagle and its participants—American and Korean—would be excluded from the U.S. occupation force that arrived in Korea only a week later, on September 8.

They were doomed to be kept out of Korea by the U.S. strategic decision to put Korea under the Pacific Theater after the war instead of the China Theater. The OSS and the China Theater under General Wedemeyer had a well-established relationship, but the OSS had no relationship at all with General MacArthur in the Pacific Theater, who as Supreme Commander for the Allied Powers in Japan would have responsibility over Korea. MacArthur had long been hostile toward the OSS, a wartime creation that was outside of the authority of the regular armed services, and he kept the OSS out of his area of responsibility in the South Pacific for the entirety of the war. An unfamiliar OSS asset from China, Project Eagle had no chance of joining the forces under MacArthur's command occupying postwar Korea.

The choice of the general to command the occupation of Korea made the loss of Project Eagle's knowledge of Korea especially significant. The plan for the postwar occupation of Japan and Korea initially made Korea the responsibility of the Tenth Army under Gen. Joseph Stilwell. Stilwell, the former commanding general in the China-Burma-India Theater, had served in China since the 1930s and had extensive experience in Asia. He also had a long history of working with the OSS, since it was the Coordinator of Information in 1942, having sponsored OSS Detachment 101 in Burma. In mid-August the plan changed to downgrade the command in Korea to one of the Tenth Army's subordinate commands, the XXIV Corps under Lt. Gen. John Hodge. Hodge was a respected combat commander but lacked experience in Asia, as did the staff and units of the XXIV Corps, which had fought in the campaign across the Pacific. They needed the knowledge of Korea that could have come from an organization that included Yi Pomsok, Clyde Sargent, and the Korean and Korean American officers under their command, but they would not have it.

While these decisions occurred in faraway U.S. military headquarters in response to the wider situation at the end of the war, the OSS in China and Yi Pomsok continued to hold out hope that their work together could continue. The OSS requested clarification from Wedemeyer on the status of Project Eagle and the future of the Koreans in it on August 31, asking whether Korea was still in the China Theater: if so, whether intelligence operations in Korea were still desired, and if not, what the disposition of Project Eagle's Korean agents should be. They emphasized the postwar importance of Gen. Yi Pomsok in the Korean Restoration Army and the Korean Provisional Government.[58] Yi Pomsok began to agitate for the continuation of cooperation immediately after he returned from Weihsien to Xian and learned about the termination of Project Eagle.

On September 1 Yi met with Lieutenant Colonel Bird—no doubt with mixed feelings after his experiences during Operation Eagle—to discuss his concerns over the end of Project Eagle and the upcoming postwar situation in Korea. Yi was already aware of the change of commanding generals in Korea from Wedemeyer to MacArthur, and he requested an opportunity to put before both generals the case for the ongoing usefulness of the Korean Restoration Army. He emphasized for them that its officers had been carefully investigated and were loyal to the ideals of independence, making them of great value to a postwar government in Korea. Having been trained by U.S. forces, they also were loyal to American ideals and would be of great aid to American forces in Korea. Moreover, the Korean Restoration Army and the Korean Provisional Government were anti-Red and could do much to combat the Communist wave that was sure to rise from Russian occupation of part of Korea.[59]

OSS leaders in China understood the importance of Yi's offer and agreed to raise it with their superiors. Bird passed Yi's statements to Heppner with a strong recommendation in favor of them.[60] Heppner agreed with Bird and on September 3 circulated Bird's message at OSS headquarters in China with the intent of raising the issue with Wedemeyer.[61]

On the day after U.S. forces landed in Korea, Yi Pomsok attempted to raise the issue again by writing to Col. Paul Helliwell, head of the OSS SI branch in China, whom he had met in June. In a letter dated September 9, 1945, Yi urged that despite the surrender of Japan and the end of the war, "I strongly feel that our work is not ended. . . . We still must 'win the peace.'" He stated, "I have done my best in the American-Korean cooperative operation because I shared the American ideal and objective of freedom and democracy, and of a world consisting of free, democratic nations. . . . In this conviction, I also represent the objectives and ideals of the Korean Provisional Government and the Korean Independence Army." He noted with great concern Russia's occupation of northern Korea and political activity in both northern and southern Korea, particularly its organization of a government in the north. Presciently he asserted that Russian actions jeopardized the freedom of Korea and its ability to develop a democratic state, and also the future position of the United States in the Far East, the peace of Asia, and, in turn, the future peace of the world.[62]

Yi requested Helliwell's assistance to enter Korea at the earliest opportunity, offering to assist the U.S. occupation force by promoting democratic principles before Communist influence could spread, encouraging the Korean people to assist the U.S. forces as they arrived, and working with the U.S. forces to help them understand the country and its people.[63] Helliwell could not act on Yi's request himself, but he passed it up the OSS chain of command with his support.[64]

The response from General Wedemeyer's China Command did not come until the middle of September, and when it did, it was predictable. On September 13 the assistant adjutant general replied that the China Theater did not require intelligence operations in Korea after the inclusion of Korea in the Pacific Theater, so what to do with the Koreans was an issue for forces of the Pacific Theater involved in the occupation of Korea. They would have the opportunity to enlist the services of Korean nationals if they chose to do so. Project Eagle therefore should be disbanded and the Korean nationals in it released.[65] Heppner passed the message to Director Donovan in Washington, with the request to offer Korean personnel to Pacific Theater forces in Korea.[66] It is unlikely that such an offer to General MacArthur ever occurred, and if it did, MacArthur did not accept it.

With no interest from higher authorities in using the OSS relationship with the Korean Provisional Government and the Korean Restoration Army to support the occupation of Korea, the liquidation of Project Eagle proceeded uninterrupted. The August 29 order to liquidate Project Eagle called for no further money to be spent and for no further official U.S.

involvement in any actions by the Koreans, with the project to wind down by October 1. All base construction in Xian would stop immediately, with further expenditures allowed only to pay for construction contracts already executed. Salaries paid to Koreans would stop on October 1. Assisting Koreans returning to Korea would be allowed, but their movements would have to be on their own, with no U.S. endorsement. Giving them equipment was permitted, but there would have to be proper receipts to make it chargeable to Lend-Lease.[67] All of these actions went ahead from the beginning of September to the end of the month.

The Americans of Project Eagle left the base in Xian over the course of August and September. They departed for other U.S. bases in China, on the first stage of their long journeys back to the United States for demobilization and then to return home. As of August 29 there were twenty-nine American officers, enlisted men, and civilians. Lt. Woon Sung Chung left on August 29, followed by two of the Korean American enlisted men on August 30. Two more officers left on September 4, followed by another on September 7 and a noncommissioned officer on September 14. The following day Capt. Ryong Chun Hahm left with eight enlisted men, six of them Korean Americans, and a civilian.

Willis Bird, whose actions had done much to discredit Project Eagle within the OSS and to discredit the United States with the Korean Provisional Government, departed by himself on September 16.[68]

Only eleven men remained after Bird's departure, and they soon became only six. Another five left on September 17, including Major Stewart, another officer, the last two Korean American enlisted men, and a civilian. During the last two weeks of Project Eagle, all that remained were Clyde Sargent and five enlisted men, whose only task was to finish shutting down the project.

The Koreans of Project Eagle went their separate way, to a different future than that of their former American comrades. As the project closed down in late August and September, they regrouped for their own journey home. Korea was over a thousand miles from Xian and over seven hundred miles from Anhui, with the Yellow Sea in between and Soviet troops blocking the overland route through Manchuria. Soviet occupation north of the 38th Parallel made a return to Pyongyang and northern Korea impossible. Even in the U.S. occupation zone south of the 38th Parallel, their fate was uncertain, because whether the new U.S. military government in Korea would permit the Korean Provisional Government and the Korean Restoration Army to enter Korea was unknown. U.S. permission and assistance would be necessary, and the United States had granted neither while Project Eagle was disbanding.

Lt. Kim Woo Chun, with the Third Detachment of the Korean Restoration Army in Anhui, experienced the end of U.S. support after the decision to terminate Project Eagle. He recalled many years later that at the end of August, he received a generous supply of U.S. military equipment—a uniform, fatigue gear, a .45 pistol, a box of ammunition, and a medical kit—and that a U.S. military flight brought him from Anhui to Chungking. It was the last assistance that he would receive from the OSS. In Chungking he rejoined the headquarters of the Korean Provisional Government, which was struggling to figure out what it was to do in postwar Korea. For him, returning to his original home in Pyongyang was not possible, and his future would have to be in the south, in whatever new Korea emerged after the end of the war. It was the start of a long road home that would not take him back to Korea until six months later.[69]

Yi Pomsok and Clyde Sargent made a final effort in late September to argue for the continuation of their wartime cooperation in postwar Korea. Sargent, officially back in charge of what was left of Project Eagle on September 17, immediately wrote to Colonel Helliwell in support of Yi's offer to take a group from the OSS and the Korean Restoration Army to support the U.S. occupation force in Korea. "I believe there is *much* merit to the proposal," he wrote. "I believe that General [Yi] with about fifteen or twenty of his men and a small group of OSS Americans . . . can greatly facilitate the work of General Hodge who, apparently, is having his headaches with the Koreans. Furthermore, General [Yi]'s very strong pro-American and very strong anti-Russian attitude will be a distinct advantage to the United States if he can get in there early and aid in molding all Korean attitudes to favor America."[70] Yi made his final attempt on September 27, again communicating through Sargent his desire to work under U.S. command in Korea.[71] Their efforts were to no avail, however, and the end came inevitably.

The OSS made the end official during the last week of September, when Colonel Helliwell sent formal farewell messages to Yi Pomsok and Kim Hak Kyu. Kim Hak Kyu in Anhui received the first one, in a letter dated September 25, which came with $5,000 as a gesture of thanks.[72] Yi Pomsok received his in a letter dated September 28, along with $10,000.[73] The perfunctory letters and monetary gifts—approximately $65,000 and $130,000 in 2015 dollars—were a petty end to a wartime relationship that had begun with high hopes and that both sides in China knew could be of pivotal importance to postwar Korea and the entire strategic balance in Northeast Asia.

On the last day of the existence of Project Eagle, Yi Pomsok and Clyde Sargent posed for a photograph that would commemorate the project that they had struggled to build together. The last five Americans with Project Eagle accompanied Sargent, all of them enlisted men, and all of them clearly happy to be finished with the war and about to go home.[74] Five Korean Restoration Army officers sat with them, looking far more serious, perhaps reflecting the uncertain future ahead of them. Yi and Sargent sat side by side with expressions of disappointment on their faces. Yi later gave a copy of the photograph to Sargent, inscribed on one side, "Commemorating First Korean and American Alliance Hsian 1945" in English, and on the other side, "Together our countries can change the world! Korea Year 27 September 30" in Korean. Commemorating a time when the two countries had failed to work together, during the twenty-seventh year of the Korean government in exile, it was a statement of solidarity but also of disappointment.

The Final Act: William Donovan and Clarence Weems in Washington

As Project Eagle came to an end in China, the final act in the brief wartime alliance between the OSS and the Korean Provisional Government played out far away in Washington. It would involve only two men, the same men who had been involved in the OSS's work with the Koreans since the early years of the war: William Donovan and Clarence Weems. Donovan saw Korea as a pivotal country in Northeast Asia that the rest of the U.S. government was ignoring, similar to his interest in Korea in the first months after the attack on Pearl Harbor, but looking ahead to the postwar world. Weems became the last man in the OSS detailed to figure out the problems with Korea and propose their solutions.

William Donovan had returned from China to Washington on August 14 facing crises both in China and at home. After his visit to Project Eagle in Xian on August 7 and the atomic bombings of Hiroshima on August 6 and Nagasaki on August 9, Soviet forces had begun to sweep across Manchuria and into Korea. In Washington, enemies of the OSS were arguing for it to be disbanded. Amid these larger events, Donovan took the risk of attempting to raise the issue of postwar Korea with President Harry Truman in an irregular way.

Donovan sent Truman a message from Kim Ku. It was the first time that an official communication from a Korean government had reached the president of the United States, and it ignored protocol, coming outside of State Department channels from a government in exile not recognized by the United States. Presented through Project Eagle after the Japanese announcement of surrender on August 15, it went to Colonel Heppner, who sent it to Donovan on August 18.[75] It was on the same day that Operation Eagle made its second attempt to fly from Xian to Seoul, to fulfill the hopes of Donovan and Heppner of heading off Soviet occupation and influence in Korea. Later that day Donovan sent a memorandum relaying the message directly to Truman's personal secretary, to be placed on the president's desk without being seen or screened by anyone else.[76]

The message from "Kim Ku, Chairman of the Korean Provisional Government" congratulated and thanked the United States and called for the continuation of U.S-Korean cooperation. It began, "Today in victory the people of Korea join the people of the United States in rejoicing with Japan's surrender and the end of the war throughout the world. Our common enemy is defeated." It continued, "In victory and freedom, we the people of Korea express our genuine and deep appreciation to the Government and the people of the United States for their achievements in defeating our enemy." Looking ahead, it declared, "With freedom and peace the Korean people now begin their important work of building an independent state and a nucleus of democracy in the Far East. . . . In our endeavors to build an independent democracy we are relying strongly on the understanding and cooperative aid of the American Government and people. It is our hope that American Korean positive cooperation initiated in China during the last few months of the war against Japan will continue and grow." Donovan added, "For your information, we have been working with him in the installation of intelligence agents in Korea."[77]

What precisely Donovan wanted to do in Korea appears not to be recorded and may never be known, but he had the intent and the means to make Korea a significant part of postwar U.S. strategy in Asia instead of a sideshow of the recently finished war against Japan. Donovan and Colonel Heppner in China were concerned about the pivotal position of the Korean peninsula between the Soviet Union, China, and Japan and the risk of Soviet domination of Korea as the Red Army entered and occupied northern Korea. Project Eagle in China connected the OSS to the Korean Provisional Government, which was waiting to return to a liberated Korea with an OSS-trained armed force. Project NAPKO, preparing in the highest secrecy in Okinawa, had the ability to insert Korean agents throughout Korea, especially in northern Korea where Soviet forces were approaching Pyongyang. The continuation of cooperation with the Korean Provisional Government and of the OSS operations prepared for Korea was almost certainly Donovan's goal when he passed Kim Ku's message to Truman.

Instead of making Truman interested in Korea and the OSS's work there, Donovan's attempt backfired. Donovan had had a close relationship with Franklin Roosevelt that made discussions of strategy outside of normal channels possible, and three and a half years earlier in January 1942, Donovan had brought the Korean Provisional Government to Roosevelt's attention in exactly the same way—with an informal memorandum sent directly to Roosevelt's desk. Donovan's relationship with

Truman was completely different, and it was distant at best. Truman had kept Donovan waiting for a month after his inauguration before meeting him for the first time, and he personally disliked Donovan, a wealthy Wall Street lawyer from New York who was completely different from the people that he had known in Missouri or even as a U.S. senator and vice president. Donovan had sent memoranda on strategic issues directly to Truman, as he had done with Roosevelt, but Truman ignored almost all of them. The message from Kim Ku became one of the few to get a reply from Truman, and it was entirely negative. On August 25 Truman sent a brief letter to Donovan telling him that any reply to Kim Ku would be inadvisable and that "I would appreciate your instructing your agents as to the impropriety of their acting as a channel for the transmission to me of messages from representatives of self-styled governments which are not recognized by the Government of the United States."[78] The thinly veiled rebuke unceremoniously cut off Donovan's attempt to discuss the fate of Korea and the continuation of the OSS's work with the Korean Provisional Government.

Truman's letter came only two days after the controversy over Lieutenant Colonel Bird's unauthorized press release about the mission to Seoul broke out, bringing Operation Eagle to a halt. The failure of Operation Eagle, followed closely by the written reprimand from the president, ended Donovan's attempts to raise the issue of the future of Korea. Preoccupied with other problems worldwide and with fighting efforts in Washington to have the OSS disbanded, Donovan turned his attention to other issues and let the liquidation of Project Eagle run its course in China.

Less than a month later, Truman signed an executive order abolishing the OSS. The September 20 executive order dissolved the OSS effective October 1 and distributed its personnel and assets to the State Department and the War Department. The Research and Analysis branch became part of the State Department's Interim Research and Intelligence Service (IRIS), under Col. Alfred MacCormack, and the rest including the Secret Intelligence and Operations branches became part of the War Department as the Strategic Service Unit (SSU), under

Brig. Gen. John Magruder. The SSU continued OSS intelligence activities in China into 1946, but Donovan's leadership role ended with the termination of the OSS on October 1, the same day as the end of Project Eagle far away in China.

A final coda to the alliance between the OSS and the Korean Provisional Government came from Clarence Weems. During September 1945, Weems traveled around China and then back to Washington on a special assignment to review the OSS's erstwhile allies. It would give him the final word on the relationship with the Koreans that he and the OSS had worked on for almost four years and that Donovan had hoped would help to ensure the postwar security of Korea and the U.S. strategic position in Asia.

The assignment took him first from one end of China to the other and back again. At the end of August, with his work in Anhui with Gen. Kim Hak Kyu and the Third Detachment of the Korean Restoration Army ended by the termination of Project Eagle, he flew west from Anhui to Chungking. There he conducted extended talks with Kim Ku, Li Chong Chon, and other leaders of the Korean Provisional Government from September 1 through September 5. He then went back east to Shanghai, where the OSS was setting up postwar operations. There he met officers of the Korean Restoration Army, who had relocated there to recruit Koreans from the dissolving Japanese forces in China after their formal surrender to Nationalist China on September 9. They included Lt. Kim Woo Chun, with whom Weems had served two weeks earlier in Anhui.[79] Weems received orders relieving him from duty in China for a new assignment in Washington on September 11. He flew back to Chungking and then to Kunming, where he caught a flight over the Himalayas to India.[80]

Weems arrived at OSS headquarters in Washington on September 25. He arrived at a confused time at OSS headquarters, five days after Truman's executive order dissolving the OSS, when IRIS and the SSU had already taken over operations, but Donovan had six days as OSS director remaining. Numerous officers who had recently served in Asia were there with no particular duties, waiting for their next assignments or for their demobilization. Among them was Willis Bird, who waited in

Washington for his release from active duty for almost the entire month of October. Weems was himself in transition, on temporary duty in Washington while awaiting reassignment. As an officer in the Research & Analysis branch, he could have been reassigned to IRIS, but he was seeking to return to Korea and soon requested immediate assignment to the U.S. occupation force in Korea as an Army civil affairs officer. Further complicating his wait at OSS headquarters was that he was preoccupied with attempting to figure out the status of his promotion to major, which Colonel Helliwell had recommended in Chungking on September 13 but still had not come though at the end of December.

Within a few days of his arrival in Washington, Weems prepared a report on the Korean Provisional Government and submitted it to Donovan. Whether Donovan requested it, or Weems prepared it on his own initiative while Donovan was too preoccupied with handling his departure from office to be concerned, is uncertain from the record.[81] Regardless of its origin, the report was the last assessment by the OSS of the Korean independence movement that it had worked with since early 1942, by the only individual in Washington with firsthand knowledge from years of involvement and over a year of experience in China. Coming only three days before the inevitable end of Donovan's time as OSS director, the report was fated to have no effect on OSS or SSU actions in Korea. Instead, it would be known only to Weems and to Donovan, who preserved a copy in his personal papers that he kept after his departure from Washington.

The report addressed the problems that the recently installed U.S. military government in Korea was experiencing and the role that the Korean Provisional Government should perform in the transition from Japanese rule to an independent Korea. It began with a brief recalling of the long history of Americans in Korea, then asserted, "They [the Korean people] favor American influence, first, because American missionaries and business men have generally made a sound impression in Korea for seventy-five years. They favor it, even more, because almost all phases of the Korean independence movement have, since 1919, been directed toward the goal of democratic government, and Koreans have felt that temporary American supervision would provide the atmosphere best suited to its achievement." The U.S. military government had encountered demonstrations opposing it, but they were the result of American miscalculations, as "This will to popular self-rule, as well as a natural hatred for Japanese control, is clearly [behind] the recent demonstrations against the continued use of Japanese administrative personnel in Korea."[82]

Weems believed that the Korean Provisional Government was the key to resolving the problems in Korea. He pointed out that there was a strong desire within Korea for the Korean Provisional Government to return from exile. He acknowledged the rivalries that existed between factions in Chungking and between Korean groups in the United States, but he explained them as frictions between cliques and personalities rather than disagreements on policy, the result of twenty-six years in exile spent trying to establish reputations as revolutionary leaders while struggling to make a living. "The problem is one of conflicting personalities which have been too closely confined with each other and which do not have enough constructive work to do." He believed that "these differences seem likely to become much less prominent if the Provisional Government is actually honored by an invitation to enter Korea and all its members are given something important to do."[83]

Weems was skeptical about the abilities of the leaders of the Korean Provisional Government, even though he regarded them as indispensable. "The 'top executives' of the Provisional Government do not seem to be, on the whole, men who can be expected to serve permanently of [sic] the administrators of a country which will have such complex problems as can be foreseen in Korea. The most important of these leaders are men of courage and good common sense, however, and they have recently been reinforced by a number of younger men who are less prominent but have a better understanding of present events and more natural ability."[84] Kim Ku, at the head of the Provisional Government, embodied their strengths and weaknesses. Weems wrote:

President Kim Ku, who is 68 years of age, was a minor official of the Provisional Government until 1932 when the tremendous success of

Yung Pong-kil's attack on Japanese officials, which Kim Ku had planned, suddenly made him the most prominent figure in the Provisional Government. He is not highly educated in accordance with modern standards and he has much of the narrowness and stubbornness which characterize the old style Korean whose youth was spent before the annexation of Korea by Japan. He has, however, the qualities of courage, sincerity and singleness of purpose, and his name is known in every section of Korea. He is not qualified to serve for any long period as the executive head of a government in Korea, but he might well serve as the chairman of an interim organization and he has all of the qualities of an elder statesman who would serve as a symbol of Korea's struggle for freedom.[85]

The Korean Restoration Army could form the basis of a Korean national police that was needed to replace the Japanese authorities that the U.S. occupation force in Korea had not yet replaced. "Training, discipline and the development of leadership are excellent in the Second and Third Detachments, which have been under our direct observation in the field since early summer," Weems observed. "These detachments provide a sound nucleus of leaders for a much larger body of men." Weems cited an estimate by Kim Hak Kyu that the Korean Restoration Army could organize a force of 30,000 in forty-five days and 100,000 in ninety days by inducting Koreans in the rapidly disbanding Japanese armed forces in China, who already had training, weapons, and equipment. "Such a body of disciplined Korean troops, moving from China into Korea, would presumably be able to take over a large part of the police and relief work required in Korea as Japanese personnel are withdrawn."[86]

More than anything else, the Korean Provisional Government would be a unifying symbol. "Greater than all the other contributions which the Korea Provisional Government might make to the national life of Korea is the name of the Korean Provisional Government itself. It forms the God-head of the Korean movement. Korean children for twenty-five years have been taught in secret that the Provisional Government was working to bring in the day of independence. It has been the one outside organization which had a general appeal to the people of Korea. The presence of this revolutionary God-head in Korea at this time would unquestionably aid the process of developing a sound Korean administration, even if the Provisional Government officials had nothing but their names to contribute."[87]

Moreover, Weems emphasized that a partnership with the Korean Provisional Government was compatible with the interests of the United States. "The Provisional Government insists that Korea can and must be independent. It favors American influence over that of any other power, as do the people within Korea if they are free to choose. Its whole political program is based on the idea of an almost pure representative system, beginning with the village and spreading to the nation. It is fearful of the effects of Russian occupation and believes that Russian influence in Korea for any extended period of time inevitably means war. It desires to make itself available to the people of Korea and let them use it according to the will of the majority. If the Provisional Government has its way, Korea will have a democratic form of government which is absolutely opposed to domination of Korea by any foreign power and which will have relations of sincere friendship with the United States."[88]

Two weeks later, in a second report on the Korean Restoration Army, Weems tried to address the threat of the Communist government that the Soviet Union was establishing in its occupation zone. He took as his starting point a September 27 message from Gen. Kim Hak Kyu in Chungking that expressed acute concern over the danger of the Soviet Union establishing a Communist regime over the north and ultimately all of Korea, first winning over people in the north and organizing Communist military units, then sending men to the south to organize underground Communist forces. It pleaded for U.S. support for the Korean Provisional Government and for permission for the Korean Liberation Army to enter Korea, expressing certainty that the Korean people would cooperate with the United States based on their long-standing relationship with the American people, who had brought religion, education, and social progress to Korea.[89]

In a report dated October 11, done on his own initiative without any claim to being an official report, Weems raised the pleadings of Kim Hak Kyu and attempted to set out a plan for putting them into action. He acknowledged that the Korean Provisional Government's proposal created a risk of sharpening the division of Korea and placing an American-sponsored regime in open conflict with a Soviet-sponsored one, but he called for aiding its army quietly and cautiously. He gave a broad range of reasons why supporting the Korean Restoration Army would serve the interests of the United States as well as Korea:

The Korean Restoration Army was intensely loyal to the principle of free democratic government for all of Korea and was preponderantly favorable to American leadership.

An enlarged Korean Restoration Army would be capable of performing the policing and relief duties being performed by Russian and American troops in Korea. While doing this work, it would exert a unifying and creative influence in favor of the U.S. approach to the final political solution in Korea.

Personnel of the Korean Restoration Army were drawn from every province in Korea and represented all social and political elements. It was a truly national force that would command respect in both North and South.

The nucleus in China was well organized and well disciplined, and it appeared capable of spreading these characteristics to between 50,000 and 100,000 trained Koreans being released from the Japanese Army in China.

If financial and other assistance were extended immediately, at least 15,000 picked men apparently could be ready for service in Korea by December, a further 15,000 by the end of January 1946, and at least 20,000 more by March. Possibly up to 50,000 more could be made available later if needed.

The availability of this force would enable the U.S.-Soviet joint commission to invite it into the entire country by providing an effective answer to any Russian argument that the continued exclusive use of Russian troops in North Korea was necessary.[90]

Recognizing the "strong possibility" that a U.S.-Soviet joint administration over Korea would fail, Weems argued that the Korean Restoration Army could be brought into the U.S. occupation zone to help bridge the gap between full U.S. military government and full Korean self-rule when failure of the joint administration became certain. With proper direction, it would be a force for the development of a sound democratic regime in the American zone, and it would be essential to the defense of the south if the conflict between the Soviet Union and a northern Communist regime and the United States and a southern democratic government were to become a reality. The Korean Restoration Army had experienced intelligence agents and organizers as well as soldiers to contribute against either a Communist underground campaign or an invasion.

Regardless of whether they were to be used in all of Korea or only in the south, Weems emphasized that the United States had "their confidence and faith right now" and "must act immediately" in order to keep it. The United States would have to act soon, and moreover it would have to act as decisively as the Soviet Union was already doing in its northern occupation zone. "We are in on the ground floor with the Korean Independence Army, which is democratic and strongly pro-American; if we use this advantage wisely and with a coldly realistic policy, we may for once be able to do as well as our practical-minded Russian friends have already done."[91]

The report described numerous actions that would be necessary both with the Koreans and internally within the U.S. command structure to make cooperation with the Korean Restoration Army effective. The United States would need to work with Nationalist China to reinforce their interest and speed the transfer of Koreans, as well as provide financial support to the Korean Restoration Army for the recruiting, training, and maintenance of its new men and for transportation to staging areas on the coast.[92] Washington would have to make clear decisions on Korea and delegate authority to work with the Korean Restoration Army. The secretary of state and the secretary of war would have to make decisions at the cabinet level on actions to be taken in Korea, instead of leaving them to MacArthur in the Pacific Theater and Wedemeyer in the China

Theater to resolve, which had left U.S. representatives on uncertain ground in August and September. After those decisions on policy, an American knowledgeable about the situation of the Koreans and with their confidence should handle the relationship along with the U.S. authorities in Korea.[93]

Weems claimed that cooperation with the Korean Restoration Army did not have to involve recognition of the Korean Provisional Government. From the beginning of cooperation between them and the OSS, both sides had understood that the purpose was military cooperation and not diplomatic recognition, and he believed that the distinction could continue. He asserted that Kim Ku, Kim Hak Kyu, and other Korean Provisional Government leaders wanted diplomatic recognition but did not actually expect it and that they would cooperate with the U.S. military government if approached by the right American—such as himself. "They will be glad to take their chances on their influence with the Korean people if they, as individuals, are given facilities for entering Korea and are able to form a joint consultative and planning group with other prominent leaders who have remained in Korea," he claimed. "It is my personal belief that if these leaders are approached by Americans who know them and their background intimately, they can be useful as an advisory group assisting American Military Government authorities during the transition period, and that they will aid rather than hinder the eventual growth in Korea of the kind of government we would like to see there."[94]

Whether or not his observations on the Korean Provisional Government and Korean Restoration Army were accurate, Clarence Weems's proposals on what to do with them ended up being little more than a pipe dream that he briefly attempted to make real. When he finished the second report on October 11, he submitted both reports to the Far East division of the SSU's Secret Intelligence branch.[95] He suggested himself for the role of liaison to the Korean Restoration Army that he had described in his second report.[96] He even personally distributed copies of his report to the State Department and to the army's Military Intelligence Service, apparently in an attempt to create interagency support for his ideas.[97] The SSU ended up rejecting them. The director of the SSU, Brig. Gen. John Magruder, sent the reports to the head of IRIS at the State Department, Col. Alfred MacCormack, stating, "These papers represent Captain Weems's personal views and are not, of course, an official dissemination of this agency."[98] Magruder filed away the report, stating in a note to his deputy at the Far East division of the Secret Intelligence branch, "I shall not disseminate this even unofficially to State Department. You may simply hold them for reference if you consider them of any value."[99]

In this way, the last word on the alliance between the OSS and the Korean Provisional Government during the Second World War immediately faded into obscurity. Weems's report on the Korean Provisional Government later appeared at the headquarters of the U.S. occupation force in Korea, but there is no evidence that it influenced the opinions or decisions of General Hodge or his staff.[100] Hodge and the U.S. forces in Korea would have to learn about Korea the hard way, as the knowledge and experience accumulated by the OSS between 1942 and 1945 were unavailable to them when they arrived in Korea. Made ignorant by the arrangements that put General MacArthur of the Pacific Theater in command over the occupation of Korea, the termination of Project Eagle, and the disbanding of the OSS after the war, the U.S. forces liberating Korea were headed toward a role in a tragedy not of their own making.

7

End of Innocence

The U.S. Military Government in Korea

The U.S. forces that landed in Korea on September 8, 1945, began the modern relationship between Korea and the United States. It was a historic mission that set the stage for the Korean War and for one of the most important alliances of both the United States and Korea. It began as only a sideshow to the occupation of Japan, however, and as an ill-prepared and almost completely uninformed one. Higher authorities in Washington and the Pacific Theater sent American troops to Korea with no knowledge of the pent-up desire of Koreans for independence and self-rule after four decades under Japan, more than half a century of American influence in Korea, or the work of the OSS with the Korean Provisional Government that was coming to an end. They arrived unprepared for the complicated situation that they would find in Korea, and the consequences would be costly for both Americans and Koreans.

The Unprepared U.S. Military Government

The U.S. military organization sent to occupy Korea was as far from being a purposely selected force as it could be. The army's XXIV Corps had been on Okinawa preparing for the invasion of Japan in early August. With its main combat units, the 7th, 27th, and 96th Infantry Divisions, it had participated in the liberation of the Philippines between October and December 1944 and then in the Battle of Okinawa from April through June 1945. Its commander, Lt. Gen. John R. Hodge, was an

infantry officer who had served in the First World War and the Guadalcanal, Bougainville, and Philippine campaigns, rising to command
over the XXIV Corps and the rank of lieutenant general during the
Battle of Okinawa. Hodge and the XXIV Corps had no prior experience
relevant to their upcoming role in Korea, and their selection happened
largely by chance. It was based solely on the shipping timetables, which
made the XXIV Corps on Okinawa the force that would be the fastest
to transport to Korea.

General Hodge's command had limited time and almost no resources
to prepare for the mission. The XXIV Corps received orders to serve
as the occupation force and military government in Korea on August
15, giving it only two weeks to prepare. The task of serving as military
government headquarters went to the Tenth Army Antiaircraft Artillery Command, which was not needed for occupation duties in Japan
and was therefore assigned to the XXIV Corps and retasked to serve as
occupation planners in Korea. The repurposed antiaircraft artillerymen
had little with which to work. The XXIV Corps embarked for Korea
with no Civil Affairs units, the army's specialists in working with civil
authorities and civilian populations. It did not receive any Civil Affairs
units until October, a month after the start of the occupation, and the
units that it received had originally been intended and trained for the
Philippines, with language instruction in Tagalog, not Korean. Having
not one soldier or interpreter who could speak the Korean language,
the XXIV Corps had to look for Koreans suitable to serve as interpreters
among Japanese prisoners of war on Okinawa. It found only six, a grossly
inadequate number for the needs of a force of 72,000 American troops
that was expected to govern and administer Korea.[1]

Knowledge of Korea beyond basic facts about geography and the
soon to be dismantled Japanese administration was almost entirely
absent. The main source of information about Korea was a Joint Army-
Navy Intelligence Study published in April 1945, called JANIS-75, with
superficial and outdated information about conditions in Korea. There
were also some reports of the interrogations of Korean prisoners of war
captured on Okinawa and a few aerial photographs of Korea that XXIV

Corps staff had been able to persuade an Army Air Forces reconnaissance squadron on Okinawa to take. The knowledge of Korea and its political movements gained by the OSS from 1942 to 1945 was unavailable, so there was a complete lack of awareness of the long and complicated history of the Korean struggle for independence and the many political factions that had been competing for leadership.[2]

General Hodge and the XXIV Corps were unready for the upcoming occupation, but they and the army as a whole hardly deserve to be singled out for criticism, because no part of the U.S. government aside from the OSS was paying any attention to Korea in August 1945. The State Department neglected to send any guidance on Korea to General MacArthur or to General Hodge. As a result Hodge and the XXIV Corps embarked for Korea without any instructions on U.S. policies toward Korean independence, removal of the Japanese administration in Korea, or Korean political groups. Hodge requested that the State Department send a political adviser to provide policy guidance, but he did not reach Okinawa until September 3, only two days before the XXIV Corps boarded its ships for Korea. The political adviser, H. Merrill Benninghoff, arrived without instructions from the State Department on U.S. policies in Korea. Benninghoff sent a request to Washington for guidance during the first week of the occupation, but the State Department did not respond with an initial directive on civil affairs administration in Korea until October 17, 1945, more than a month after the XXIV Corps arrived in Korea.[3] Hodge and Benninghoff were repeating, probably unknowingly, the experience of the first U.S. ambassador and military attaché in Seoul six decades earlier in 1883–87, Lucius Foote and Ens. George Foulk, who were practically ignored by the State Department in Washington.

General Hodge and his troops arrived unprepared for the role that they would perform in Korea, and part of the tragedy was that they did not have to be that way. OSS assets in Asia could have provided them with knowledge of Korea and connections to Korean leaders that might have made a difference. Project Eagle in China had Gen. Yi Pomsok pleading for authorization to join the U.S. occupation force, as well as

Americans from Korea with considerable knowledge of the country: Capt. Clarence Weems, in Anhui with the Korean Restoration Army; Capt. Ryong Chyun Hahm, Project Eagle's intelligence officer, with the Operation Eagle mission to Seoul; and Horace Horton Underwood, one of the last Americans to leave Korea in 1942 and the planner of the Presbyterian Church's return to Korea. On Okinawa, only a short distance from where General Hodge and his staff of antiaircraft gunners turned occupation planners were struggling with almost no knowledge of Korea, Project NAPKO had considerable information about Korea and highly trained Korean agents with networks of relatives and associates throughout the country. Douglas MacArthur's refusal to work with the OSS made them unavailable to Hodge and his staff.

Little of the expertise on Korea accumulated by the OSS reached the U.S. occupation force, and the individuals who joined it succeeded in doing so only after lengthy journeys through the vast bureaucratic administration of the U.S. armed services, months after the occupation began—too late to affect its crucial early actions. Ryong Chyun Hahm left the OSS's successor, the SSU, to join the staff of the U.S. military government in Korea in November 1945.[4] Clarence Weems joined the staff even later, in early 1946, despite his requests to be sent to Korea as a Civil Affairs officer as soon as possible. After he spent September and October 1945 at OSS headquarters attempting to draw attention to the Korean Provisional Government, the army assigned him to its School of Military Government in Charlottesville, Virginia, to teach classes on Korea to Civil Affairs personnel preparing for Korea. He was there from November 1945 to February 1946, while the American military government in Korea struggled to deal with the leaders of the Korean Provisional Government and could have used his knowledge and contacts.[5]

Clyde Sargent did not make it to Korea until 1947, after two years in China and the United States. After disbanding Project Eagle, Sargent stayed with the U.S. Army in China as a newly promoted major on a special assignment that would affect the fate of the 1.5 million Koreans living in China. From October to December 1945, he visited the Korean communities in Shanghai, Beijing, Tianjin, and other areas of northern

China, tasked with assessing what assistance the United States should offer them. His assessment was crucial to the U.S. decision in December 1945 to provide transportation for any Koreans choosing to leave China and return to their homeland. With that task completed, he returned to the United States in January 1946. After his discharge from the SSU and the army, Sargent attended Columbia University to complete the doctorate in Far Eastern studies that he had left unfinished in 1940, interrupted by the war for six eventful years.[6] As Dr. Clyde Sargent, he finally went to Korea in 1947 to serve as political adviser to the U.S. delegation to the U.S.-USSR Joint Commission on Korea.

The strangest odyssey back to Korea by veterans of the OSS was that of the Korean agents of Project NAPKO. Deployed overseas from California to Okinawa with maximum secrecy earlier in 1945, they returned to the United States for the disbanding of the project before being repatriated to Korea. Those who had volunteered from the prisoner of war camp at Camp McCoy, Wisconsin, faced the hardest road home. Officially recorded as escaped POWs in U.S. military records and reported as such to the Red Cross, they were serving in the OSS with no legal status under the Geneva Conventions. Compounding the problem was that they had been living and training in the United States and then deployed overseas using U.S. passports that the OSS had obtained illegally using false information. To avoid the complications of their legal status, the OSS had them smuggled from Okinawa back into the United States and then placed with Japanese POWs being shipped home.[7] U.S. records do not document how these Koreans reacted to returning home as Japanese POWs after their extraordinary wartime service with the OSS, or whether they suffered any harm from other POWs after rejoining them in what must have been suspicious circumstances.

A further handicap to the U.S. military government in Korea was that the leading American experts on Korea serving outside of the armed services at the end of the war never joined it, instead leaving the U.S. government entirely. Horace Horton Underwood left his civilian role with the OSS and returned to Korea with the Presbyterian Church, to resume his position in Seoul as a university president. George McCune resigned from his position as the Korea desk officer at the State Department in October 1945, his always precarious health near collapse. By 1945 his heart problems left him debilitated, unable to climb stairs without stopping to rest. The outcome of the war for Korea, with the United States and Soviet Union discussing joint trusteeship over Korea instead of independence and dividing Korea into separate occupation zones, left him profoundly depressed. On the advice of his physician, he left government service and took almost a year off to recuperate in California. McCune's disability deprived the State Department of its main expert on Korea, who could have made a difference as the Korea desk officer in Washington or as the political adviser to the military government in Korea.

Knowing almost nothing about what to expect, U.S. soldiers began their mission blind and without any orders telling them what to do. Neither the State Department in Washington nor General MacArthur in the Pacific bothered to send them any plans or policies aside from a general instruction from MacArthur to administer Korea in the same way as Japan. As a result, a nation eager to be liberated by Americans was supposed to be treated in the same way as the defeated common enemy. The Korean people and the U.S. forces sent to govern them both deserved better.

The U.S. Military Government and the Korean Provisional Government

The second American era in Korea began with misunderstandings and mistakes that would permanently change the relationship between Koreans and Americans, and General Hodge would become the main target of criticism from all sides. Hodge has been a vilified figure in Korea for his role in the difficult U.S. occupation, and American historians judging him in hindsight have been quick to find mistakes in his decisions. A fairer view of Hodge's situation shows him in a different light. Hodge was a capable and conscientious officer trying to carry out a mission for which no one had prepared him, and the task of governing Korea put him in a position in which it was almost impossible to succeed.

The arrival of the XXIV Corps set a tone for the confused U.S.

occupation. As a military operation, it proceeded with few problems, demonstrating the operational and logistical skill for moving large forces over long distances that the U.S. military had developed during four years of war. It began on August 31 with the establishment of radio contact with the only known authorities in Korea, the Japanese military command.[8] The arrival in Seoul of an advance party in B-25 bombers followed on September 4, just over two weeks after the misadventures of Operation Eagle at the same airbase. The lead elements of the XXIV Corps sailed from Okinawa on September 5 and landed at Inchon on September 8, led by a regiment of the 7th Infantry Division. Problems immediately arose when they set foot in Korea. A cheering crowd had gathered to meet them at the port, but a force of Japanese police kept Koreans away from the troops. As soldiers of the XXIV Corps moved from Inchon into Seoul and began to set up the military government, their almost total lack of knowledge and language skills impaired their efforts. They found that more than seventy political parties had already formed in the south, but they were unable even to tell most of them apart, finding many of their names translating identically and complaining that no system for romanization of the Korean alphabet existed to help—unaware that George McCune had developed one seven years earlier.[9]

The new U.S. Army Military Government in Korea (USAMGIK) soon found that the outgoing Japanese authorities had created a significant problem for it. In mid-August 1945, with the surrender of Japan announced and Soviet forces driving into northern Korea, the governor-general of Korea had created a Committee for the Preparation of Korean Independence in Seoul. Koreans eager for independence soon formed numerous "people's committees" around the country in emulation of the committee in Seoul. The Japanese commanding general in Korea sent a brief warning about them to General Hodge in a radio message on September 1, saying, "There are Communists and independence agitators among Koreans who are plotting to take advantage of this situation to disturb peace and order here," but it was only one sentence in a lengthy radio message about arrangements for September 8, justifying a request to have a minimal Japanese military presence at the landing.[10]

On September 6 the committee in Seoul renamed itself the Korean People's Republic, claiming to be the provisional government of Korea.

The main leader of the Korean People's Republic was Yo Un Hyong, a Presbyterian born in 1886 with a long history as a Korean nationalist. He had studied at the Paejae School in Seoul as a teenager in 1900, and in his twenties he attended the Union Presbyterian Theological Seminary in Pyongyang, the Sinhung Military Academy in Manchuria, and a university in Nanjing, China, where he studied English literature. He had participated in Korean nationalist movements in China and Russia in the 1910s and in the founding of the Korean Provisional Government in 1919. He returned to Korea from Shanghai as a captive of Japanese agents and spent three years in Seodaemun Prison. After his release in 1932, he continued his resistance activities as a newspaper publisher and an underground activist.[11] In 1945, at the age of fifty-nine he had four decades of experience resisting Imperial Japanese rule, had lived in China, Japan, and the Soviet Union, and had worked at various times with the Chinese Nationalist Party, the Korean Communist Party, and the Soviet TASS news agency in Shanghai. He was already a relic of a past era when Koreans of many ideologies could cooperate. He and the Korean People's Republic loosely brought together ideas from the left and right, and both sides soon would violently oppose them.

General Hodge rejected the claim of the Korean People's Republic to be the provisional government, following U.S. occupation policies for Japan that ruled out working with self-proclaimed government authorities. Nevertheless, the Korean People's Republic continued as a moderate left-wing political party called the People's Party of Korea, founded by Yo Un Hyong in November 1945. Some historians have criticized General Hodge for his refusal to accept the Korean People's Republic's claim to be the government of Korea, declaring it to have been part of an anti-Communist agenda, but Hodge was equally opposed to the Korean Provisional Government that was the Communists' main opponent in Korea. Hodge's limited instructions from General MacArthur did not allow the formation of competing authorities in his area of responsibility, and in the early days of his command he had no reason to disagree. The tragic flaw of the U.S. military government in Korea was that its orders from above put it on a collision course with all of the political factions of Korea, each of which had an equal hunger for immediate independence after a generation of rule by Japan.

The national police soon created another problem for Hodge. They were widely hated for their longtime role of enforcing Japanese rule, and demands came from every direction to disband them and other holdovers of the Japanese administration. Hodge instead kept them in place, a decision for which he has been criticized in hindsight. What else he could have done is unclear, though, as he needed help from somewhere to govern Korea. Part of the reason was military logistics. Units of the XXIV Corps were slow to arrive because U.S. transport ships were in limited supply, and landing U.S. occupation troops in Japan and in China at Shanghai were higher priorities. A month after the first landing at Inchon, only half of the XXIV Corps was in Korea, and its units were still in the process of establishing a presence in all of the major cities and provinces. Not until December was its full strength in place. With limited U.S. personnel available and knowledge of Korea and its language almost nonexistent, Hodge needed existing organizations to rely on. The national police and other leftover Japanese authorities were available, so Hodge retained them.

Retaining Japanese in positions throughout the administration was deeply unpopular among Koreans. The Japanese had admitted few Koreans into government or industry, resulting in a complete absence of Koreans from public administration and few capable of running railroads and other essential services. Hodge promised to replace Japanese with Americans as soon as possible, then replace Americans with Koreans, but violent protests forced him to accelerate dismissals of Japanese and their replacement with Koreans. Almost 75,000 Koreans had been hired to replace Japanese in government positions by December 1945. With its Japanese commanders and Korean rank and file who were seen as collaborators, the national police was one of many institutions requiring massive turnover.

The formation of a new police force did not begin until late in 1945, and it barely existed through the end of 1946. In November 1945 Army Chief of Staff George Marshall and General MacArthur discussed plans for raising a Korean police force, and the U.S. military government enacted a law authorizing a Korean constabulary on November 13. In early December an officer training academy opened, with its first cadets a mix of former officers of the Korean Restoration Army and Koreans who had served as officers in the Imperial Japanese Army. The first constabulary battalion formed in Seoul in January 1946, followed by more units in each of the south's eight provinces later in the year. At the end of November they numbered only five thousand, slightly more than the strength of a single U.S. Army infantry regiment, and at the end of 1947 they were still less than twenty thousand. This small force eventually became the army of the Republic of Korea instead of a police force.

Events could have been different if the Korean Restoration Army had been available to the U.S. military government early in the occupation. The small force that existed in September 1945 could have provided Hodge with an organization of Koreans whose leaders already had experience working with Americans through Project Eagle and were eager to advise and assist the liberation and occupation of Korea. The plan of Gen. Kim Hak Kyu to expand the Korean Restoration Army with Koreans from the Imperial Japanese Army and use it to support the U.S. occupation force in the south, which Clarence Weems had attempted to promote in Washington in his reports on September 28 and October 11, could have been an early start to the creation of a new Korean police and defense force to replace the existing national police. But it was never an option that Hodge could have chosen.

The Korean Provisional Government was far away in China when U.S. forces landed at Inchon on September 8, and its leaders faced a long wait before they could return to Korea. The political leaders were in Chungking, and the Korean Restoration Army was scattered in Xian, Anhui, and other locations, winding down its involvement with the oss in Project Eagle. It was uncertain when and how they would return to Korea and what their relationship with the United States would be. Dissolving the entire government was a possibility discussed in the legislative assembly until Kim Ku persuaded them to keep it together and return to Korea to present it before the people. To ease its return, the Korean Provisional Government asked the U.S. embassy in Chungking for U.S. aircraft to fly its leaders to Korea.

Responding to this request involved providing not only an airplane but also the appearance of official endorsement by the United States, so the U.S. response was cautious and time-consuming. The issue went all the way to Washington in mid-September, and at the end of the month the State Department decided that it would allow such flights only if Korean Provisional Government leaders returned to Korea as individuals, not as officials of a provisional government, with equal privileges and facilities for members of all Korean factions.[12] The State Department issued an official press release on this policy on October 16, stating that the U.S. military government in Korea had "initiated a policy of seeking advice on local matters from representative Koreans in their individual capacities" and that "the opportunity is now open to Koreans who are interested in rendering service to their countrymen," with the State Department accepting applications for travel permits.[13] The response crushed the Korean Provisional Government's plans, but despite the disappointment, they decided to accept returning to Korea as private individuals.

The first Korean leader to return under this policy was not from the Korean Provisional Government in Chungking; it was Syngman Rhee. The seventy-year-old Rhee, who had been living in the United States for twenty years since leaving the Korean Provisional Government in Shanghai in 1925, flew into Seoul on October 16, on the same day as the State Department's press release. The State Department, including George McCune as the Korea desk officer, had long disliked Rhee, but he had a prominent supporter in Col. M. Preston Goodfellow, former deputy director of the OSS, who had been involved in OSS relations with Rhee in Washington since 1942. Now a War Department adviser, Goodfellow arranged to have Rhee flown from Japan to Korea in General MacArthur's personal airplane. Accusations that the United States set up Rhee to take power in Korea have followed ever since, but in reality he was one of many Korean leaders in exile that various U.S. authorities brought to Korea. Kim Ku and the Korean Provisional Government in Chungking also flew to Korea in a U.S. plane a month later.

The Korean Provisional Government took its time moving from Chungking to Seoul, retracing steps that its surviving members had taken since 1919. They spent weeks closing down their offices and the lives that they had lived in Chungking for seven years since their long journey from Nanjing in 1937–38. Not until November 5 did Kim Ku, the cabinet, and other officials board U.S. aircraft that flew them to Shanghai.[14] It was thirteen years since they had fled Shanghai after the Japanese assault on the city and the bombing campaign that Kim Ku had organized in 1932. There Kim Ku visited his wife's grave and the graves of compatriots in Shanghai's French concession. On November 23 U.S. aircraft flew the group from Shanghai to Seoul's Kimpo Airport. Almost twenty-seven years had passed since Kim Ku had left Korea to join the Korean Provisional Government in 1919, and others had been in exile even longer. The flight from Shanghai to Seoul took them back in only three hours. "With a heart throbbing with both joy and sadness, I stepped on the soil of my motherland and breathed its fresh air for the first time in twenty-seven years," Kim Ku recalled later in his memoirs.[15] When they arrived, they were greeted by a parade through Seoul attended by huge crowds and a lavish welcoming banquet attended by General Hodge and other U.S. officials.

The Korean Restoration Army faced an even longer path back to Korea. In September Gen. Kim Hak Kyu and officers of his Third Detachment, including Kim Woo Chun, relocated from their wartime post in Anhui to Shanghai. Gen. Yi Pomsok and officers of the Second Detachment in Xian joined them after the end of Project Eagle on September 30. In Shanghai they succeeded in recruiting several thousand Koreans from the surrendering Japanese forces, but they lost many to desertion as months passed and winter set in. With funds and supplies inadequate to support several thousand men, the Korean Restoration Army could not hold on to most of its recruits, who wanted above all to return Home.[16] In December, more than one thousand revolted and asked U.S. military authorities in China to repatriate them after not receiving the food, clothes, and shelter that the Korean Restoration Army had promised since September.[17] In February 1946 the Korean Restoration Army officially disbanded, which finally allowed its men to return to Korea under the U.S. rules against repatriation of organizations.[18]

The former soldiers of the Korean Restoration Army became a few thousand souls in vast movements of Koreans who returned from exile in China, Japan, and all around the Pacific after the war. The repatriation of Japanese in Korea to Japan and of Koreans in Japan to Korea was an immediate priority of the U.S. occupation authorities, and the U.S. military government in Korea drafted a repatriation plan within a week after the initial landing at Inchon. The withdrawal of Japanese military personnel was completed by November 1945, and Japanese civilians were repatriated by March 1946. More than 1 million Koreans had returned to the U.S. occupation zone from Japan by the end of 1946, mostly in a fleet of Landing Ship Tank (LST) amphibious assault ships that shuttled regularly across the Sea of Japan, transporting thousands each day. Repatriation of Koreans in China from the ports of Shanghai, Tianjin, and Qingdao by ships of the U.S. Seventh Fleet began in late January 1946, after Clyde Sargent's recommendation in December 1945.[19] By June 1946 approximately 600,000 had departed for Korea, including the former members of the Korean Restoration Army. Thousands more came from Formosa, the Philippines, Southeast Asia, and Pacific islands, where Japanese forces had taken them and they had been stranded at the end of the war.

Refugees crossing the 38th Parallel further swelled the population of the south. The Korean Christians of Pyongyang and northern Korea faced intimidation by the Soviet occupation force and the Korean Communists who followed them, then outright persecution, and many uprooted themselves and fled south. Hundreds of thousands of non-Christians left the north as well, escaping Soviet occupation and a new regime that treated landowners, merchants, and anyone considered to have collaborated with Japan as enemies. Approximately 750,000 people fled to establish new lives in the south between 1945 and 1950. Approximately 300,000 Japanese military personnel and civilians also moved across the 38th Parallel, seeking repatriation to Japan. Most of the Korean Christians and other refugees from the north passed through Kaesong, once the Methodist mission station and home of Clarence Weems and his family, which was now located just south of the 38th Parallel and used by the U.S. military government as a center for receiving and caring for refugees from the north.

The 1.6 million people repatriated from Japan and China and approximately 750,000 refugees from the north placed a heavy burden on the south, which already faced an economic crisis after the division of Korea. A legacy of Korea's colonization was uneven economic development, in which the south with its more favorable geography for agriculture produced most of the country's food, while the north had most of its industry, based on hydroelectric power from dams and reservoirs in its mountainous regions—including the Chosin Reservoir, soon to become known to Americans as the location of one of great battles of the U.S. Marine Corps. The south had little industrial output, and Seoul relied almost entirely on power plants north of the 38th Parallel for its electric power. The division of Korea disrupted the economies of both occupation zones and left the south with little ability to provide work and livelihoods for the millions of refugees arriving from abroad, often destitute, who mostly stayed in Seoul and other urban areas. They became a significant part of the population of the south, which had just over 16 million people in September 1945, and their discontents contributed to making the south a tinderbox soon after its liberation.

The leaders of the Korean Provisional Government returned from exile to this situation of division and turmoil. The 38th Parallel had become a hostile border between the U.S. and Soviet occupation forces, and Kim Ku from Haeju and others originally from north of the 38th Parallel were unable to visit their hometowns in the Soviet occupation zone. In the U.S. occupation zone, there was widespread unrest over plans for a period of trusteeship over Korea that the United States and Soviet Union were discussing. Koreans universally expected that liberation would bring them independence, and as talks between Washington and Moscow dragged on, with reports of plans to defer Korean independence until after years of foreign trusteeship, outrage against foreign occupation rose. Syngman Rhee and Kim Ku on the right, the People's Party of Korea on the left, and practically all other Korean political groups denounced trusteeship and demanded immediate independence.

General Hodge and the U.S. military government in Korea had no role in the discussions over trusteeship, and as they learned more about Korea, a rift opened between them and their superiors in Washington. A key adviser to Hodge during this period was William Langdon, who arrived in October 1945 to serve as his acting Political Advisor. Unknown to most Americans, including most historians, a Political Advisor from the State Department is a central part of a U.S. military command overseas, the primary adviser to the commanding general on the politics of the host country and on the foreign policy decisions of the State Department. Langdon had served as the U.S. consul in Korea before the war and had some familiarity with the country, unlike his predecessor, H. Merrill Benninghoff, who was sent back to Washington to report to the State Department on the situation in Korea.[20] As early as November 10, Hodge and Langdon urged the State Department to abandon the idea of trusteeship as repugnant to Koreans of all political factions.[21] They recommended considering immediate Korean independence, by recognition of the Korean Provisional Government or establishment of a Korean government in the south using the Korean Provisional Government as a nucleus.[22]

Langdon repeated these recommendations at greater length on November 20. He reported to the State Department that its discussion of trusteeship was disrupting what had begun as an amicable relationship between Koreans and the U.S. military government. Trusteeship violated Koreans' universal demand for "their country to themselves in their lifetime," without "any form of foreign tutelage to attain an alien standard of nationhood," and should be abandoned. He further asserted that avoiding becoming associated with the Korean Provisional Government, under the State Department's policy of abstaining from any action that might interfere with Koreans' ability to choose their own form of government, did not make sense. He reported that all parties and factions recognized the Korean Provisional Government, still waiting in Shanghai for its return to Korea, as "quasi legitimate" and with "no rival for first government of liberated Korea," and that "jubilance prevails over its impending return and widespread arrangements are being made for a triumphal welcome." Kim Ku was the key figure, with "wide esteem" that "offers us an opportunity for attempting a constructive Korean policy that can hardly be resented or traduced."[23]

Langdon laid out a plan for Korean independence, under the leadership of Kim Ku and the Korean Provisional Government, and the withdrawal of U.S. and Soviet forces as soon as possible. Kim Ku would form a governing commission that first would integrate with the military government and then would replace it. The governing commission then would hold a national election to select a head of state to form a government. Before the election there would be negotiations with the Soviet Union for the mutual withdrawal of U.S. and Soviet troops and for extension of the authority of the governing commission into the Soviet occupation zone. If the Soviet Union refused to participate, the United States would proceed with the plan in its occupation zone south of the 38th Parallel.[24]

The State Department rejected Langdon's recommendations in a message sent on November 29, after Kim Ku's arrival in Seoul, its reply pointing out that its primary concern was the ongoing trusteeship discussions with the Soviet Union. The State Department responded that it gave "careful consideration" to Langdon's suggestions, but it regarded trusteeship as possibly necessary to secure elimination of the boundary at the 38th Parallel. Ending discussion of trusteeship would be possible if the United States could obtain adequate specific guarantees from the Soviet Union for the unification and independence of Korea. It disapproved of the governing commission plan, believing that attempting to introduce such a new idea would jeopardize negotiations with the Soviet Union. The State Department recognized that Kim Ku was already preparing to form a provisional government within days of his return to Korea, but it urged Langdon and Hodge not to deviate from existing policies and not to cooperate with Kim Ku.[25]

Washington's policies were set, and the recommendations of U.S. military and civilian officials in Korea would not change them. Hodge and Langdon urged their superiors to reconsider their policies on Korea far more stridently in mid-December, but their messages again received little attention. Langdon repeated their opposition to trusteeship on December 11, recommending again that the State Department raise the governing commission plan with the Soviet Union. He criticized the State Department, War Department, and Navy Department in Washington for ignoring "the present mood of the Korean people: impatient of spoon feeding, conscious of independence and eager to exercise it." "We [Hodge and Langdon] believe that only by making important concessions to this mood can the situation be kept in hand, conflict avoided, and cooperation obtained in our zone. . . . [W]ith Kim Koo and all national leaders at last gathered in Seoul, political fever is running high and expectations are great. But without offices to fill or fight for, it will soon be realized that all Korean political activity is mummery, and resentment will follow frustration."[26]

Hodge followed several days later with a lengthy, blistering report on his conclusions after three months in Korea:

> In south Korea the U.S. is blamed for the partition and there is growing resentment against all Americans in the area including passive resistance to constructive efforts we make here. No explanation can reach through to the people since it is counteracted by the existing facts. Every day of drifting under this situation makes our position in Korea more untenable and decreases our waning popularity and our effectiveness to be of service. The word pro-American is being added to pro-Jap, national traitor, and Jap collaborator. . . . Every Korean knows full well that under the dual occupation any talk of real freedom and independence is purely academic. It will be extremely difficult, if not impossible, ever to establish unity of spirit in the Koreans until they see the present Thirty Eighth Parallel barrier removed. Every day of delay fosters further and permanent division of the people.

Hodge recommended that the United States seriously consider an agreement with the Soviet Union for mutual withdrawal of forces from Korea and "to leave Korea to its own devices and an inevitable internal upheaval for its self purification."[27]

The rift between General Hodge in Korea and his superiors in Washington finally came to a head at the end of December, when news about the Moscow Conference on the postwar dispositions of numerous countries in Europe and Asia reached Korea. The conference, held from December 16 to December 26, produced agreements on Italy, Romania, Bulgaria, Hungary, Finland, Japan, China, and Korea. Its declarations on Korea called for establishing a Joint Commission of representatives of the U.S. and Soviet military commands, which would form a democratic Korean provisional government and govern Korea with the participation of the provisional government under a four-power (the United States, the Soviet Union, China, and the United Kingdom) trusteeship for "a period of up to five years"—the policy that Hodge and Langdon had urged against as certain to be angrily opposed by all Koreans.[28] Hodge and Langdon proved to be right. When the announcement about trusteeship reached Korea on December 27 through foreign news sources, there was immediate mass outrage in Seoul. Demonstrations began in the streets and continued to rage into the new year. Korea's political factions maneuvered to take advantage of the unrest, and Hodge labored to contain it while engaging in a war of words with Washington.

Kim Ku and some leaders of the Korean Provisional Government used the crisis to declare Korean independence and attempt to seize power. They organized mass demonstrations in Seoul after news of the Moscow Conference arrived on December 27, and on the evening of December 31 Kim Ku made a series of speeches denouncing the U.S. military government and declaring himself to be in power in Korea. This weak attempt at claiming power, sometimes called a coup but hardly deserving to be called one, was a dismal failure, as Hodge suppressed it easily and on New Year's Day summoned Kim Ku to his headquarters for a stern talk.

What exactly Kim Ku was thinking when he spoke up in this way is not clear. He left the events of December 1945 out of his memoirs entirely, leaving no thoughts on what happened and why he acted in the way that he did. Regardless of his exact motivations, his actions were those of a sixty-nine-year-old man recently returned from twenty-six years in exile, after half a century of resistance activity. After a month back in Korea with discontent with the U.S. military government growing, followed by mass outrage over the trusteeship announcement and the excitement of the protests in the streets of Seoul, he may have simply acted emotionally and irrationally. It is possible that he had heard from a source at U.S. military government headquarters that Hodge disapproved of trusteeship and believed that he should lead a Korean government replacing the U.S. military government and he badly miscalculated what Hodge would do in response to his actions, but it is unlikely that any evidence of this scenario can ever be found.[29]

Kim Ku was not the only figure in Korean politics to act peculiarly during the crisis, as the Korean Communist Party did so as well. Revived in Seoul in October 1945 after being dormant since 1928, the Communist Party at first joined the popular protests against trusteeship. On January 3 it suddenly reversed its position and demonstrated in favor of trusteeship, on the instructions of Moscow. This about-face against the practically universal will of the Korean people widely discredited the Communist Party in the south.

The demonstrations fulfilled the warnings of Hodge and Langdon earlier in December that attempting to impose trusteeship on Korea would collide with the desire of the Korean people for independence and cause irreparable damage to the U.S.-Korea relationship. The leaders of the demonstrations had been Kim Ku, Syngman Rhee, and others who had been friendly toward the United States and whom the U.S. military government favored for leadership roles in Korea. Hodge struggled to contain the protests in Seoul and calm them down, partly with arrests of protestors by Korean national police and partly with radio messages worked out with the State Department that clarified the terms of the Moscow Conference announcement on trusteeship, emphasizing that it was intended to make Korean unification and full independence possible and terminate in no later than five years.[30] The unrest subsided toward the end of January, but it flared up again as a result of a Soviet press release on January 25 that blamed the United States for trusteeship, claiming that Americans had insisted on a term of ten years or more that the Soviet Union had argued against.[31]

The crisis left Hodge thoroughly frustrated with Washington's handling of Korea.[32] Inattention toward the U.S. military government in Korea had been apparent in November, after the resignation of George McCune from the Korea desk in October, when the State Department gave instructions to Langdon about how to handle Kim Ku based on a story in the *New York Times* instead of Langdon's reports, and the instructions used "Koo" as his last name.[33] The State Department had disregarded warnings from Hodge and Langdon and it had failed to inform them about trusteeship developments at the Moscow Conference despite repeated demands to be kept informed in order to prepare for reactions in Korea, resulting in Koreans learning about developments first from news reports.[34] Hodge declared in a message to MacArthur on February 1 that the State Department had "paid little attention either to the information painstakingly sent in from those actually on the ground as to the psychology of the Korean people or the repeated urgent recommendations of the Commander and State Department political advisers." He concluded, "I do not know who have been the experts on Korea who have advised and guided the State Department in their disregard of my recommendations. It certainly has not been anyone who has seen and really knows Korea since the war."[35]

In the aftermath of the crisis over trusteeship, the relationship between the United States and Korea had changed permanently. The United States and the Soviet Union proceeded with the arrangements agreed upon at the Moscow Conference, forming the Joint Commission of representatives from their military commands in Korea and holding its first meeting in Seoul on March 20, 1946. The Joint Commission would meet twenty-four times from March 20 through May 6 but would fail to reach agreement on terms for the formation of a provisional Korean government.[36] It was the start of a year of fruitless negotiations over the future of Korea by U.S. officials overseas carrying out policies devised in Washington, the first of many in the years to come. In Korea, Hodge and Langdon faced the loss of the only Korean leader whom they believed could lead an independent Korea. Kim Ku's failed bid at seizing power on December 31 had ended their idea that he could lead a transitional governing commission, and no one else who had been with the Korean Provisional Government in Chungking had his stature.

Syngman Rhee became the beneficiary of Kim Ku's mistakes. He proved to be far more adept than Kim Ku at exploiting the controversy over trusteeship and Koreans' desire for immediate independence. After the January demonstrations against trusteeship, Rhee spent the spring of 1946 outside of Seoul on a speaking tour of the provinces that boosted his popularity throughout the south, then in June outmaneuvered Kim Ku to take over control of the National Society for the Rapid Realization of Independence (NSRRI), the leading right-wing political organization, which Rhee had founded after his arrival in Korea in October 1945. Taking over the NSRRI enabled Rhee to set the agenda for a broad coalition of right and center parties and gave him control over an organization with offices throughout the south. By the autumn of 1946, Rhee had displaced Kim Ku as the leader of the right wing and the remnants of the Korean Provisional Government and established himself as the front-runner to become the head of a future independent Korea.

Syngman Rhee and Kim Ku could not have had less in common, although they were born only a year apart and within a few miles of each other, in Haeju just north of the 38th Parallel. Kim Ku had no formal education, spent his early years with the Korean independence movement far from Seoul in provincial northern Korea, and had never seen the world outside of Korea and the Korean exile communities in China. Syngman Rhee had been educated at the Paejae School in Seoul, obtained further degrees from George Washington University, Harvard University, and Princeton University, spent his early years with the Korean independence movement in Seoul with Philip Jaisohn's elite Independence Club, and had lived in the United States on and off since 1904 and traveled to Europe representing the Korean independence cause.

Rhee was a strange figure in Korea, in exile since 1912 and living among Koreans for the first time in twenty years. He returned speaking Korean with an American accent and with an Austrian wife, Franziska Donner, who was a key part of his political inner circle. All that Syngman Rhee and Kim Ku shared were their place of birth, conversions to Christianity, and status as former presidents of the Korean Provisional Government.

Syngman Rhee was an outsider in Korea, and in the unusual situation that existed after the liberation, his outsider status proved to be a political asset—probably the first and last time for such an occurrence in Korea. With many Korean political factions divided by personal rivalries between their leaders more than by ideology, Rhee's lack of preexisting ties became an advantage instead of a disadvantage, making him acceptable to many parties as a compromise leader. His years living in the United States also gave him some experience dealing with American politics and U.S. government officials, unlike Kim Ku and others who had lived in Korea and China. Rhee's experience and his ability to speak English gave him an advantage over his rivals, although his relationship with the State Department, General Hodge, and many other U.S. authorities was tense and often hostile.

The support of "youth" groups that became a significant part of the violent politics of the south was also crucial to the rise of Syngman Rhee. The leaders of the political factions had already surrounded themselves with security entourages to prevent attempts at assault or assassination by rivals. Assassinations nevertheless claimed the lives of many, including Korean People's Party leader Yo Un Hyong, who was assaulted numerous times and finally killed by a gunman in July 1947. Even Kim Il Sung in Pyongyang was the target of assassination teams sent from the south in the spring of 1946.[37] By late 1945, left- and right-wing parties alike had gone further and created mass "youth" organizations to fight their political battles by intimidating leaders of opposing parties and breaking up their demonstrations. The youth groups were paramilitary organizations of young men from their teens to their thirties, who were easily recruited in large numbers from the masses of unemployed young men in the cities. Refugees from the north violently opposed to Communism especially swelled the ranks of the right-wing youth organizations, making up the entire membership of one of the most extreme groups, the Northwest Youth. Founded in November 1946, the Northwest Youth developed an organization throughout the south and even an underground network in the north. It and other right-wing youth groups backed Syngman Rhee as the leader of the right in 1946.

Yi Pomsok became the leader of the largest and most important youth group, the Korean National Youth Corps. It was a strange twist of fate for Yi Pomsok, arguably the foremost soldier among Koreans in 1945. After thirty years of military service in exile, concluded as the Korean co-commander of Project Eagle, he should have returned to Korea with honors, to become a protector of the newly independent Korean state for which he had struggled since his teenage years. Instead, after Operation Eagle failed and U.S. authorities turned down his offers to advise and assist the U.S. military government in Korea, he went in a different direction. He stayed in Shanghai as one of the leaders of the Korean Restoration Army in its ongoing exile, remaining there as one of the last holdouts after most of its men returned to Korea in March 1946. At one point after Kim Ku's attempted "coup," General Hodge ordered him prohibited from returning to Korea in January 1946, viewing him as a potential threat as a staunch supporter of the Korean Provisional Government.[38] Hodge eventually relented and in March 1946 offered to make Yi the first minister of defense under the U.S. military government, but Yi turned it down, declining to work under U.S. command. Yi finally returned to Korea in June 1946, nine months after the end of the war, at the invitation of Syngman Rhee.

An alliance between Syngman Rhee and Yi Pomsok was an unnatural combination that occurred because of the way that Korea had been liberated. They shared nothing aside from Korean nationalism and hostility toward Communism. A generation younger than Rhee, Yi did not share the Christian school education and American intellectual influence of Rhee and other leading Korean political figures. Yi had learned his hostility toward the Soviet Union and Communism through firsthand experience living in the Soviet Union in the early 1920s, reinforced in the 1930s by his service in the Nationalist Chinese Army, fighting both Japan and the Chinese Communists. He emerged from the war with unique leadership experience and his own ideas on the need to organize and educate the Korean people after their decades under colonial rule. The ongoing lack of Korean independence and the threat of Communism in the north and within the south drew him into an alliance with Syngman Rhee and into using his three decades of military experience in partisan politics.

The result was the Korean National Youth Corps. Yi joined the Korean constabulary as an adviser in July 1946, but he became dissatisfied with the presence of numerous leftists in its ranks and resigned in November.[39] He then founded the Korean National Youth Corps as an intensely nationalist anti-Communist paramilitary organization. He made it the largest of the youth groups, with at least 200,000 members and organizations in cities and villages throughout the south.[40] It became a significant influence on the emerging security services of the south as it fed thousands of men into the national police and the constabulary, then into the army of the Republic of Korea that the constabulary became. The organization made Yi the second most influential leader in the south after Syngman Rhee. Yi and his movement received support from the U.S. military government, leading to them being seen as American surrogates, but in reality they were beyond American control, cooperating with U.S. authorities when useful to them but pursuing their own agenda.

Hodge and Langdon considered Rhee to be a divisive figure who was destroying any possibility of establishing a government in the south that would be broadly accepted by all political groups, and they hoped to find an alternative to Rhee. They favored Kim Kyusik, a centrist who had been educated in the United States and had a long history as a unifying figure in the Korean nationalist movement. In 1935 he had founded a united front party in Shanghai with Kim Wonbong, the Communist leader who later reconciled with Kim Ku and allied with the Korean Provisional Government, and during the war he had served as the Korean Provisional Government's vice president. In September 1946, at Kim Kyusik's suggestion, Hodge and Langdon even went to the length of requesting that the State Department approach eighty-two-year-old Philip Jaisohn, the pioneer of the reform and independence movement in Korea half a century earlier, with a request to return to Korea to serve as a special adviser to the U.S. military government, hoping that he could become a rival to Rhee.[41] The elderly Jaisohn returned to Korea but proved to be as incapable of checking Rhee's influence as Kim Ku, Kim Kyusik, or anyone else, and Hodge found himself forced to work with Rhee even though he considered him unacceptable.

By April 1946 Hodge believed that the U.S. military government could not effectively govern the south because of opposition from both Korean nationalists and Communists and should be withdrawn as soon as possible. He reported to MacArthur on April 2, "Although they know we are trying to help them, they are highly suspicious of United States final motives, resent the need for help as well as any controls and blame all their national ills on anyone handy who is not Korean." He recommended that if the Joint Commission succeeded in establishing a provisional government, the United States should propose to the Soviet Union that both countries withdraw their forces no later than January 1947, and that if the Joint Commission did not make definite progress within a month, it should close and the issue of Korean independence should be resolved by the United Nations or by negotiations with the Soviet Union.[42] On April 27, with the concurrence of his senior commanders, staff officers, and advisers, Hodge formally recommended that preparations begin for the withdrawal of U.S. and Soviet occupation forces at the earliest possible date after the establishment of a provisional government. He recognized that his proposal was a radical departure from policies set in Washington, but he insisted that it was the only sound basis for a successful conclusion of the mission in Korea and the best chance for Korea to develop as a nation.[43]

The views of Hodge and his advisers in Korea had little or no influence on decisions made regarding Korea in Washington, however, and Hodge and the U.S. military government had to continue their work governing the south and the futile Joint Commission negotiations with their Soviet counterparts. After the failure of the Joint Commission to reach agreement on terms for the formation of a provisional government from March through May 1946, the U.S. military government continued for another year. It faced an increasingly assertive right-wing nationalist leadership in Seoul under Syngman Rhee and rising unrest in rural areas that flared up in major uprisings in 1946 and 1947.[44] The first in the fall of 1946 forced Hodge to declare martial law at a time when the U.S. forces in Korea had fallen to only 43,500 and had little ability to deal with the unrest. A second, much larger wave of violence raged in the summer and fall of 1947, as peasants revolted in the southwestern province of Cholla and other areas, and Communists in the south sought to take advantage of the disturbances. Right-wing youth groups and the national police fought the uprisings in what was becoming a civil war within the south. Joint Commission meetings, which resumed on May 22, 1947, and continued into August, took place in this setting of violence and insurgency.

As the United States and the Soviet Union made no progress in the second series of Joint Commission meetings, Korea was headed inexorably toward permanent division. The south was approaching it with a U.S. military government and a Korean nationalist movement barely able to cooperate and with the countryside where most of its people lived in a state of disorder and Communist insurgency. The north, meanwhile, was assembling a regime and an army that in a few years would be able to launch an overwhelmingly powerful invasion of the south. They were products of a Soviet occupation of the north whose organization and decisiveness were a stark contrast to the U.S. occupation of the south. The difference and the war in 1950 that it made possible would cost the lives of more than 36,000 Americans and 2.5 million Koreans.

The Creation of the North Korean Regime

The Soviet Union wasted little time creating a regime to take over control of its occupation zone. While the U.S. military government in the south struggled with lack of knowledge, planning, and rational policies from Washington, Soviet authorities in the north proceeded with the clear objective of creating a Korean state under their influence. By 1950 the client state that they created would be prepared to go to war against the south with an overwhelming blitzkrieg.

Behind the Red Army force that entered Pyongyang on August 24, under the command of the Twenty-Fifth Army of the First Far Eastern Front, arrived a political organization different from anything in the U.S. military and U.S. government. The Communist Party of the Soviet Union oversaw the Red Army using a vast organization of political commissars, officers with military ranks who were political officers answering to the party, whose primary role was to shadow military commanders to ensure the political reliability of officers and their units. In Korea the political commissars became the de facto rulers of the country. The first was the political commissar of the Twenty-Fifth Army, Maj. Gen. Nikolai Georgievich Lebedev. When a Soviet Civil Administration officially took over authority in northern Korea on October 3, its head was Maj. Gen. Andrei Alekseyevich Romanenko, previously the political commissar of the First Far Eastern Front's Thirty-Fifth Army in Manchuria. Over both Lebedev and Romanenko was Col. Gen. Terentii Fomich Shtykov, the political commissar of the First Far Eastern Front, equivalent in rank to a U.S. four-star general. Shtykov became the supreme authority in Korea, the creator of the state of North Korea, and the first Soviet ambassador to North Korea.

The political commissars and the Twenty-Fifth Army arrived in Korea initially as unprepared as the U.S. Army's XXIV Corps. The Soviet Union had paid little attention to Korea before and during the war, and Soviet actions before the war had further handicapped it. The Soviet Union's large population of Koreans had included numerous Communist Party members, military officers, and Communist International (Comintern) members, but Stalin's Great Purge of 1936–38 had annihilated most of them, and in 1937 the entire Korean population of the Soviet Far East— over 170,000 people—had been deported to remote areas of Central Asia on the suspicion that they could become a fifth column for Imperial Japan. Thousands died during the deportations, which dumped them in arid regions of Kazakhstan and Uzbekistan, and not until 1956 would the Soviet government allow them to leave their internal exile and join mainstream Soviet society. Many served as draftees in the Red Army during the war, but there was no special effort to place them in the Twenty-Fifth Army before the occupation of Korea. In August 1945 the Twenty-Fifth Army had little information about Korea and lacked Korean interpreters. Like General Hodge and his advisers, the Soviet authorities in Korea would have to learn on the job about the country and the Koreans with whom they would work.

Shtykov and his fellow political commissars found that the north was almost devoid of any Communist movement and had political leaders opposed to Communism. In Pyongyang and other cities, they encountered people's committees inspired by the Committee for the Preparation of Korean Independence in Seoul. The leader of the people's committee in Pyongyang was Cho Man Sik, a Presbyterian convert who was influenced by Mohandas Gandhi's concepts of nonviolent resistance and national self-sufficiency. He had participated in the March First Movement of 1919 and led nonviolent resistance to Japanese rule in Korea for a quarter of a century. Seeking to construct a client regime in the north in one way or another, Shtykov attempted to co-opt Cho to serve as a non-Communist but compliant leader in the north. Shtykov kept the people's committees and Cho in place while putting them under the authority of the Soviet civil administration, a military organization of Red Army personnel, officially created on October 3. At the same time, he brought in groups of Korean Communists to create Communist organizations as alternatives.

The Korean Communists brought into the north became several competing factions. The largest was several thousand who had left Korea in the 1920s and 1930s and ended up joining the Chinese Communists, called the Yanan Faction after the city that had been the wartime Chinese Communist headquarters. The Yanan Faction returned to Korea in October 1945 and founded the New People's Party in February 1946. A smaller group, the Soviet Faction, consisted of Koreans born or raised in the Soviet Union who had survived the Great Purges and the deportations to Central Asia in 1937–38. Although they had little or no personal experience with Korea, the Soviet Union trained them and sent them to Korea to serve the Soviet Civil Authority. The smallest faction, the Guerilla Faction, consisted of Koreans who had fought as guerillas in Manchuria and then fled to the Soviet Union to escape Japanese retribution. Drafted into the Red Army, they became part of a unit of former guerillas from Manchuria called the 88th Independent Brigade, created in 1942 and based near Khabarovsk, eight hundred miles from Korea. They were fewer than two hundred in a unit composed primarily of Chinese. After three uneventful years guarding the border with Japanese-occupied Manchuria, the Koreans of the 88th Independent Brigade were sent to Korea in September 1945. They became the core of the North Korean Bureau of the Communist Party of Korea, created in October 1945 as a northern substitute for the Communist Party of Korea headquartered in Seoul.

When Cho Man Sik proved to be unwilling to follow Soviet orders, Shtykov had him and the people's committees replaced with a Communist-led governing body. Shtykov did it gradually but decisively, while in the south the U.S. military government had to fight Koreans over trusteeship and Koreans fought each other. Cho opposed the imposition of Communism in Korea and on November 3 started his own nationalist political movement, the Chosun Democratic Party. When Cho opposed the Moscow Conference decision on trusteeship, Red Army soldiers arrested him on January 5, 1946, placing him under house arrest in a Pyongyang hotel.[45] A purge of the main leaders of the Chosun Democratic Party followed. With Cho and other well-known Korean nationalists out of the way, on February 8, 1946, Shtykov created a new Korean governing body called the Provisional People's Committee for North Korea. For its chairman, Shtykov chose Kim Il Sung, an officer in the 88th Independent Brigade who was only thirty-three years old and almost unknown in Korea, whom he had made the head of the North Korean Bureau of the Communist Party of Korea in December 1945.

Shtykov's choice of Kim Il Sung began the creation of the totalitarian dynasty that would rule North Korea for multiple generations into the twenty-first century, starting with a previously insignificant figure. Kim Il Sung's life before 1945 was and still is an enigma. His father had moved the family to Manchuria in 1920 and then died in 1926, when the son was fourteen. As a teenager he dabbled with Communist ideas and organizations while in school, then in 1931 joined the Communist Party of China. He spent the 1930s in various guerilla bands in Manchuria, numbering in the tens or few hundreds, which were among many small Korean groups attempting to fight Japan in northern China. His actions during this period were minor, but they played two important roles in his life: they created a basis for an extensive future hagiography about him as a guerilla fighter, and during them he renamed himself Kim Il Sung.

The future totalitarian leader was a product of the fortunes of war. In 1940, fleeing Japanese retribution in Manchuria like many other Korean resistance fighters, Kim Il Sung crossed the border into the Soviet Union. The Red Army inducted him and made him an officer commanding the small Korean battalion in the 88th Independent Brigade in 1942. He lived a quiet life as a Red Army officer in the Far East, distant from the Soviet war against Nazi Germany. His only noteworthy achievement during the war was fathering a son whom he gave the Russian name Yuri and the Korean name Jong Il, who would succeed him as ruler of North Korea half a century later. In 1945 Kim Il Sung was somewhat like a younger and lesser version of Yi Pomsok, who had stayed in the Soviet Union because of his political inclinations.

Kim Il Sung returned to Korea for the first time since 1920 in late September 1945, a month after Soviet forces occupied Pyongyang. He arrived at Wonsan on a Soviet transport ship from Vladivostok with a group of veterans of the 88th Independent Brigade. At that moment, he most likely had no idea that the Soviet political commissars ruling the north would soon set him up as the leader of North Korea.

Soviet-directed moves also set up the Communist party organizations that would run North Korea. The Provisional People's Committee for North Korea was initially a coalition of four Communist and non-Communist parties: the North Korean Bureau of the Communist Party of Korea, the New People's Party, the purged and intimidated Chosun Democratic Party, and the Friends Party, created in February 1946 by followers of the Cheondogyo religion that had emerged from the Tong-hak Movement in the 1890s, which still had over 1 million followers in the north in 1945.[46] In the spring the North Korean Bureau became a separate Communist Party of North Korea, headed by Kim Il Sung. In July a popular front called the United Democratic National Front formally subordinated all political parties to the Communist Party of North Korea, which merged with the New People's Party to form the Workers' Party of Korea. Kim Il Sung began as the deputy chairman of the Workers' Party at its founding conference in August, reflecting his status as one of many Korean Communist leaders in a system that he had not yet risen to dominate.

To create a veneer of legitimacy for the regime that it was creating, the Soviet Civil Administration held elections in 1946–47. Elections for regional, provincial, and city people's committees were held in November 1946 with only the United Democratic National Front as a "yes" or "no" choice, followed by Shtykov setting representation in the First Congress of People's Committees at 35 percent for the Workers' Party, 15 percent each for the Chosun Democratic Party and the Friends Party, and 35 percent deputies without any party affiliation, with preestablished numbers for women, workers, peasants, and other social groups.

Measures for social and economic reform and state control of the economy proceeded under Soviet guidance during this period of government formation. Land reform enacted by the Provisional People's Committee of North Korea in March 1946, generally credited to Kim Il Sung but drafted by the Soviet Civil Administration, confiscated all land owned by Japanese or by landlords and distributed it to peasants, a measure that proved widely popular with impoverished tenant farmers given their own land for the first time. Nationalization of industry followed under Soviet Civil Administration guidance in August 1946. It technically confiscated only industries owned by Japanese or by their Korean collaborators, but with all but the smallest businesses having had to collaborate with the Japanese authorities before or during the war, the state effectively took over all industry in the north. The Provisional

People's Committee of North Korea issued its first economic plan in February 1947, before the official creation of the North Korean state.[47]

The land reform and nationalization of industry added to the flight of over 1 million people from the north to the south between 1945 and 1953. The March 1946 land reform confiscated all Korean landholdings exceeding five *chongbo*, approximately five hectares or just over twelve acres, which dispossessed all but the smallest landowners. Business owners similarly found themselves expropriated. Many of those who had lost everything to the hostile regime fled to the south to rebuild their lives. They joined most of the north's Christians, who faced persecution by the Soviet authorities and then by the newly created regime in the north. By 1950 approximately 750,000 people had fled to the south, and during the Korean War (1950–53), another 650,000 escaped. The exodus represented approximately 15 percent of the north's population of just over 9 million in 1945.

The flight of Christians erased Pyongyang's Christian community and ended the city's historic role as Korea's main center of Christianity. Christians were approximately one-sixth of Pyongyang's population of 300,000 in 1945, and they were a considerable part of the educated class and political leaders in the north. The Soviet occupation authorities first cut them off from the outside world by prohibiting the return of American missionaries, who in the south were reopening their old missions, as far north as Kaesong on the 38th Parallel. Soviet and Korean Communist authorities then suppressed Christian political organizations and acted to control and intimidate the churches. A Christian Social Democratic Party and Christian Liberal Party had emerged in 1945 as part of the people's committee in Pyongyang, but the Soviet Civil Administration excluded them. Seeing the Presbyterian and Methodist churches founded by Americans as especially threatening to Communist authority, in November 1946 the Provisional People's Committee for North Korea created an organization called the Federation of Christians that all church officials were required to join. Imprisonment was the fate of church leaders refusing to submit to state control. Confiscation of churches and church properties followed. Christians fled persecution in an exodus to the south, ending organized Christianity in the north and making Seoul its new center. The "Jerusalem of the East" that American Christians had helped to build came to an end, soon to be forgotten in a succession of tragic events that followed in Korea.

The building of the North Korean war machine that would bring about these tragic events went ahead at the same time as the creation of the regime. The north had only half of the south's population of 16 million, little military industry, and no military organization of its own in 1945, but the Soviet Union began the creation of a Korean armed force immediately and built it into a formidable force far more powerful than the army of the south. In October 1945 the first Soviet-trained police units were formed, and a full range of units of a modern mechanized army followed. On February 8, 1948, the Korean People's Army officially formed, months before the official creation of the North Korean state. By 1950 North Korea would have entire divisions of veteran troops with years of combat experience and an arsenal of modern weapons that had been the Red Army's mainstays in its war against Nazi Germany.

The north's army benefited from the civil war in China between 1945 and 1949, in which tens of thousands of its soldiers fought on the side of the Chinese Communists and gained combat experience against the army of Nationalist China. Koreans fought in the People's Liberation Army in large numbers, making up most or all of several entire divisions as well as irregular guerilla forces. Between 1948 and 1950, veteran units of Koreans withdrew from former battlefronts in China and went to North Korea, to be reconstituted as divisions in the Korean People's Army.[48]

The Soviet Union further increased North Korea's military superiority by providing tanks, combat aircraft, and training that enabled an armor-led offensive with air support. The Korean People's Army received T-34/85 tanks that were impervious to the small and obsolete antitank guns that the south's army possessed. The north also possessed an air force of Yakovlev Yak-9 fighters and Ilyushin Il-2 "Shturmovik" ground attack aircraft that gave it complete air superiority and the ability to strike the south's forces from the air with impunity. The United States provided the south with no combat aircraft, no tanks, and only 37mm antitank guns that were almost identical to the German 37mm antitank guns that had been hopelessly inadequate against the T-34 in 1941. By June 1950 North Korea was ready to unleash an assault that South Korea was unprepared to resist.

The Division of Korea

When the U.S.-USSR Joint Commission meetings resumed in May 1947, with the United States struggling to govern the south and watching it descend into insurgency and civil war and with the Soviet Union steadily creating a Communist client state in the north, the discussions went nowhere and set the stage for the permanent division of Korea. By September the United States had completely given up on negotiating with the Soviet Union and referred the situation to the United Nations General Assembly on September 23. On November 14, the UN General Assembly approved a resolution supporting a U.S. proposal that free elections occur in both the north and south by March 31, 1948, overseen by a UN Temporary Commission on Korea (UNTCOK), and that all foreign troops withdraw. The Soviet Union refused to participate in the vote or to cooperate with the resolution or with UNTCOK, so the election for the government of an independent Korea proceeded in the south alone. Just over two years after the liberation of Korea in two occupation zones, the final steps were in place for the permanent division of the country in 1948, 1,280 years after its original unification.

The prospect of dividing the country was widely unpopular throughout Korea, and in the south even some anti-Communist leaders were willing to meet with the emerging Communist regime in the north in order to attempt to avoid it. Protests occurred in the south, including on Cheju Island—known later as a tourism destination—where a violent uprising that lasted for over a year began in early April 1948. Kim Ku and his wartime vice president Kim Kyusik quickly led a group of southern political leaders on a delegation to Pyongyang to attend a conference on reunification organized by the Provisional People's Committee of North Korea. The meeting in Pyongyang brought together leaders who had cooperated with each other across the ideological divide a decade earlier in China, with one of the North Korean Communist leaders being Kim Wonbong, who had allied with the Korean Provisional Government under Kim Ku and Kim Kyusik for the war against Imperial Japan. No cooperation was possible this time with the Soviet-created Communist regime under Kim Il Sung, however, and the conference on April 19–23 produced nothing. Its purpose had been to disrupt the election and government formation process in the south, and it accomplished its goal.

Meeting with the North Korean regime in Pyongyang became the final step in the fall of Kim Ku and the defeat of the political outcome sought by the U.S. military government in Korea. Kim Ku and Kim Kyusik became pariahs among leaders concerned with the threat from North Korea after their return from Pyongyang. Syngman Rhee and Yi Pomsok made the meeting in Pyongyang their final breaking point with Kim Ku, after more than two years of political rivalry. The election went ahead without the participation of Kim Ku and Kim Kyusik, the mainstays of the wartime Korean Provisional Government and the leaders that General Hodge had most favored for principal roles in an independent postwar Korea.

The election held on May 10, 1948, was the first step to forming a constitutional government for a new Republic of Korea, electing a National Assembly that would draft and adopt a constitution and then elect a president, and its results reflected the primacy of Syngman Rhee in the south's politics but also the diversity of its parties and factions. Over 7.8 million votes were cast, a turnout of 95.5 percent of eligible voters. The National Society for the Rapid Realization of Independence coalition headed by Syngman Rhee finished first with 26 percent of the vote, giving it 55 out of 200 seats. Other parties received 34 percent of the vote and 60 seats, and independents received 40 percent of the vote and 85 seats. It was a sharp contrast to the elections engineered by Soviet political commissars in the north in 1946, which had formalized arrangements devised by Colonel-General Shtykov and his subordinates.

The Republic of Korea founded after the May 1948 election was a creation filled with contradictions, a continuation of the Korean Provisional Government derived from the March First Movement of 1919, which had been inspired by ideas brought by American Christians, whose origins went unrecognized by the United States. The constitution that the National Assembly adopted on July 17, 1948, enshrined democracy as the governing principle of Korea and declared the nation's adherence to the cause of the Korean Provisional Government, born of the March First Movement. For the United States and the rest of the world, which knew little or nothing about the earlier struggles of the Korean people, the creation of the Republic of Korea was part of the emerging rivalry between the United States and the Soviet Union, and the events of the preceding decades were of little or no concern. Attention went instead to the emerging authoritarian rule of Syngman Rhee and to the Communist regime that the Soviet Union had already formed in the north.

Syngman Rhee took over leadership of the new Republic of Korea with a remnant of the Korean Provisional Government that was unrecognizable as the organization that the OSS had made an ally three years earlier. The National Assembly elected Rhee as president on July 20, with 180 out of 196 votes, with Kim Ku receiving only 13 votes. Rhee's inauguration occurred on August 15. Yi Pomsok, as a key supporter of Rhee, became second in importance in the new government, serving as both prime minister and minister of defense. Kim Ku, Kim Kyusik, and other longtime leaders of the Korean Provisional Government retired from politics soon afterward, weakened by age after decades of struggle in Korea and in exile and unwelcome in a political system dominated by Rhee. The Republic of Korea was on its way to becoming an authoritarian state under Rhee, then a series of military dictators, its original ideals inherited from the Korean Provisional Government and the March First Movement deferred for decades.

While the south prepared for its election and then undertook the creation of a government, the formation of a separate state in the north proceeded as steadily under Soviet supervision as the creation of the Communist regime had during the preceding years. The drafting of a constitution for a Democratic People's Republic of Korea (DPRK) had begun in the north in the fall of 1947, and in February 1948 the Soviet Politburo became involved in reviewing the draft. Approval of the draft constitution came from Stalin and the Politburo on April 24, the day after the end of the conference in Pyongyang attended by Kim Ku, and the People's Assembly in the north formally ratified the constitution on April 28, almost two weeks ahead of the election in the south on May 10. The constitution did not recognize the existence of a separate state in the south, and it declared Seoul to be the capital of the DPRK, not Pyongyang. The DPRK's election waited until after the inauguration of Syngman Rhee. The DPRK officially came into existence on September 9, 1948, formalizing the division of Korea into two states.

Almost exactly three years after the first U.S. soldiers landed at Inchon on September 8, 1945, beginning the second era in Korea for Americans, the final division of the country into separate states marked the failure of the U.S. mission in Korea in 1945-48. The United States had sought to bring about a unified and democratic Korea, free of Soviet influence. The result in 1948 was a divided country, ruled in the north by a Soviet-created Communist regime, and with a government in the south that was democratic in form but becoming authoritarian in substance. The United States also did not prepare the Republic of Korea adequately to stop an invasion from the north, as shown by the rapid defeat of the ROK Army by the north's invasion on June 25, 1950. Even worse, the consequences permanently altered the reputation of the United States in Korea. Viewed almost entirely favorably in Korea before 1945, as a result of six decades of missionary work by American Christians, the United States became associated soon afterward with the division of the country and with support for a right-wing dictator.

General Hodge, sent to Korea by chance, had done his best to fulfill his mission and make a unified and democratic Korea possible. After spending almost three years of his life in Korea, dealing with crisis after crisis, he left Korea as soon as possible after his mission ended with the creation of the Republic of Korea. He asked to be relieved of his position as commanding general in Korea before the inauguration of Syngman Rhee, and he left Korea within two weeks after attending the inauguration ceremony with General MacArthur. The withdrawal of U.S. troops began soon afterward on September 15 and finished by June 30, 1949, leaving only a small group of 500 U.S. military advisers. They would be the only U.S. troops in the country a year later when the North Korean army stormed across the 38th Parallel on June 25, 1950.

Hodge never received widespread recognition in the United States for his work in Korea. The army recognized that he had taken on a difficult mission and fulfilled it as well as could have been expected, however, and he continued to serve in senior commands and received a fourth star in 1952. He retired a full general in 1953 and passed away in 1963.

Six years after Americans raised in what had become North Korea had gone to Washington to participate in U.S. actions involving Korea during the world war, neither of the two who had served in leading roles with the OSS were in Korea to witness the final division of the country. For each of them, this period was when the Korea that they had known, and their own lives, both fell apart.

Clarence Weems had worked for the U.S. military government in Korea in 1946–47, and during those difficult times he and his wife, Jennie, were expecting their second child. Jon Jordan Weems was born in 1947 but died soon after his birth. After burying him in Yanghwajin Foreign Missionary Cemetery in Seoul, Clarence and Jennie Weems left Korea, and their marriage ended soon thereafter.[49]

George McCune had gradually recuperated from the collapse of his health during the war, but in 1948 his health broke down again. He joined the faculty of the University of California at Berkeley in July 1946 as a lecturer in the history department and was promoted to assistant professor in 1947 and then associate professor in February 1948. After two academic years of teaching and prolifically publishing scholarship on Korea about both its history and its current situation under U.S. and Soviet occupation, he became bedridden and confined to his home in February 1948. With the assistance of his wife, Evelyn, a Korea scholar in her own right, he continued to supervise the work of graduate students and publish scholarship on Korea through the autumn of 1948, and his courses continued with Evelyn lecturing from his notes. From afar, he followed the division of Korea and the formation of the Republic of

Korea and the DPRK. He died on November 5, 1948, two months after the declaration of the DPRK that signified the final division of Korea.[50] As his father, George Shannon McCune, had not outlived the era of the American Christian missions in Korea, George McAfee McCune did not long survive the disappearance into North Korea of the city of Pyongyang where he had been born.

8

After the Mission

The key figures in the OSS-Korean alliance during the Second World War diverged widely in how their lives went after the foundation of the Republic of Korea and the division of Korea in 1948. The differences show how thoroughly the American role in Korea after the war left behind what had existed earlier, and they illustrate the vast gap between the ways that Koreans and Americans have remembered their shared history.

Kim Ku did not live long after Syngman Rhee's rise to power in Korea. On June 26, 1949, Ahn Du Hui, a lieutenant in the ROK Army, found him reading at his home in Seoul and shot him four times.[1] Kim Ku died soon afterward. The assassination is widely believed to have been a conspiracy, ordered by Rhee to eliminate his main rival.[2] It was the end of a remarkable life that began seventy-three years earlier in a rural village north of the border dividing Korea, bound by poverty and stultifying traditions. In it he had joined the struggle for the survival of Korea in the modern world, embraced a new religion and a new identity, led resistance to Korea's occupier by any means necessary during a quarter of a century in exile, and returned to continue the struggle for independence and unity in the postwar world. His funeral, held in Seoul on July 5, 1949, drew hundreds of thousands of mourners, saying farewell to a man who embodied much of the tragedy of the Korea of their time.[3]

In the years that followed, Kim Ku became a universally respected symbol of the struggle for Korean independence and unity. Despite the terrible suffering of the Korean War of 1950–53 and other events that made his direct relevance recede into the past, Kim Ku became an even more popular figure after his death. A leader of the anti-Communist right, he became equally esteemed by the left in the Republic of Korea, all sides respecting his will to fight for Korean independence and unity during the darkest times. After the authoritarian rule of Syngman Rhee ended with his resignation of the presidency in 1960, the Republic of Korea in 1962 posthumously awarded Kim Ku the highest grade of its highest national award, the Order of Merit for National Foundation, and later designated his autobiography as a cultural treasure of Korea. Today Kim Ku routinely is the first choice in any selection by people in the Republic of Korea of the greatest leader and historical figure of Korea. Even North Korea has paid respect to his memory, awarding him its National Reunification Prize in 1998.

Kim Ku is almost completely unknown in the United States, however, and the difference reflects the difficulty that Americans have in understanding Korea or any country overseas. Having died before the Korean War, Kim Ku simply does not exist in any events that Americans have as part of their historical memory. Even Americans familiar with Korea often have not heard of him. He receives little attention from academic historians, among whom it is not unusual to write an immense volume about the history of Korea that barely mentions his existence at all.[4] Lacking awareness of him and other parts of Korea's past is a significant handicap for the United States in its relations with Korea, a country where historical memories matter a great deal. Meanwhile, the People's Republic of China recently has cultivated its ties to Korea by creating a common history of resistance to Japan based on the actions of Kim Ku and the Korean Provisional Government. China has constructed museums to the Korean Provisional Government in Shanghai and Chungking, and in 2014 it added a memorial in Harbin to Ahn Chunggun, the friend of Kim Ku who assassinated Ito Hirobumi in 1909. Each year hundreds of thousands of Koreans visit these sites, where China contributed little to the cause of Korean independence other than being the place where events happened.

Yi Pomsok continued as a leading political figure in Korea but left a mixed legacy. As minister of defense, he attempted to build up the armed forces quickly to match the north's army, presiding over the expansion of the ROK Army from 25,000 at the beginning of 1948 to 95,000 by June 1950. He became associated heavily with Syngman Rhee and his authoritarian regime, however, and it overshadowed his other actions over the years. Rhee alternated between using Yi Pomsok's support and fearing that he was becoming too powerful. Rhee removed him as minister of defense and prime minister and sent him abroad to political exile in Taiwan as ambassador to Nationalist China in April 1950, then recalled him to Korea after the North Korean invasion on June 25. Yi served as interior minister and led the political party that supported Rhee's campaign for reelection as president in 1952. Since his passing in 1972, Yi has rarely appeared in American historical accounts except when connected to the actions of the Korean National Youth Corps, the national police, and the ROK Army in suppressing insurgency and political opposition, often simplistically portrayed as little more than a fascist copying the worst aspects of Nationalist China.

The brief cooperation between the OSS and Yi Pomsok in 1945 may have been a significant lost opportunity for the United States. Guided by U.S. military commanders, his leadership qualities could have been a significant asset to the United States in the creation of a new state in Korea. Clyde Sargent and the OSS had already earned his trust during six months of working together on Project Eagle. Instead, Yi experienced disappointment with the United States, first in being dismissed by the OSS in September 1945, then in being kept out of Korea for six months with the Korean Restoration Army. It may have equaled Yi's disappointment with the Soviet Union from 1922 through 1925. As a result, Yi threw his support behind Syngman Rhee and used his leadership skills to aid the creation of Rhee's regime and then support it during the 1950s.

The relationship between the OSS and the Korean Provisional Government as a whole was certainly a lost opportunity. At the end of the Second World War, the Korean Provisional Government led by Kim Ku had waited for a quarter of a century to work with the United States. Its main leaders were Christian converts, embracing American political ideas of democracy and representative government, who had decades of familiarity with Communist movements throughout Asia. Instead of using the Korean Provisional Government as a partner in postwar Korea, the United States excluded it, despite the recommendations of Clarence Weems during the last days of the OSS and of General Hodge as head of the U.S. military government in Korea. Leadership of the Republic of Korea ended up in the hands of a remnant of the Korean Provisional Government that had changed beyond recognition, altered by three years of political conflict, led by Syngman Rhee instead of its real leaders in exile. The three years were also lost in preparing the south for its inevitable conflict with the north, which contributed to leaving the Republic of Korea unprepared for the North Korean invasion in 1950.

Yi Pomsok and Clyde Sargent remained friends after 1945 despite the problems that Yi had with the United States over the years. As a sign of their friendship, Yi gave Sargent a gift during an official visit to Washington in 1953: a German Shepherd puppy, believed to be descended from Yi's German Shepherd in Xian that he had taught to understand commands in Russian. It was the Sargent family dog during the 1950s and a living link in the United States both to Project Eagle and to Yi Pomsok's years in exile in China and the Soviet Union.

Sargent ceased to have any involvement with Korea after the end of his role in the U.S. delegation to the U.S.-USSR Joint Commission in 1947. He instead made a career as a China scholar in the postwar intelligence community. The Central Intelligence Agency hired him to create its foreign language and foreign affairs training program, and he served as the CIA's director of foreign area and language training from 1948 to 1965. He returned to academic roles after 1965, becoming a professor of history with the East Asian Institute at Oakland University in Michigan in 1966–67 and then director of the George Washington University Center at the Naval War College in Newport, Rhode Island, in 1968.[5] After a long career teaching U.S. intelligence officers and military officers about Asia, he passed away in 1981 at the age of seventy-one.

It is unlikely that any of the agents in Clyde Sargent's program at the CIA, and certain that none of his students after 1965, ever knew much about his pioneering work with the OSS in China and about the times in 1945 when the future of Korea relied heavily on him. Project Eagle and many other operations of the OSS in China remained secret long after the war, their classified information stored in the archives of the CIA and their veterans remaining silent about their wartime actions. Not until almost half a century later did the U.S. government complete the declassification of the OSS records and free those who had participated in long-secret OSS operations in China to talk about their experiences. It occurred too late for Sargent, who had already passed away, taking with him the only memories of the entirety of Project Eagle.

Project Eagle and Project NAPKO both disappeared almost completely even after the declassification of remaining information about them. In the United States, only a few paragraphs scattered in books and articles about OSS intelligence operations in Asia have mentioned them.[6] In Korea, where U.S. classification did not prevent talking or writing about wartime actions with the OSS, Project Eagle appeared in the autobiographies of Kim Ku, Yi Pomsok, and Kim Woo Chun. Their experiences with the OSS in 1945 were only brief moments in long lives spent serving Korea, however, and the story became lost in the far larger arc of the history of Korea. In neither country does any significant memory of these actions exist.

Only one artifact of either OSS operation with Koreans is known to exist in the United States or Korea: one of the GIMIK boats built for Project NAPKO. It sits in a corner of the Battleship Cove naval museum at Fall River, Massachusetts, little noticed in a display of warships that includes the battleship USS *Massachusetts* and the National PT Boat Museum. A small item in the vast inventory of leftover U.S. military equipment worldwide at the end of the war, the GIMIK boat had last been seen in Okinawa in the fall of 1945. It somehow ended up abandoned in a U.S. Navy storage yard in Newport, Rhode Island, where it was discovered in 1972. Its unusual design and lack of documentation led to the belief that it was a captured Japanese suicide explosive boat, and the museum put it on display as a curiosity among its PT boats. Not until 2007 did the museum learn its true identity, when a retired U.S. Navy officer recognized it from a reference in Carl Eifler's autobiography. The GIMIK boat now sits properly identified but still little known, like a long-lost child that remains as evidence of the coming together of two nations in wartime over seventy years earlier.

Clarence Weems, like Clyde Sargent, returned home to a country that could not understand his experiences during the war. He resumed the doctoral studies on Korea that he had started and abandoned during the 1930s, this time at Columbia University. During the Korean War his expertise on Korea became useful to a military research project on behavior and psychological warfare supported by the Human Resources Research Institute (HRRI), an Air Force–funded think tank used by the armed services and the intelligence community, for which he worked on a report on Korea in 1950-51.[7] Weems's background in Korea fell in importance after the war, however, and unlike Sargent as a China scholar at the CIA and the Naval War College, Weems never found an academic home after the completion of his doctorate in 1954.[8] He spent the 1950s and 1960s at a series of universities on the east coast—Fairleigh Dickinson in New Jersey, Mansfield in Pennsylvania, George Washington in the District of Columbia, New York University in New York City—staying at each for only a few years. Little interest in Korea existed in the United States after the end of the Korean War, and Weems's career reflected it.

Despite the lack of interest in Korea in the United States, Weems stuck to it as his field. It was almost a field of one after the death in 1948 of its main scholar, George McCune, and the passing of Homer Hulbert in 1949, during his first visit to Korea since his expulsion by Japan in 1907.[9] His most noteworthy achievement came in 1962, when he edited and published a revised edition of Hulbert's *History of Korea*, which had been the standard text on the history of Korea in the English-speaking world since its original publication in Seoul in 1905.[10] Clarence Weems died in 1996 and rests in an unmarked grave in Bloomfield, New Jersey, buried literally without a trace along with his wartime work with the Korean Provisional Government for the OSS.

The only memory of Clarence Weems's work for the OSS that survived was in Korea with his wartime comrade Kim Woo Chun. He had returned to Korea in March 1946 on an American LST after the disbanding of the Korean Restoration Army, and he continued serving the Korean Provisional Government, working first for Kim Ku and then for the Republic of Korea's National Assembly. He and Weems remained friends after the war, even though they disagreed about many things that had happened between the United States and Korea. The friendship extended to Kim's son, who attended Princeton Theological Seminary not far from Weems's residence in New Jersey, after joining the Presbyterian Church like many in postwar Korea. In 2015, on the seventieth anniversary of the liberation of Korea, Kim Woo Chun attempted to get recognition in Korea for Clarence Weems and his other wartime American comrade, John Birch, by nominating them for the same award that Hulbert and McCune had received in 1963, the Order of Merit for National Foundation.[11] The awards did not occur, denying Weems and Birch of recognition in Korea for their wartime actions, as they had been denied recognition in the United States.

As Clarence Weems and other Americans born and raised in the north passed away, almost no one in the United States remembered them.[12] The entire American presence from 1882 to 1942 in what is now North Korea became a forgotten episode in the remote past, buried without a trace just as Clarence Weems had been. Pyongyang has become known to the world only as the capital of North Korea, which it has been since 1948 except for a brief period of control by ROK Army and UN forces in 1950 during the Korean War. Kaesong, the hometown of Clarence Weems, changed hands three times in 1950–51 and was the only city in the south permanently lost to the north. With all signs of the American presence and of Korean Christianity eliminated from these cities and throughout North Korea, the American presence and its influence on the people of Korea became completely forgotten. American attention during the Cold War focused almost solely on the Communist regime in North Korea, with anything before it ignored as irrelevant. The same attitude prevails in the United States and worldwide long after the Cold War.

In Korea the historic American presence in the north has never become irrelevant, as its legacy remains alive in the Republic of Korea. The south, once overshadowed by Pyongyang as the center of Christianity in Korea, experienced a surge of interest in Christianity after the flight of Christians and their churches from North Korea. It has developed into one of the most heavily Christian societies in the world, with Christians outnumbering followers of all other religions, most of them in the Presbyterian and Methodist churches brought by Americans in the late nineteenth century. It has established one of the most vibrant representative democracies in Asia, embracing the western political ideas also brought to Korea by American Christians long before the arrival of U.S. military forces and diplomatic influence in 1945. Along with the rapid economic development that has propelled the Republic of Korea into the ranks of the world's wealthiest countries, these developments have become defining features of Korea, and they are likely to outlive by far the U.S. military presence that has been central to the U.S. role in Korea since 1945. They are a better tribute to the actions of Americans in Korea from 1882 to 1942 than any old buildings or monument would be.

Memories of the American Christians who lived in Korea and struggled on its behalf have faded in the Republic of Korea, however, eroded by the passage of time and the great changes that have occurred since 1945. Only a few Americans connected to the era from 1882 to 1942 have remained in Korea as living links to the past, foremost among them the Underwood family, who continued to serve as professors and administrators at Yonsei University in Seoul until the passing of Horace Grant Underwood II in 2004 and the departure of his son Horace Horton Underwood II later in the same year. The Republic of Korea's rapid economic and social transformations have made the era before Korean independence an increasingly forgotten past, with few remembering a time when Americans were a significant presence in the country. Other than the Underwood family, few Americans continue to be remembered. One of few is Homer Hulbert, who has been the subject of a resurgence of interest, led by Koreans who rediscovered and revived the story of his contributions to Korea.[13]

The American Christian presence in Pyongyang and other areas of North Korea became especially obscure, with all reminders of it long since disappeared. The Rev. George McCune, its leading figure in Pyongyang, is remembered only by historians with an interest in that now long-ago era.[14] The stories of his lesser-known contemporaries and the Second World War generation that followed them have completely escaped notice, remaining undiscovered in both Korea and the United States. The author hopes that this book becomes the start of a broader rediscovery of a remarkable but forgotten group of Americans who helped to shape the destiny of Korea.

In North Korea, the ongoing existence of the regime of the Kim Il Sung family and the misery that it inflicts on its own people give continued relevance to the long-forgotten era of American Christians in North Korea. Long after the last American missionaries departed Pyongyang and North Korea eradicated the practice of Christianity in its territory, Korean Christians continue to be a significant factor in North Korea. Efforts to rescue refugees from North Korea have been largely the work of Korean Christians from the churches brought to Korea by Americans. Inside North Korea, underground Christians live in unknown numbers, never completely eliminated by the North Korean regime and seen as an existential threat to it, as an enduring community of dissent against the totalitarian state. They are a remnant of the destruction of the Jerusalem of the East by the Soviet Union and the North Korean regime. Americans were part of this history from its beginning, through the forgotten American missionary communities of Pyongyang and other cities in North Korea. Americans today should not forget them or the brief period during the Second World War when their children attempted to guide the United States in its first actions with Koreans.

For a reminder of the American past in North Korea, one need look no further than Kim Il Sung Square, the huge open space in the center of Pyongyang where North Korea regularly conducts mass spectacles, including parades of its soldiers, tanks, and missiles. The square lies next to what was once the Union Christian College campus and the Presbyterian mission station in Pyongyang, which began at what is now the northern edge of the square. There, George McCune worked to educate a generation of Koreans and defied the authority of Japan, George McAfee and Evelyn Becker McCune were born, and numerous Korean Christians including the father of Kim Il Sung received their educations. The land became part of a broad stretch of Pyongyang on the west bank of the Taedong River that the Kim Il Sung regime leveled to build vast monuments to itself starting in 1954. The complete obliteration and replacement of Union Christian College and the Presbyterian mission are a microcosm of the larger fate of North Korea and its historic American and Christian presence. Americans and Koreans alike should remember both the past and present embodied in this place and their ongoing significance to the future of Korea and of the role of the United States in Northeast Asia.

Fig. 23. Gen. William Donovan. Photo courtesy of National Archives.

Fig. 24. GIMIK submersible. Photo courtesy of the National Archives.

Fig. 25. GIMIK at full speed. Photo courtesy of the National Archives.

Fig. 26. Clyde Sargent in his office in his official cover position as special assistant to the U.S. ambassador to China, Chungking, 1942–43. Photo courtesy of Robert Sargent.

Fig. 27. George McCune in 1946. Photo courtesy of the University of California Archive.

Fig. 28. Clarence Weems Jr., Jennie Weems, and son, William, in 1945.
Photo courtesy of Jonathan Weems.

Fig. 29. Capt. Clarence Weems (*center*) with General Kim Hak Kyu (*holding hat*) and soldiers of the Third Detachment of the Korea Restoration Army at the entrance to the unit's headquarters in Anhui in August 1945. Photo courtesy of the National Archives.

Fig. 30. Capt. Clarence Weems (*right rear*) and Lt. Woon Sung Chung (*right front*) of the OSS, and an unidentified woman from the OSS, with Lt. Kim Woo Chun (*left front*) and Lt. Chung Yun Sung (*left rear*) of the Korea Restoration Army. Photo courtesy of Kim Woo Chun.

Fig. 31. Yi Pomsok as a general in the army of Nationalist China. Yi wears the German-style uniform and helmet used by senior officers and elite units of the Nationalist Chinese army. Photo courtesy of Robert Sargent.

Fig. 32. Yi Pomsok with his German Shepherd, who understood only Russian language commands. Photo courtesy of Robert Sargent.

Fig. 33. Yi Pomsok with his revolver and German Shepherd. Photo courtesy of Robert Sargent.

Fig. 34. Communications training. Photo courtesy of Robert Sargent.

Fig. 35. William Donovan in Xian, discussing Project Eagle with Capt. Clyde Sargent (*right*), Capt. Ryong Chyun Hahm (*left*), and Gen. Yi Pomsok (*left, facing away*). Photo courtesy of the U.S. Army Center of Military History.

Fig. 36. Kim Ku and OSS director William Donovan at the conclusion of their meeting in Xian on August 7, 1945. Photo courtesy of the U.S. Army Center of Military History.

Fig. 37. Gen. Yi Pomsok, three officers of the Korean Restoration Army, and Capt. Clyde Sargent preparing to take off on the Operation Eagle prisoner of war rescue mission to Seoul on the morning of August 18, 1945. Photo courtesy of Robert Sargent.

Fig. 38. Gen. Yi Pomsok and Capt. Clyde Sargent with Chinese military and civilian officials at the airfield at Weihsien in the Shandong Peninsula, before returning to Xian at the end of Operation Eagle. Gen. Li Wenli is to the right of Yi and Sargent, holding a white hat. Photo courtesy of Robert Sargent.

Fig. 39. Commemorative group portrait of Yi Pomsok, Clyde Sargent, five officers of the Korea Restoration Army, and the last five Americans serving under Sargent with Project Eagle on September 30. The Korean caption reads, "Together our countries can change the world! Korea, Year 27, September 30." Photo courtesy of Robert Sargent.

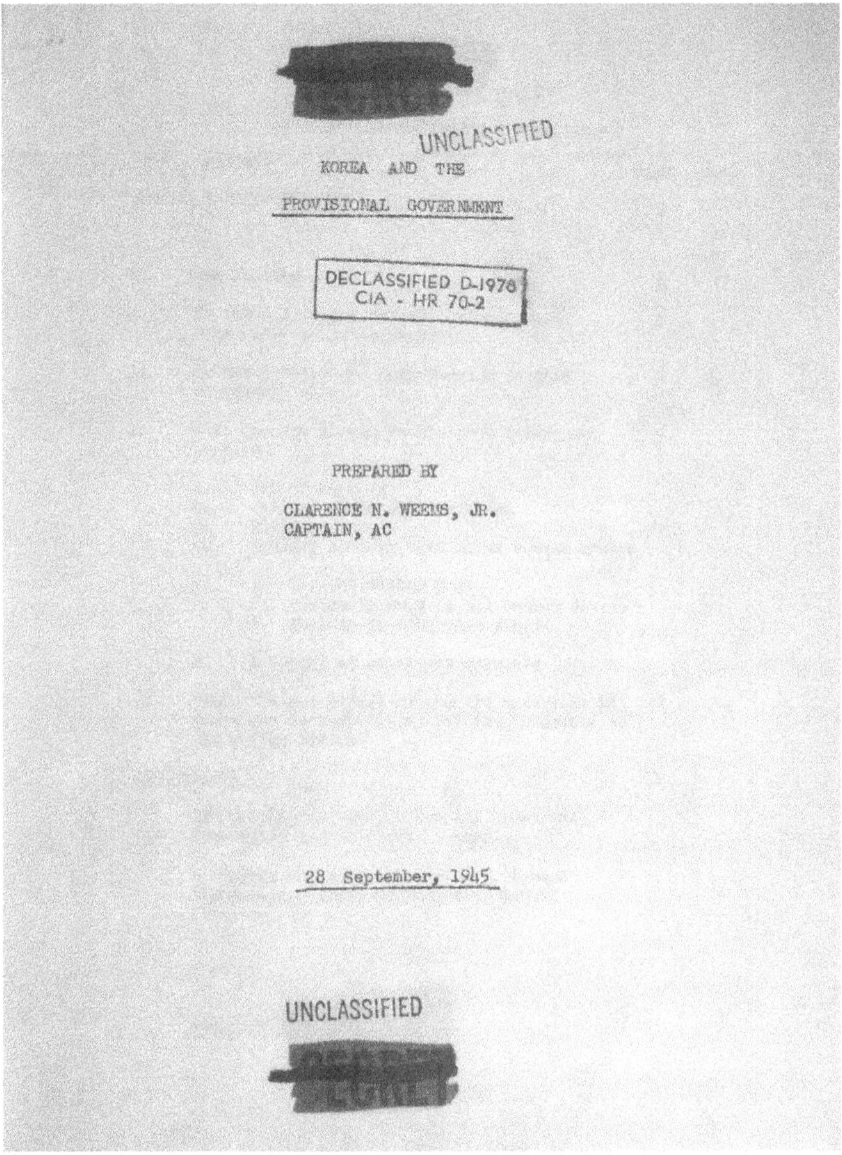

UNCLASSIFIED

KOREA AND THE

PROVISIONAL GOVERNMENT

DECLASSIFIED D-1978
CIA - HR 70-2

PREPARED BY

CLARENCE N. WEEMS, JR.
CAPTAIN, AC

28 September, 1945

UNCLASSIFIED

Fig. 40. Clarence Weems's report on the Korean Provisional Government, prepared for OSS director William Donovan. Photo courtesy of the Army Historical Center, Collection of General William J. Donovan.

Fig. 41. American soldiers of the 7th Infantry Division marching past the Government-General Building in Seoul on September 8, 1945, met by Koreans cheering their liberation. Photo courtesy of the National Archives.

Fig. 42. Korean police, still under Japanese command, restraining crowds celebrating the arrival of the American forces on September 8, 1945. Photo courtesy of the National Archives.

Fig. 43. British and Australian prisoners of war from a camp near Seoul, whom Operation Eagle had sought to liberate, greeted by Koreans during their evacuation. Photo courtesy of the National Archives.

Fig. 44. Maj. Clyde Sargent during his survey of the Korean communities in Shanghai, Beijing, and Tianjin, October–December 1945. Photo courtesy of Robert Sargent.

Fig. 45. Syngman Rhee and Kim Ku meeting Lt. Gen. John Hodge,
November 1945. Photo courtesy of the National Archives.

Fig. 46. Col. Gen. Terentii Fomich Shtykov with Lieutenant General
Hodge at the first meeting of the U.S.-USSR Joint Commission on Korea.
Photo courtesy of the National Archives.

Fig. 47. Kim Ku at a rally against trusteeship over Korea in late 1945.

Fig. 48. Kim Ku addressing the first meeting of the Korean Representative Democratic Council, with Kim Kyusik to the left and Syngman Rhee between them, on February 14, 1946. Photo courtesy of the National Archives.

Fig. 49. Lt. Gen. Hodge, Syngman Rhee, and Yi Pomsok at the farewell ceremony for Hodge on August 26, 1948. John Muccio, first U.S. ambassador to the Republic of Korea, stands next to them. Photo courtesy of the National Archives.

Fig. 50. GIMIK boat from Project NAPKO at the National PT Boat Museum at Battleship Cove in Fall River, Massachusetts.

Fig. 51. Kim Il Sung Square in Pyongyang, looking north toward the former location of the Presbyterian mission and Union Christian College. West Gate Church, Presbyterian Theological Seminary, and the buildings and athletic field of Union Christian College were located just beyond the buildings at the northern side of the square.

NOTES

1. Genesis, 1882–1919

1. During its occupation of Gangwha Island in 1866, the French expeditionary force seized a library dating from the fourteenth to the nineteenth century, which became the foundation of the Korea collection of the Bibliothèque nationale de France. In 2011 France returned the collection to Korea, where it is now in the National Museum of Korea.

2. The *General Sherman* incident was an exceptional case in a history of friendly relations between American sailors and Korea. During the 1850s and 1860s, American merchant sailors shipwrecked in Korea during voyages to China and Japan had received good treatment and repatriation, and a U.S. Navy gunboat had made a friendly visit to Pusan in 1853.

3. Internet sensationalism in America has further embellished the story by confusing the *General Sherman* with the *Sherman*, a similarly named ship that was also a Confederate blockade runner captured by the U.S. Navy, converted into a gunboat, and renamed after William Tecumseh Sherman. The *Sherman* sank near Myrtle Beach, South Carolina, in 1874, and its wreck has become a popular scuba diving destination. Incorrect stories have circulated that describe the *General Sherman* as having been raised, put back into service, and then sunk again off South Carolina.

4. Fifteen sailors and marines received the Medal of Honor for their actions in the fighting on Gangwha Island, the first such awards for an overseas action.

5. McCune and Harrison, *Korean-American Relations,* 1:3.

6. Foote to Frelinghuysen, no. 32, October 19, 1883, in McCune and Harrison, *Korean-American Relations,* 1:53.

7. Frelinghuysen to Foote, no. 14, November 6, 1884, in McCune and Harrison, *Korean-American Relations,* 1:57.

8. A sign of the disregard for the Korean request is that the State Department has continued to leave it out of its official histories of relations with Korea, even in classified histories for internal U.S. government use. See, e.g., "United States Policy regarding Korea, 1834–1941," 5–7.

9. One of the witnesses to the murder of Queen Min was William Dye, who lived in the Gyeongbokgung Palace and attempted to rally the surviving palace guards to protect the royal family. Dye remained in Korea with the royal guard until failing health forced him to return to the United States in May 1899. He died six months later.

10. "United States Policy regarding Korea, 1834–1941," 35.

11. Hulbert, *The History of Korea*; Hulbert, *The Passing of Korea*.

12. For more on the life of Homer Hulbert, see Dong Jin Kim, *Crusader for Korea*.

13. Dong Jin Kim, *Crusader for Korea*, 33–34.

14. For more about the pre-1884 Christian believers in Korea, see Chung, *Syncretism*, 13–16.

15. Buswell and Lee, *Christianity in Korea*, 292.

16. Arthur Brown, *The Korean Conspiracy Case*, 7.

17. The denominations, and the various nationalities of each denomination, divided Korea into separate territories where each would conduct mission activity. The Methodist Episcopal Church, South had most of central Korea north of Seoul, as far north as Wonsan; the Methodist Episcopal Church, North had a belt across Korea south of Seoul and pockets in northwestern Korea; the Presbyterian Church of the U.S.A. had Pyongyang and most of northwestern Korea, parts of the Seoul area, and North Kyungsang Province, including the city of Taegu, in the south; and the Presbyterian Church in the U.S. (South) had North and South Cholla Provinces in the southwest, including Cheju Island. Australian Presbyterians had Pusan and South Kyungsang Province in the southeast, and Canadian Presbyterians had northeastern Korea, extending down to the Wonsan area.

18. Clarence Weems Sr. provided a firsthand account of the growth of the Methodist Church in Korea during the 1920s, the emergence of a unified Korean Methodist Church, and the ordination of women in a series of articles that he published in an American magazine in 1933. See C. N. Weems, "Early Days in Korea," *World Outlook,* July 1933, 8–9, 32–33; C. N. Weems, "Centenary Days in Korea," *World Outlook,* August 1933, 8–9, 34; C. N. Weems, "Building a Church in Korea," *World Outlook*, September/October 1933, 4–5, 34.

19. This mission lasted for thirty-five years until 1957, not closed until almost a decade after the foundation of the People's Republic of China. Chung, *Syncretism*, 17.

20. Clark, *Living Dangerously in Korea*, 121–25.

21. Children of missionary families in China educated in Pyongyang included Ruth Bell Graham, daughter of Presbyterian missionaries in Shanghai, who later married the Rev. Billy Graham.

22. Chairyung Station to Dr. Brown, confidential letter, April–June 1, 1919, Presbyterian Historical Center, RG 140, box 16, folder 16-13.

23. Park Eun-sik, *The Bloody History of the Korean Independence Movement.*

24. The most notorious atrocity occurred on April 15 in a village named Jeam-ri, south of Seoul near the city of Suwon. There Japanese troops responded to an attack on a police station by herding the men of the village into a church that they set ablaze, killing everyone inside, and burning the village and others nearby. The massacre at Jeam-ri became known through the efforts of a Canadian missionary doctor, Francis Schofield, who visited the village with a group of American missionaries. Further evidence came to light with the publication of the journal of Gen. Utsunomiya Taro, the commander of the Japanese forces in Korea, who described the incident and the cover-up by the Japanese forces afterward.

25. Rhee later earned a bachelor's degree from George Washington University, a master's degree from Harvard, and a doctorate from Princeton.

26. Incident no. 22, The Norabawie Massacre; Incident no. 23; Incident no. 26, The Murder of Colporteur Yi Sun Sik and Four of His Fellow Villagers; Incident no. 28, West Kando Shares Chientao's Fate, Presbyterian Historical Society, RG 140, box 16, folder 16-20.

27. The U.S. government enjoined Americans in Korea from participation in Korean political affairs during the March First Movement, and it refrained from any encouragement of Korean nationalists. "United States Policy regarding Korea, 1834–1941," 43–44. The State Department filed all requests for assistance and recognition without acknowledgment.

2. Kim Ku and the Korean Liberation Movement

1. Kim Ku, *Paekpom Ilchi*, 23–30.

2. Kim Ku, *Paekpom Ilchi*, 33–47.

3. Kim Ku, *Paekpom Ilchi*, 47–54.

4. Kim Ku, *Paekpom Ilchi*, 75–80.

5. Kim Ku, *Paekpom Ilchi*, 79n144.

6. Kim Ku, *Paekpom Ilchi*, 80–93.

7. Kim Ku, *Paekpom Ilchi*, 97–100.

8. Kim Ku, *Paekpom Ilchi*, 93–97.

9. Kim Ku, *Paekpom Ilchi*, 110–17.

10. Kim Ku, *Paekpom Ilchi*, 117–26.
11. Kim Ku, *Paekpom Ilchi*, 136–39.
12. Kim Ku, *Paekpom Ilchi*, 147–55.
13. The Korean martial art of Taekwondo commemorates Ahn Chunggun in the name of its sixth pattern, usually rendered as Joon Gun.
14. Kim Ku, *Paekpom Ilchi*, 160–62.
15. Kim Ku, *Paekpom Ilchi*, 162–91, 331–32.
16. Kim Ku, *Paekpom Ilchi*, 192–93. Prior to this time, Kim used the name Kim Ku, but with Ku standing for the word for turtle to symbolize long life, and the pen name Yonha.
17. Kim Ku, *Paekpom Ilchi*, 213–16.
18. Kim Ku, *Paekpom Ilchi*, 216–20.
19. When Kim Ku was police commissioner, Yi Tonghwi approached him to obtain his support for the Communist faction, but Kim Ku refused, objecting to subordinating the Korean independence movement to the Communist International. Kim Ku, *Paekpom Ilchi*, 222.
20. Kim Ku, *Paekpom Ilchi*, 232.
21. "United States Policy regarding Korea, 1834–1941," 36–37.
22. Kim Ku avoided jail when Japanese police swept the French concession for Koreans suspected of involvement with the assassination attempt with the assistance of French police, who escorted him when Japanese police detained him and refused to allow them to question or jail him. Kim Ku, *Paekpom Ilchi*, 214–15.
23. While visiting Shanghai in 1925, Na had sold his clothes at a pawn shop to buy food for a birthday celebration for Kim Ku, who could not afford one for himself or for his mother's sixtieth birthday in 1919. In commemoration of this gesture, Kim Ku never celebrated his birthday again. Kim Ku, *Paekpom Ilchi*, 207.
24. Kim Ku, *Paekpom Ilchi*, 234–39. Yi Pongchang became part of the pantheon of Korea's national heroes for his attack on Hirohito. After Korea achieved independence, Kim Ku buried his remains in Hyochang Park in Seoul, alongside those of two presidents of the Korean Provisional Government. A statue of Yi Pongchang throwing a hand grenade stands in the park. He also received the posthumous honor of being one of the first recipients of the Order of Merit for National Foundation when the Republic of Korea created it in 1962.
25. Kim Ku, *Paekpom Ilchi*, 240–41.
26. The U.S. State Department's representative in Shanghai reported the incident as a "bombing outrage . . . seriously injuring the Japanese representative, Mr. Shigemitsu," with the result that "further progress in the negotiations was delayed." It would be a quaint description five years later, with an all-out war

raging between China and Imperial Japan. "Summary of Situation at Shanghai—January 20–March 31, 1932," 66, National Archives and Records Administration (NARA), General Records of the Department of State, RG 59, NARS A-1, entry 397, Far Eastern Division: Records Relating to the Crisis in Manchuria, 1931–34, box 1 of 3.

27. Yun Ponggil, like Yi Pongchang, received high honors after Korea achieved independence. In 1946 Korean residents in Japan disinterred his remains and sent them to Seoul, where they are buried in the Korean National Cemetery. The Republic of Korea made him, along with Yi Pongchang, an original recipient of the Order of Merit for National Foundation in 1962.

28. For the full story of George and Geraldine Fitch, see Fitch, *My Eighty Years in China.*

29. Kim Ku, *Paekpom Ilchi*, 241–48.

30. Kim Ku, *Paekpom Ilchi*, 248–49.

31. Kim Ku, *Paekpom Ilchi*, 260–61.

32. Kim Ku, *Paekpom Ilchi*, 267.

33. Kim Ku, *Paekpom Ilchi*, 273.

34. Kim Ku, *Paekpom Ilchi*, 263–70.

35. Kim Ku, *Paekpom Ilchi*, 270–73.

36. Kim Ku, *Paekpom Ilchi*, 273–75.

37. Kim Ku, *Paekpom Ilchi*, 335–36.

38. One Korean draftee, Yang Kyoungjong, endured a seven-year odyssey that saw him forced to serve in the Imperial Japanese Army, the Soviet Army, and the German Wehrmacht. Drafted into the Imperial Japanese Army in 1938 at the age of eighteen, he was taken prisoner at the Battle of Khalkin Gol in 1939, survived three years in a Soviet labor camp, was drafted into the Red Army in 1942, survived a year of combat until taken prisoner by the Germans in the Third Battle of Kharkov in early 1943, and then found himself drafted into a German Army unit of Soviet prisoners of war serving in Normandy, where he was captured by the U.S. Army. After a period in a prisoner of war camp in the United Kingdom, he settled in the United States and died in Illinois in 1992. His experiences during the war formed the basis of the story in the Korean motion picture *My Way*, produced and directed by Kang Jegyu.

39. The State Department official was Alger Hiss, who became famous after the war when he was accused of being a spy for the Soviet Union during the 1930s and 1940s. "United States Policy regarding Korea, Part III, December 1945–June 1950," 2–5.

40. "United States Policy regarding Korea, Part II, 1941–1945," 8.

41. "United States Policy regarding Korea, Part II, 1941–1945," 9–10.

42. "United States Policy regarding Korea, Part II, 1941–1945," 13–14.
43. "United States Policy regarding Korea, Part II, 1941–1945," 15–17.
44. "United States Policy regarding Korea, Part II, 1941–1945," 22.

3. Americans of Korea

1. Van Tassel, "The Legend Maker."
2. Weems Family Genealogy, Weems-Botts Museum.
3. "Life of Clarence Norwood Weems," ca. fall 1951, personal papers of Peter Weems.
4. Clarence N. Weems, "Some Difficulties I Have Faced in Life," August 1951, 2–3, and "The Logan-Tate Affair, a True Story," ca. 1951, both in personal papers of Peter Weems.
5. Minutes of the First Annual Meeting of the Korean Mission of the Methodist Episcopal Church, South, Held at Seoul, Korea, December 8, 1897, iii–v, United Methodist Archives and Historical Center (UMAHC).
6. Minutes of the First Annual Meeting of the Korean Mission of the Methodist Episcopal Church, South, i; Minutes of the Thirteenth Annual Meeting of the Korean Mission of the Methodist Episcopal Church, South, Held at Seoul, Korea, September 2–6, 1909, UMAHC.
7. Journal of the Korean Annual Conference, Methodist Episcopal Church, South, Thirteenth Session, Chongkyo Church, Seoul, Korea, September 24–30, 1930, UMAHC.
8. Rev. C. N. Weems, United Methodist Church Mission Biographical Series, roll 70, UMAHC.
9. Minutes of the Meeting of Missionaries, Korean Mission, Methodist Episcopal Church, South, Thirty-Fourth Session, Wonsan Beach, Korea, August 21–25, 1930, 8–9, UMAHC.
10. Journal of the Korean Annual Conference, Methodist Episcopal Church, South, Thirteenth Session, Chongkyo Church, Seoul, Korea, September 24–30, 1930, UMAHC.
11. Weems, Biographical Series, roll 70.
12. P. H. Yu and C. K. Lee, "The Biography of Rev. C. N. Weems," in *In Commemoration of Thirty Years of Missionary Service of Rev. C. N. Weems*, Wonsan, Korea, 1939, 1–6, UMAHC.
13. Dae Young Ryu, "Understanding Early American Missionaries in Korea (1884–1910)."
14. Clarence N. Weems to Bill Weems, August 27, 1951, personal papers of Peter Weems.
15. Weems, "Some Difficulties I Have Faced in Life," 12.

16. Weems to Weems.

17. "United States Policy regarding Korea, 1834–1941," 48.

18. Weems, Clarence Norwood (Rev. and Mrs.), 1941, roll 147, Missionary Files: Methodist Church, 1912–49, UMAHC.

19. Matriculation Card, David Askew Weems, Emory University Archives.

20. Weems, David, Korea, 1926–37, Missionary Files: Methodist Church, 1912–49, UMAHC.

21. William's interest in machines began during periodic family furloughs from Korea in Arkansas, when he and several friends would buy old Model T Fords and tinker with them. Being only thirteen years old, he and his friends drove these cars illegally without licenses, and one time in Little Rock a police officer caught him and charged him with driving under age, without a license plate, with no lights, with no horn, and with no inner tubes in the tires. It was a terrifying experience, but no formal charges resulted. William R. Weems, "William Rupert Weems' Story," 1991, 4, personal papers of Jonathan Weems. Another brief problem occurred during his first entry into the United States by himself in 1927, when he was traveling from Korea to Atlanta to attend preparatory school at Emory University Academy. After twelve hours on a train from Kaesong to Pusan, a twelve-hour ferry ride from Pusan to Shimonoseki in Japan, a train ride to the port of Kobe and a two-day wait there, and finally a three-week sea voyage to San Pedro, the port of Los Angeles, he arrived with no form of identification other than a Japanese police permit, which had been sufficient in previous entries with the entire family, but which his father mistakenly believed would be sufficient to enter the United States without a parent with a passport. He spent the night in a jail cell pending confirmation of his previous entries into the United States. "William Rupert Weems' Story," 6–7.

22. "William Rupert Weems' Story," 15–19; A Progress Report of Georgia Tech's Part in the War, Submitted to President Blake R. Van Leer and The Board of Regents, University System of Georgia by John A. Griffith, Georgia School of Technology, October 20, 1944, 17, Georgia Tech Archives.

23. William Weems worked on economic development projects in numerous other countries, including Zambia, Malawi, and Nepal. He eventually settled down in the Washington DC area, where he worked for the U.S. Agency for International Development until he retired in 1974 and lived in a house at 6821 Broyhill Street in McLean, Virginia, within walking distance of the author's house in McLean. He did handyman work until he moved into a retirement home in 1991. "William Rupert Weems' Story," 29–38.

24. Benjamin Weems, *Reform, Rebellion, and the Heavenly Way*. This was originally

written as a master's thesis when he obtained a degree in international affairs from Georgetown University.

25. For more about Benjamin Weems, see "Obituary: Benjamin Burch Weems (1914–1986)," and C. N. Weems, "Benjamin Burch Weems: May 28, 1914–January 31, 1986."
26. Matriculation Card, Clarence Norwood Weems Jr., Emory University Archives.
27. *The 1930 Commodore, Being the Year Book of Vanderbilt University*, Nashville, Comet Series XLIV, Commodore Series XXII.
28. C. N. Weems Jr., "Japan's Acquisition of Korea from the Treaty of Shimonoseki (1895) to the Annexation of Korea by Japan (1910)."
29. He lived in the Dupont Circle area and worked as a typist at the Reconstruction Finance Corporation, a government agency created in 1932 to alleviate economic hardships of the Great Depression.
30. Coursey, *Who's Who in South Dakota*, 5:230–33; S. McCune, "The Testing of a Missionary."
31. One of the Rev. Cleland McAfee's daughters, Mildred Helen McAfee Horton, became president of Wellesley College in 1936 and director of the WAVES (Women Accepted for Volunteer Emergency Service) in the U.S. Navy during the Second World War. McAfee Hall at Wellesley College and Horton Hall at the University of New Hampshire each are named in her honor.
32. Rev. G. S. McCune, D.D., LL.D, "Fifty Years of Promotion by the Home Board and Home Church," Jubilee Papers, Korea Mission, Presbyterian Church, U.S.A., 21, reprinted in G. S. McCune, *American Support of Presbyterian Missions in Korea*.
33. A third American on board was Floy Donaldson, a young graduate of Coe College, who was traveling to Korea to become a missionary and marry Dr. Edwin Koons, head of the Presbyterian academy in Seoul. Coursey, *Who's Who in South Dakota*, 5:226–30.
34. *Who Was Who in America*, 1950, 2:358.
35. After the mass conversions of the Great Pyongyang Revival, the Presbyterian mission in Korea more than doubled from forty-six members in 1907 to ninety-three in 1921. "Fifty Years of Promotion by the Home Board and Home Church," 27.
36. Brown, *The Korean Conspiracy Case*, 7. In October 1950 Sunchon became the location of a major massacre of American prisoners of war by the North Korean regime. North Korean guards killed over a hundred American prisoners in a railway tunnel near the city, an act sometimes called the Sunchon Tunnel Massacre. See Avery and Faulkner, *Sunchon Tunnel Massacre Survivors*.
37. Letter from Severance Hospital, Seoul, March 18, 1912, Presbyterian Historical Society, RG 140, box 16, folder 16-9.
38. Letter from Severance Hospital, 16.

39. Letter from Severance Hospital, 17. For more about the experiences of George McCune during the Conspiracy Case of 1911, see S. McCune, "The Testing of a Missionary."

40. G. S. McCune, "Fifty Years of Promotion by the Home Board and Home Church," bibliographical notes 1 and 2.

41. George McCune frequently faced accusations by the Japanese police that he used the Bible and his preaching to incite Koreans to resist Japanese rule. The accusations against him in the Conspiracy Case had included teaching a Bible study class with the story of David and Goliath, appearing to promise Koreans victory over Japan. Brown, *The Korean Conspiracy Case*, 8. These accusations recurred from the Conspiracy Case of 1911 to the 1930s.

42. A panel that convened on October 11, 1912, included Seth Low, former president of Columbia University and mayor of New York and chairman of the American Section of the Edinburgh World Conference Commission on the Relations of Missions and Governments; John W. Foster, former secretary of state and grandfather of John Foster Dulles, secretary of state under President Dwight Eisenhower; Charles W. Eliot, former president of Harvard University; Arthur Hadley, president of Yale University; and James Brown Scott, international law adviser of the United States at the Hague Peace Conference. Adm. Alfred Thayer Mahan was invited but unable to attend because of illness. Minutes of the Confidential Conference on the Situation in Korea at the Aldine Club, New York, October 11, 1912, Presbyterian Historical Society, RG 140, box 16, folder 16-10.

43. Extract of letter from the Rev. Geo. S. McCune, dated SonSen, Korea, January 18, 1915; "Mr. McCune Warned," *Seoul Press*, January 16, 1915, Presbyterian Historical Society, RG 140, box 16, folder 16-12. Japanese police appear to have used an agent provocateur planted at a Korean newspaper to publish stories about McCune, praising actions by him in support of Korean independence in Korea and the United States that were disinformation intended to provide the police with evidence for accusing McCune of attacking Japanese authority. They included making speeches in the United States that spread propaganda in support of Korean nationalists and against Japanese rule and meetings in Philadelphia with Philip Jaisohn and associates of Syngman Rhee. Translations made from the *Korea National Herald*, nos. 375 and 376, November 4, 1914, Presbyterian Historical Society, RG 140, box 16, folder 16-12. The newspaper issued a retraction of this reporter's stories that declared him to be an agent of Imperial Japan. Translation of an article that appeared in *Korea National Herald*, no. 397, January 17, 1915, Presbyterian Historical Society, RG 140, box 16, folder 16-12.

44. M. Komatsu to Dr. Arthur Brown, April 12, 1915; Brown to His Excellency M. Komatsu, director of foreign affairs, May 18, 1915; Brown to the Rev. George S. McCune, May 19, 1915, Presbyterian Historical Society, RG 140, box 16, folder 16-12.

45. Charles Sharp, chairman of the executive committee of the Korea Mission of the Presbyterian Church in the U.S.A., to Dr. A. J. Brown, July 8, 1915, Presbyterian Historical Society, RG 140, box 16, folder 16-12.

46. H. G. Underwood to Brown, June 24, 1915, Presbyterian Historical Society, RG 140, box 16, folder 16-12.

47. Dr. Robert E. Speer to Dr. Brown, September 20, 1915, Presbyterian Historical Society, RG 140, box 16, folder 16-12.

48. Letter from Syenchun, Korea, March 5, 1919, Presbyterian Historical Society RG 140, box 16, folder 16-15.

49. Too many stories of arrests and torture to mention are preserved in the archives of the Presbyterian Historical Society, RG 140, box 16, folders 16-13, 16-14, and 16-15.

50. Helen McCune may have sheltered students as Eli Mowry had done. Shannon McCune recalled that the family's children had been forbidden to look in the attic of their house for several days, with no explanation, while Japanese police were searching the town and conducting mass arrests of students. S. McCune, "The Mansei Movement," 7–8.

51. Translation, Criminal Case no. 299 of 1919, Presbyterian Historical Society, RG 140, box 16, folder 16–18. The sentence was reduced to four months and suspended for two years on May 17, and Mowry won an appeal on August 18.

52. McCune, "The Mansei Movement," 15–18.

53. Coursey, *Who's Who in South Dakota*, 5:234.

54. Huron College, founded as Presbyterian University of South Dakota in 1883, became part of Sri Tanka University–Huron under Cheyenne River Sioux Tribe ownership in 2001 but closed in 2005. The City of Huron purchased the campus and later demolished it in 2011 to replace it with a city park.

55. McCune, "The Mansei Movement," 37. Saito Makoto had served as governor-general from 1919 to 1927 and 1929 to 1931, then as prime minister of Japan from 1932 to 1934. He died on February 26, 1936, assassinated by young ultra-nationalist Imperial Japanese Army officers staging an attempted coup.

56. George Shannon McCune to Dr. A. J. Brown, February 17, 1927, Presbyterian Historical Society, RG 140, box 16, folder 16-39.

57. *Who Was Who in America*, 1950, 2:358.

58. G. S. McCune, "Fifty Years of Promotion by the Home Board and Home Church," bibliographical note 3.

59. S. McCune, "The Mansei Movement," 19; G. S. McCune, "Fifty Years of Promotion by the Home Board and Home Church," bibliographical note 7.

60. McCune, "The Mansei Movement," 3. George McAfee McCune had received the Korean name Yun An-Gul.

61. McCune, "The Mansei Movement," 5–7.

62. George McCune's master's thesis was a 241-page work entitled "Manchuria as an Agent in Japan's Rise to Dominance in Asia," which examined the internal power struggle in Japan between the military and civilian parties. "George McAfee McCune (1908–1948) and His Works," 35.

63. George McCune had to teach primarily European history as a young instructor and assistant professor. The courses that he taught at Occidental College included ancient history, Europe during the Middle Ages, modern European history, and the Pacific Ocean in history. "George McAfee McCune (1908–1948) and His Works," 35–36.

64. G. McCune, "The Yi Dynasty Annals of Korea," "The Exchange of Envoys between Korea and Japan during the Tokugawa Period," and "The Japanese Trading Post at Pusan." Discussed in "George McAfee McCune (1908–1948) and His Works," 36–39.

65. For more about Evelyn Becker McCune and her marriage, see Thompson and Blackwood, *A Daughter's Journey*.

66. See S. McCune, *Korea's Heritage, a Regional and Social Geography*, *Korea: Land of Broken Calm*, "The Testing of a Missionary," and "The Mansei Movement, March 1, 1919," in G. S. McCune, *American Support of Presbyterian Missions in Korea*. Shannon McCune also collected rare Korean maps that can be found in the Geography and Map Division of the Library of Congress.

67. For more biographical information, see Kim Han-Kyo, "Shannon McCune and His Korean Studies."

68. George McAfee McCune to "Bill," May 15, 1938, papers of Heather McCune Thompson.

69. Conversation with Antoinette McCune Bement, February 2, 2016.

70. "United States Policy regarding Korea, 1834–1941," 49.

71. In addition to the departures, fifteen Presbyterian missionaries experienced expulsion from Korea in October 1941 for attempting to organize a day of prayer for peace on February 28, 1941. Presbyterian Historical Society, RG 140, box 16, folder 16-25.

72. Underwood to Hooper, October 14, 1940; Underwood to Hooper, October 23, 1940, Presbyterian Historical Society, RG 140, box 16, folder 16-23.

73. The Japanese ocean liner *Asama Maru* earlier had been the center of a diplomatic dispute when the British cruiser *Liverpool* intercepted it off the coast of Japan

on January 21, 1940, and removed passengers believed to be German sailors. The *Asama Maru* was later sunk by the U.S. submarine *Atule* in the South China Sea on November 1, 1944.

74. The U.S. State Department chartered the Swedish passenger liner MS *Gripsholm* from 1942 to 1946 for the exchange and repatriation of civilians, under the protection of the Red Cross. The *Gripsholm*, the first diesel-powered transatlantic passenger liner when built in 1924, served the Gothenburg–New York run before the war. From 1942 to 1946 it made twelve round-trips on repatriation missions, carrying 27,712 passengers.

75. Chosen Mission Executive Committee Meetings, June to August 1942, Presbyterian Historical Society, RG 140, box 16, folder 16-26.

76. Presentation by Dr. Horace H. Underwood; paper presented at Conference by Dr. Harry A. Rhodes, Korea and the War; paper presented at Conference by Mr. D. N. Lutz, Our Responsibility to Rural Korea, Presbyterian Historical Society, RG 140, box 16, folder 16-26.

77. A Suggested Plan for the Reoccupation of Korea, Presbyterian Historical Society, RG 140, box 16, folder 16-35.

78. A firsthand account of the history of the Air Ground Aid Section (AGAS), *MIS-X Top Secret*, which describes the role of Max Becker in its creation and operations, was published in 1997 by the founder and commander of AGAS, Lt. Col. A. R. Wichtrich. AGAS operations were classified during and after the war and were not declassified until the 1990s, after the records of AGAS were destroyed in a fire at the U.S. National Archives.

79. U.S. War Department, General Staff, G-2 Division, *A History of the Military Intelligence Division, 7 December 1941–2 September 1945*, 129, 380.

80. Information from Heather McCune Thompson and Helen McCune. McCune described his travels in Korea, Japanese-ruled Manchuria, China, and Siberia in 1919 in a letter that included detailed descriptions of Japanese surveillance in Korea, military installations in Manchuria, and seaports, railroads, and airbases in Korea and Manchuria. McCune to "Bill," May 15, 1938, papers of Heather McCune Thompson.

4. The OSS and the Korean Provisional Government

1. Often called the "Father of American Intelligence," William Donovan had been a distinguished Wall Street lawyer, a New York National Guard colonel awarded the Medal of Honor for his service in the infantry in the First World War, and a candidate for governor of New York.

2. Anthony Brown, *Wild Bill Donovan: The Last Hero*, 20.

3. Ruth Donovan to her mother, on stationery from the Chosen Hotel, June 26, 1919, Buffalo History Museum Research Library, B86-6, William J. Donovan Papers, box 3, folder 2, Siberia Trip, 1919.

4. Diary: Visit to the Orient, Donovan Collection, U.S. Army Heritage and Education Center, box 132A, Diaries and Reports from 1910 to 1919.

5. Memorandum for the president from William J. Donovan, no. 186, January 24, 1942, Franklin D. Roosevelt Presidential Library and Museum, Papers as President, President's Secretary's File, 1933-45.

6. The Rev. James Gale amassed a collection of classical Korean literature that he donated to the Library of Congress in 1927. Gale also wrote frequently in the Western press on affairs in Korea. See, e.g., Gale, "Count Terauchi, Governor of Chosen."

7. Sarah Anne H. Gale, "My Recollection of a Korean-English Dictionary in Preparation."

8. For further information about Dr. Gale's work in China, see his autobiography, *Salt for the Dragon.*

9. Memorandum for the president from William J. Donovan, no. 186, January 24, 1942.

10. Memorandum for Colonel Donovan: Subject—Scheme "Olivia," January 27, 1942, Millard Preston Goodfellow Papers, 1942-1967, Hoover Institution Library and Archives. Lieutenant Colonel DePass and his staff developed the Olivia plan at the training camp in Canada of the United Kingdom's intelligence organization, the Special Operations Executive (SOE). The COI lacked its own training center and facilities and used the SOE's camp in Canada. Another plan for operations in China and Korea appears to have been submitted earlier in January by two COI officers named Larsen and Underwood, whose identities are uncertain, but it appears to have been on their own initiative and not related to DePass's Olivia plan. Chinese Scheme, January 7, 1942, Goodfellow Papers. The army also began to consider the potential of U.S.-Korean cooperation in early 1942. The Army MIS issued an assessment of the Korea liberation movement in March 1942, in which its Psychological Warfare Division proposed that the United States could broadcast propaganda to Koreans in Korea, China, and Japan and support Korean armed forces that had organized in China and the Soviet Union. Such operations offered the potential to attack Japanese interests in Korea and China and eventually take the fight into Japan itself. Joint Psychological Warfare Committee, Proposed Plan for Using Koreans against Japan, March 21, 1942, RG 226, microform M1642, roll 6, frames 33-62.

11. Memorandum to Colonel Donovan, February 17, 1942, RG 226, microform M1642, roll 51, frame 9.

12. Memorandum for the president from William J. Donovan, no. 186, January 24, 1942.

13. The Korean Liberty Conference in Washington DC, February 27–March 1, 1942, was a nationwide gathering of Korean immigrants and expatriates and Americans who supported the Korean cause. The Korean-American Committee, the leading Korean immigrant organization in the United States, organized the meeting with support from the Korean-American Council. Held on the anniversary of the March First Movement, the conference had about two hundred attendees, including Homer Hulbert and Syngman Rhee. Coordinator of Information, Far Eastern Section, Situation Report no. 2, "The Korean Liberty Conference, Washington DC, February 27–28 and March 1," March 9, 1942, Donovan Collection, U.S. Army Heritage and Education Center, box 49, Korea Miscellaneous. Also in RG 226, entry NM 54–8, container 2, folder R&A #253: Korean Liberty Conference.

14. McCune admitted when he submitted his reports that he had limited information about Korean actions in China, as State Department cables from China were vague about them, and Koreans in the United States gave information that was often contradictory. Interoffice memo from G. M. McCune to Dr. Remer, Subject: Report on "Potentialities for Korean Help against Japan," April 24, 1942, RG 226, entry NM 54–8, container 6, folder R&A #629b: Potentialities for Korean Help against Japan.

15. Interoffice memo from G. M. McCune to C. F. Remer, Subject: Korean "Recognition," March 7, 1942, RG 226, entry NM 54–8, container 2, folder R&A #253: Korean Liberty Conference.

16. McCune's 1942 reports were among a handful of documents about Korea that OSS Director William Donovan would retain and use through the end of the war. Donovan Collection, U.S. Army Heritage and Education Center, box 49, Korea Miscellaneous.

17. Having witnessed the March First Movement at the age of eleven, George McCune had deep personal impressions of Koreans' desire for independence. He later recalled having witnessed a Korean childhood friend being beaten and bayonetted by Imperial Japanese troops. "George McAfee McCune (1908–1948) and His Works," 35.

18. Coordinator of Information, Far Eastern Section, Report 41, "The Korean Independence Movement," April 25, 1942, Donovan Collection, U.S. Army Heritage and Education Center, box 49, Korea Miscellaneous. Also in RG 226, entry NM 54–8, container 6, folder R&A #629a: Korean Independence Movement. This report oversimplified the differences between the Provisional Government and the Korean Volunteer Corps, however, as it overlooked the role of Kim

Ku in organizing the 1932 terrorist bombings and Nationalist Chinese military support for both the Provisional Government and the Korean Volunteer Corps between 1932 and 1937.

19. Coordinator of Information, Far Eastern Section, Report 41a, "Potentialities for Korean Help against Japan," April 25, 1942, 1–2, Donovan Collection, U.S. Army Heritage and Education Center, box 49, Korea Miscellaneous. Also in RG 226, entry NM 54-8, container 6, folder R&A #629b: Potentialities for Korean Help against Japan.

20. "Potentialities for Korean Help against Japan," 3–4.

21. State Department cables from Chungking also did not report the integration of the Korean Volunteer Corps into the Korean Restoration Army when it occurred in June 1942, requiring McCune to depend on reports on Nationalist Chinese radio and information from Korean sources instead. Coordinator of Information, Far Eastern Section, Situation Report no. 7, "Unification of Korean Independence Groups," June 15, 1942, Donovan Collection, U.S. Army Heritage and Education Center, box 49, Korea Miscellaneous. Also in RG 226, entry NM 54-8, container 2, folder R&A #298: Unification of Korean Independence Groups.

22. "Unification of Korean Independence Groups," 4–5.

23. Within the U.S. government, lack of knowledge of Korea would continue to be a problem. For example, the Office of Naval Intelligence (ONI), unlike the COI/OSS and the Army Military Intelligence Service, had no specialist on Korea in 1942 and had to assign other staff to review Korean issues when the need arose. As a result, the ONI's Far Eastern Section mishandled George McCune's reports on Korea from April 25, 1942, accidentally accepting and substituting a paper with the same date written by S. K. Hahn, a leader of one of the Korean factions in the United States. Interoffice memo from G. M. McCune to C. F. Remer, Subject: Conversation with Commander McCollum, June 8, 1942, RG 226, entry NM 54-8, container 2, folder R&A #298: Unification of Korean Independence Groups.

24. For a detailed description of the development of OSS organization and operations in China, see Yu, *The OSS in China: Prelude to Cold War*, 31–157.

25. Syngman Rhee to Leo Crowley, September 29, 1943, RG 226, microform M1642, roll 66, frames 257–60.

26. Memoranda, November 4, 1943, November 5, 1943, and November 10, 1943, RG 226, microform M1642, roll 66, frames 250–52.

27. Memoranda, October 22, 1943, October 29, 1943, November 20, 1943, and November 23, 1943, RG 226, microform M1642, roll 66, frames 253, 255–56, 263–66.

28. Memoranda, December 21, 1943, December 22, 1943, and December 24, 1943,

RG 226, microform M1642, roll 66, frames 249, 261–62. The OSS's inaction with respect to the Koreans came under criticism from Senator Elbert Thomas of Utah, who inquired of Donovan whether the OSS was taking advantage of opportunities presented by the availability of the Koreans. Donovan to Ellery C. Huntington Jr., RG 226, microform M1642, roll 115, frames 33–36.

29. Korea Project memorandum, November 3, 1942, RG 226, microform M1642, roll 45, frame 771.

30. Memorandum on Project FE-4–Korean Group, November 10, 1942, RG 226, microform M1642, roll 66, frame 224.

31. Donovan to Col. Charles Y. Banfill, April 23, 1943, and Banfill to Donovan, April 28, 1943, RG 226, microform M1642, roll 79, frames 122–24.

32. Certificate of Medical Examination, March 14, 1943, RG 226, entry 224, container 501, folder of George M. McCune.

33. For more biographical information, see "George McAfee McCune (1908–1948) and His Works," *Journal of Modern Korean Studies* 2 (December 1985): 34–46.

34. Personal data, Clarence N. Weems Jr., RG 226, entry UD 92, container 289, folder 21.

35. Military record of Weems, Clarence Norwood, SN AO-912806, NARA, National Personnel Records Center.

36. Memoranda, May 4, 1943, and July 27, 1943, RG 226, entry UD 92, container 289, folder 21.

37. Memorandum from Edward E. Mason, acting director of R&A Branch, September 10, 1943, RG 226, entry 224, box 794, Personnel File of Weems, Clarence.

38. Carl Eifler became a legendary figure in the history of the OSS. Massively built at over 6 feet and 250 pounds, he had lied about his age to enlist in the army at the age of fifteen during the 1920s, then lied about his age again to become a seventeen-year-old police officer in the Los Angeles Police Department. In 1928 he joined the U.S. Customs Service, where he served as an officer on the California-Mexico border, did undercover work in Mexico, and rose to chief inspector in Hawaii in 1936. He had enlisted in the Army Reserve after turning eighteen and become a commissioned officer through a correspondence course. The army called him to active duty in March 1941 to command a military police company in Honolulu, where he experienced the attack on Pearl Harbor. The COI recruited Eifler a month later, and in June 1942 the OSS sent him to command its mission in Burma. Promoted to colonel, the intrepid Eifler successfully recruited and trained a force of Kachins and established a network of camps in northern Burma from which they spied on and harassed the Imperial Japanese Army. For a detailed account of Carl Eifler's exploits with the OSS, see his somewhat self-promotional

autobiography written with one of his former subordinate officers. Moon and Eifler, *The Deadliest Colonel*.

39. For his intelligence work, Birch received the Legion of Merit in 1944. General Chennault also posthumously nominated Birch for the Distinguished Service Cross, which was not awarded, and recommended nominating him for the Medal of Honor. The nomination for the Distinguished Service Cross described Birch's service in 1942–45 in this way: "Without any previous training in ground-air coordination, and with practically no guide materials or instruction, Birch, over a period of two years, during which he was almost continually in the field, living under the most primitive conditions and constantly in close proximity to the enemy, achieved phenomenal success. From 25 May 1944 until the end of the war Captain Birch operated almost exclusively behind the lines. His job was at all times extremely hazardous. Due to his outstanding ability in gathering intelligence and organizing intelligence nets, he was an extremely valuable member of the Allied Forces and he contributed immeasurably in bringing the war in China to a successful conclusion."

40. By mid-1944 the OSS assessed Korea to be an increasingly important area for intelligence operations. A July 1944 report identified numerous areas where operations in Korea could contribute significantly to intelligence collection: tapping of communication cables running through Korea to intercept Imperial Japanese Army communications avoiding the use of radio; monitoring of shipping as the IJN retreated to its home waters; and monitoring of air operations, rail traffic, and industrial production in Korea. Korean laborers would be in positions where they could sabotage shipping and industries, and eventually a revolution against Japanese rule might be possible. The presence of Korean laborers in Japan offered similar opportunities for intelligence collection and sabotage in Japan. For a study of the potentialities of OSS operations in Korea and through Koreans in Japan, see Office of Strategic Services, Research and Analysis Branch, R&A no. 2310, July 5, 1944, RG 226, entry UD 92, container 521, folder 2.

41. Colonel Eifler appears to have had no idea that the Korean Provisional Government in China existed. In his autobiography he describes Project NAPKO at length but mentions the existence of a Korean government in exile only once, and he believed that it was in Washington DC under Syngman Rhee. Moon and Eifler, *The Deadliest Colonel*, 168.

42. Carl F. Eifler, Colonel, Infantry, to Brig. General William J. Donovan, February 1, 1944, RG 226, entry UD 92, container 521, folder 2.

43. Qualifications of Personnel Assigned to Field Experimental Unit, June 17, 1944, RG 226, entry UD 92, container 521, folder 2.

44. According to Eifler, Project NAPKO staff recruited prisoners of war from Camp McCoy with only the camp commander and adjutant general informed of their activity. Korean POWs selected for the project went to the camp hospital for fictitious health problems, at which point Project NAPKO staff moved them to the Sherman Hotel in Chicago, then to the Biltmore Hotel in Los Angeles, and finally to Catalina Island for their training. Moon and Eifler, *The Deadliest Colonel*, 217.

45. Report on activities of FEU for period beginning April 4, 1945, and ending April 30, 1945.

46. Induction and Assignment of Richard Underwood (Inductee) to the Office of Strategic Services, Washington DC, June 22, 1945; Subject—Request for Procurement of Military Personnel, June 12, 1945, RG 226, entry 224, container 794, folder of Richard Underwood.

47. Report on Korean Underground and Resistance Potential, July 17, 1945, RG 226, entry UD 92, container 521, folder 3.

48. Report on Korean Underground and Resistance Potential, July 17, 1945.

49. Col. Carl F. Eifler, Infantry, Field Experimental Unit, Office of Strategic Services, Washington DC, to Maj. Gen. William J. Donovan, Office of Strategic Services, Washington DC, Napko Project, March 7, 1945, RG 226, entry UD 92, container 521, folder 1.

50. The business was a chain of pharmacies that may have been named New Ilhan & Co. In his autobiography Eifler identified a chain of pharmacies as the business owned by the leader of the Project NAPKO team that would operate in Seoul. Moon and Eifler, *The Deadliest Colonel*, 220, 225. A group photograph of employees of a drug wholesale distributor named New Ilhan & Co., dated 1940, appears in the OSS archives, G 226-P, Prints: OSS Personalities 1941–45, Japan-Korea, box #22, OSS-P-113A and OSS-P-113B.

51. Napko Project, 6–14, Annex A, Immediate Missions; 42–48, Annex I, Additional Information on EINEC and CHARO Plans. Eifler in his autobiography incorrectly described these four men as having farming backgrounds, possibly intentionally to obscure their identities after the war, when they may have returned to their home regions in North Korea. Moon and Eifler, *The Deadliest Colonel*, 225.

52. Napko Project, 6–14, Annex A, Immediate Missions, 42–48.

53. The islands around Mokpo include Jindo Island, the site of a major victory of Adm. Yi Sun Shin in 1597 in which he defeated a Japanese fleet of 133 ships with a force of only 13 ships. Jindo Island was the home of the author's maternal grandfather.

54. Napko Project, 15–16, Annex B, Follow Up Missions. The plan called for the use of approximately 450 U.S. Army personnel as it matured, estimated to be after one year of operation. Recruitment of Koreans would continue among Korean

civilians in the territory of Hawaii and the Philippines, Korean prisoners of war, and Korea itself, until potential recruits were completely exhausted. Napko Project, 24, Annex D, (1) Approximate United States Personnel (2) Recruitment of Korean Agents.

55. The design of the submersibles followed these specifications: Length: approximately 18 feet; Beam: 36 inches; Depth: 40 inches; Surface speed: 9.5-10 knots; Maximum range: 100 miles; Crew and passenger compartments: operator facing forward, passengers facing aft; Propulsion: two cylinder gasoline; Approximate weight: 2,500 pounds. GIMIK and BEEBE, Projects, April 18, 1945, NARA, Records of the Office of Strategic Services, RG 226, entry UD 92, container 521, folder 3.

56. An online article has incorrectly reported that the boats could submerge to a depth of up to thirty feet to be cached at a destination for up to three or four weeks. http://covertshores.blogspot.se/2010/07/lost-in-plain-sight-gimik-and-oss_19.html. This mistake was likely the result of confusion with the Central Intelligence Agency's postwar "Skiff" submersible, based on the same design, which had this capability. A Skiff is on display at the CIA Museum in Langley, Virginia. https://www.cia.gov/about-cia/cia-museum/experience-the-collection/text-version/collection-by-subject/directorate-of-science-and-technology.html. The article also stated that the boat had a radius of 110 miles, which was its maximum range; the operational radius was 50 miles.

57. George McCullough, "GIZMO #1 and GIZMO #2," August 25, 2003 (unpublished manuscript), 3.

58. G. J. Fannon, Major, QMC, SSO Supply Officer, to Mr. M. I. McHugh, Army Intelligence Boats, July 2, 1945, RG 226, entry UD 92, container 521, folder 5.

59. Napko Project, 25-33, Annex E, Schools and Training.

60. George McCullough, "GIZMO #1 and GIZMO #2," 1. McCulloch incorrectly identifies all of the Korean trainees as former prisoners of war. The OSS probably did not inform him of the real backgrounds of the Koreans with whom he was training, given the highly compartmentalized handling of the Project NAPKO teams.

61. McCullough, "GIZMO #1 and GIZMO #2," 2, 4. George McCulloch was still alive and living in Houston, Texas, in 2015.

62. McCullough, "GIZMO #1 and GIZMO #2," 4.

63. McCullough, "GIZMO #1 and GIZMO #2," 5.

64. Moon and Eifler, *The Deadliest Colonel*, 218-20.

65. Colonel Eifler was eager to start landings in Korea as soon as possible, and he devised a plan for an operation before the Battle of Okinawa had ended. Named "Mooro," the plan called for occupying a small island off Korea, with

only eighteen inhabitants, and using it as the first base for smuggling teams into Korea. Eifler notified Donovan of the Mooro plan on May 1, 1945, but the plan went unfulfilled. Moon and Eifler, *The Deadliest Colonel*, 226–27.

66. McCullough, "GIZMO #1 and GIZMO #2." The base for Project NAPKO probably was on the island of Kerama Retto, approximately twelve miles southwest of the main island of Okinawa. Kerama Retto had a network of caves where U.S. forces discovered a large cache of Japanese suicide boats with large explosive charges, designed to destroy ships. The caves would have been ideal places to hide the GIMIK boats.

67. The Eagle Project for SI Penetration of Korea, Prepared by SI Branch, OSS, China Theater, February 24, 1945, Annex 4, "Korean Personnel for the Eagle Project," 17, RG 226, entry A1 154, container 167, folder 2887.

68. "Korean Personnel for the Eagle Project," 17.

69. Kim Woo Chun, *Kim Ku Sonsaengue Salmul Daraso*, 66–69.

70. Memorandum to Lt. Col. W. E. Walker, SI Branch from Maj. C. W. Culp, PPB, Subject: Your Requisition #827, January 3, 1945, NARA, RG 226, entry 224, container 304, folder Hahm, Ryong C.

71. Kim Woo Chun, *Kim Ku Sonsaengue Salmul Daraso*, 62.

72. Kim Ku, *Paekpom Ilchi*, 282.

73. Kim Ku, *Paekpom Ilchi*, 283n139.

74. Clarence N. Weems Jr., Captain, Air Corps, to Lt. Col. Willis H. Bird, February 3, 1945, RG 226, entry A1 148, container 9, folder 149. Weems canceled the luncheon because of a conflict that the Korean side had with the date. Weems to Bird, February 6, 1945, RG 226, entry A1 148, container 9, folder 149. The Sino-Korean Cultural Association was a department of the Korean Provisional Government where Ahn Pyongmu, who recorded Weems's words to Kim Ku on January 31, 1945, worked as the secretary.

75. Immediate Intelligence Directives, Korean Interrogation—Week of April 1, 1945; Items of Particular Interest to the American H.Q., April 19, 1945, RG 226, entry A1 148, container 9, folder 149.

76. The Eagle Project for SI Penetration of Korea, Prepared by SI Branch, OSS, China Theater, February 24, 1945, RG 226, entry A1 154, container 167, folder 2887.

77. Memorandum from William F. Davis, Colonel, FA, Operations Officer, to Chief, Office of Strategic Services, China Theater, March 1, 1945, RG 226, entry A1 154, container 167, folder 2887.

78. Memorandum from Willis H. Bird, Lt. Col., Ord., Deputy Chief, OSS, C.T. to Commanding General, USF, China Theater, through G-5 (for Colonel Heppner), March 13, 1945, RG 226, entry A1 154, container 167, folder 2887.

5. Project Eagle

1. The Eagle Project for SI Penetration of Korea, 2, 16.
2. The Eagle Project for SI Penetration of Korea, 11. The plan referred to these areas by their Japanese language names: Shingishu, Seishin, Heijo, Keijo, and Fusan, respectively.
3. Organization Plan, RG 226, entry E154, container 201, folder 3414. Each of the five areas had two or three groups, each with two or three agents, to operate in specific localities. The groups in each area covered: in the northwestern border area, Sinuiju (Shingishu) (three agents) and Ryongchon (Tashito) (three); in the northeastern border area, Chongjin (Seishin) (three) and Rason (Yuki) (three); in north-central Korea, Pyongyang (Heijo) (three) and Wonsan (Genzan) (three); in south-central Korea, Seoul (Keijo) (three) and Inchon (Jinsen) (three); and on the southern coast, Pusan (Fusan) (two), Jinhae (Chinkai) (two), and Mokpo (Moppo) (two).
4. The operation would be under the command of the OSS's SI branch in China, supported by Communications and Services, with cooperation from R&A and S&T. The Eagle Project for SI Penetration of Korea, 3, 8, 15, 24–25.
5. The Eagle Project for SI Penetration of Korea, 8, 17, 22–23.
6. R. Harvey Sargent's journey across China is the subject of a traveling exhibition, *China: Exploring the Interior, 1903–04*, curated by Robert Sargent, grandson of R. Harvey Sargent and son of Clyde Sargent. See http://www.chinaexhibit.org/index.html.
7. Extracts from letters from Chengtu, China, from Clyde Sargent, Professor, Language School, Cheloo University, to his wife and mother, ca. October and November 1941, 5–7, Hoover Institution Library and Archives, Clyde Sargent Letter Extracts, 1941–47.
8. Chester Cooper, a staff sergeant with Project Eagle whose doctorate degree studies had been interrupted by the war and who after the war served in the Central Intelligence Agency, the National Security Council, and the State Department, wrote in 2005 that "Lee was about fifty years old, much younger than Kim Ku and his other political bosses. He looked and behaved like a character from central casting for a grade B, made-in-Bombay movie. Unlike the officials of the provisional government, he was neither heartsore nor tired. He did not walk; he marched. He did not nibble; he devoured. He did not sip; he gulped. He was short, ramrod straight, trim, bald, and energetic. He cultivated a thin, neat mustache. His revolver, swagger stick, and menacing German Shepherd dog were ubiquitous accompaniments during his every waking hour." Chester L. Cooper, *In the Shadows of History*, 72–73. Cooper provides the only published firsthand account of Project Eagle by an American with the OSS. Unfortunately,

many details of Cooper's memories of Project Eagle were wildly inaccurate, reflecting the passage of sixty years before he wrote and published them.

9. Aide memoire for Korean file by Clyde B. Sargent, Captain, AUS, undated, RG 226, entry A1 154, container 167, folder 2887.

10. Aide memoire for Korean file by Clyde B. Sargent, Captain, AUS, April 3, 1945 (first of three), RG 226, entry A1 154, container 167, folder 2887.

11. Aide memoire for Korean file by Clyde B. Sargent, Captain, AUS, April 3, 1945 (first of three).

12. Aide memoire for Korean file by Clyde B. Sargent, Captain, AUS, undated, RG 226, entry A1 154, container 167, folder 2887.

13. "Personal Data, Clarence N. Weems Jr.," RG 226, entry UD 92, container 289, folder 21. Earlier, in December 1944, Duncan C. Lee had described Weems and another officer to Lt. Col. Paul Halliwell as "excellent men on Korea" and recommended asking for Weems to be transferred to SI for operations work. Instead, Weems remained with R&A as an analyst. Memorandum from DCL to Lt. Col. Helliwell and Major Lee, December 23, 1944, RG 226, entry UD 92, container 289, folder 21. Helliwell instructed in July 1945 that "Weems is not repeat not to engage in operational planning or conduct of operations since he has a tendency to go off half cocked. Furthermore he is anathema to certain important Koreans with whom we are working." Det. 202 Communications Outgoing, from Helliwell to Drummond, July 3, 1945, RG 226, entry A1 154, container 201, folder 3414.

14. Memorandum on Eagle Project from Lt. Col. Paul E. Helliwell, Chief, SI Branch, to Maj. Gustav Krause, July 15, 1945; Memorandum on Eagle Project from Maj. Gustav Krause to Lt. Col. Paul E. Helliwell, Chief, SI Branch, July 23, 1945, RG 226, entry A1 154, container 208, folder 3542.

15. Clyde B. Sargent to Gustav Krause, June 11, 1945, RG 226, entry A1 154, container 208, folder 3543.

16. Monthly Report for May: Eagle Project, May 30, 1945, RG 226, entry A1 154, container 167, folder 2887; container 208, folder 3544.

17. Monthly Report for May: Eagle Project, May 30, 1945.

18. Memorandum from Richard P. Heppner, Colonel, FA, Chief, OSS, China, to Commanding General, United States Forces, China Theater, March 3, 1945; with annotation by Edwin O. Shaw, Lt. Col., A.C.D., Adjutant General, Headquarters, United States Forces, China Theater, to Chief, OSS, China Theater, approving by command of Major General Chennault, RG 226, entry A1 154, container 167, folder 2887.

19. Monthly Report for May: Eagle Project, May 30, 1945.

20. Monthly Report for June: Eagle Project, June 29, 1945.

21. Monthly Report for May: Eagle Project, May 30, 1945. Project Eagle also lacked a medical officer until July. Sargent recruited Dr. Hou Pao-chang, dean of the Cheloo College of Medicine, whom he had known for twelve years and who already had two sons working for the OSS. Sargent began working on obtaining approval to hire him in early June but did not get final approval until July 6. Documents related to employment of Dr. Hou Pao-Chang, a medical officer for American personnel, RG 226, entry A1 154, container 208, folder 3542.

22. Monthly Report for May: Eagle Project, May 30, 1945.

23. Monthly Report for May: Eagle Project, May 30, 1945.

24. General Outline of Course; Class Schedule: 4 to 9 June 1945; 1st Week: 4 June to 9 June 1945; 2nd Week: 11 June to 16 June 1945; 3rd Week: 18 June to 23 June 1945; 4th Week: 25 June to 30 June 1945, RG 226, entry A1 154, container 208, folder 3544.

25. Official Weapons Training Class: 13 June to 16 June 1945, RG 226, entry A1 154, container 208, folder 3544.

26. Kim Woo Chun, *Kim Ku Sonsaengue Salmul Daraso*, 74–77.

27. A Korean Code Employing Korean Alphabet, June 6, 1945, RG 226, entry A1 154, container 208, folder 3544. The one time pad, invented in 1917, was an encryption system using duplicate paper pads printed with random number groups, each with a serial number. A page would be used to encode a message, which would be sent with the serial number of the page. The recipient would reverse the encryption using the page with the same serial number in his duplicate copy. The pages in each pad would be destroyed after use, hence the name "one time pad."

28. Proposed Sub-base for Eagle to Be Located on Shantung Peninsula, July 8, 1945, RG 226, entry A1 154, container 208, folder 3544.

29. Morale Operations Program (Tentative), July 8, 1945, RG 226, entry A1 154, container 208, folder 3547.

30. Boa Plan, July 31, 1945, RG 226, entry A1 154, container 208, folder 3547.

31. Monthly Report for May: Eagle Project, May 30, 1945.

32. Monthly Report for May: Eagle Project, May 30, 1945.

33. Eagle Project, Monthly Report, June 1945, June 29, 1945, RG 226, entry A1 154, container 208, folder 3544.

34. Training Conference Held at EAGLE PROJECT on July 7, 1945, RG 226, entry A1 154, container 208, folder 3544.

35. The most prominent Korean American officer during the Second World War was Young Oak Kim, who rose to the rank of captain as an infantry company commander in the Japanese American 442nd Infantry Regiment. He became a colonel after service as an infantry commander again in the Korean War. See Woo Sung Han, *Unsung Hero*.

36. Letter from Mervin S. Gross, Brigadier General, U.S.A., Acting Chief of Staff, Headquarters, United States Forces, China Theater, May 26, 1945, RG 226, entry A1 148, container 9, folder 149. Woon Sung Chung's army personnel file in the National Personnel Records Center was lost in the 1973 fire that destroyed millions of Second World War military personnel files, and his OSS personnel file in the OSS archive in the National Archives is almost completely empty, so further information about his military service is unavailable.

37. Clyde B. Sargent, Captain, AUS, Field Commander, Eagle Project, to Captain Ryong C. Hahm, on assignment of duties at Eagle, August 1, 1945, RG 226, entry A1 154, container 208, folder 3542. Korea University was the first university founded by Koreans, in 1905, the first not founded by American Christians.

38. Hahm's wife, Myrtle Ruth Reidling, was from St. Vincent, Arkansas. As of the time of writing, it was not apparent whether there was any connection between Clarence Weems Sr. and Myrtle Ruth Reidling that contributed to her meeting Hahm. She passed away in 2008 in Arkansas at the age of one hundred.

39. Alien's Personal History and Statement, RG 226, entry 224, container 304, folder Hahm, Ryong C.

40. Hahm, Ryong C., Captain, USA, RG 226, entry A1 154, container 208, folder 3543.

41. Memorandum from Personnel Officer, SI to Chief, PPB, Subject Mr. Ryong C. Hahm, November 17, 1944; Appointment in the Army of the United States, February 15, 1945; Job Description and Justification in the Case of Ryong C Hahm; Application Form for Commissions in Army, Navy, or Marine Corps, RG 226, entry 224, container 304, folder Hahm, Ryong C.

42. Memorandum, July 21, 1945, Hsian 071, RG 226, entry A1 154, container 167, folder 2887.

43. RG 226, entry 224, box 794, Personnel File of Underwood, Horace H. Underwood joining the OSS had been a subject of discussion between the OSS in Washington and China at least since early May 1945. Message from Helliwell to Lee, Chungking 754/Washington 961, May 11, 1945, RG 226, entry A1 148, container 9, folder 129.

44. The OSS also attempted to obtain the transfer of Horace Underwood III in May 1945, but the Navy rejected the transfer. RG 226, entry 224, box 794, Personnel File of Underwood, Horace H.; Memorandum, May 11, 1945, RG 226, entry A1 154, container 167, folder 2887.

45. The nine arrivals on August 1 were Pvt. Chester Kim, Pvt. David Kim, Pvt. Shoon Kul Kim, Pvt. Chang Hei Lee, Pvt. Frank Lee, Pvt. 1st Class Harry Lee, Pvt. Kyung Sun Lee, Pvt. Peter Namkoong, and Pvt. Sang Pok Surh. The arrival on August 21 was Cpl. James Kang.

46. The nine August 1 arrivals also increased Project Eagle's staffing to twenty-three

Americans: five officers, fifteen enlisted men, and three civilians. Roster of American Personnel on duty with this Headquarters as of 2400 hours, August 7, 1945, August 8, 1945, RG 226, entry A1 154, container 208, folder 3543.

47. Clarence Weems had been an influence on the life of the most professionally accomplished among the ten enlisted men, Peter Namkoong, a certified public accountant from Hawaii with a private practice in Oahu. Originally from Kaesong, he had attended Songdo Higher Common School when Weems Sr. was the principal and Clarence Jr. was a teenager. Namkoong, Peter Park, Private, USA, ASN13139644, RG 226, entry A1 154, container 208, folder 3543.

48. S&T Weekly Report for Period 30 July through 4 August 1945, August 5, 1945, RG 226, entry A1 154, container 208, folder 3544.

49. Memorandum from Richard F. Heppner, Colonel, FA, Strategic Services Officer, to Commanding Officer, OSS Southern Command, Commanding Officer, OSS Central Command, and Commanding Officer, OSS North Eastern Command, "Areas of Command," August 2, 1945, RG 226, entry A1 154, container 167, folder 2887.

50. Assessment, Eagle Project, RG 226, entry A1 154, container 199, folder 3379.

51. Willis H. Bird, Lt. Col., Ord., Deputy Chief, OSS, China to Colonel Richard F. Heppner, SSO, OSS, China Theater, April 27, 1945, RG 226, entry A1 148, container 16, folder 237.

52. Incoming message from 109 to Heppner and Doering, Chungking 867/Kunming 1228, May 6, 1945, RG 226, entry A1 148, container 16, folder 237.

53. Incoming wire from Heppner to 109, 911 Washington, 662 Chungking, May 8, 1945; Incoming wire from 109 to Heppner, 1263 Kunming, 902 Chungking, May 9, 1945, RG 226, entry A1 148, container 16, folder 237. Later in May, the OSS command in China raised further objections based on the logistical burden of Project NAPKO. Incoming wire from Heppner to 109, 963 Washington, 756 Chungking, May 11, 1945, RG 226, entry A1 148, container 16, folder 237. OSS headquarters acknowledged that Project NAPKO, based in Okinawa and using special maritime equipment, would require a first movement of 48 bodies and 35 tons of gear using 2,552 cubic feet, and a second movement 27 bodies and 13 tons of gear using 1,626 cubic feet, while Project Eagle based in China with the same number of bodies would require a first movement of 11 tons using 1,316 cubic feet, and a second movement of 10 tons using 1,187 cubic feet. Incoming wire from 109 to Heppner, 1371 Kunming, 1010 Chungking, May 18, 1945, RG 226, entry A1 148, container 16, folder 237.

54. Outgoing wire from Davis to Heppner, 518 Kunming, August 9, 1945, RG 226, entry A1 148, container 16, folder 237.

55. Aide memoire for Korean file by Clyde B. Sargent, Captain, AUS, April 3, 1945 (third of three), RG 226, entry A1 154, container 167, folder 2887.

56. Aide memoire for Korean file by Clyde B. Sargent, Captain, AUS, April 3, 1945 (second of three), RG 226, entry A1 154, container 167, folder 2887.

57. Memorandum for Record, Visit of Representatives of Korean Provisional Government, Headquarters, United States Forces, China Theater, Chungking, China, April 17, 1945, RG 226, entry A1 154, container 148, folder 148.

58. The plan presented to General Wedemeyer made ambitious but unrealistic requests for U.S. reinforcement of the Korea Restoration Army. In addition to requesting training in guerilla warfare and for regular military operations, it requested the transfer to the Korea Restoration Army of Koreans serving in the U.S. armed forces or living in the United States, as well as Korean prisoners of war. He even requested the organization of a Korean air force, using Koreans serving in the U.S. and Chinese air forces. Ministry of Foreign Affairs, Provisional Government of the Republic of Korea, Chungking, "An Outline of the Suggestions Relating to the Military Aid Requested to the U.S. Authorities," RG 226, entry A1 154, container 148, folder 148.

59. Yi Pomsok's requests also included OSS assistance to establish direct radio communication between himself in Xian and Kim Hak Kyu's Third Detachment of the Korea Restoration Army in Anhui, as well as promotions for American officers serving with Project Eagle, to make their ranks more equal to those of their Korean counterparts. For example, he was a general in the Korean Restoration Army while Clyde Sargent was only a captain in the U.S. Army. Lee Bum Suk, Commander, Second Detachment, Korean Independence Army, to Colonel Helliwell, June 16, 1945, RG 226, entry A1 154, container 208, folder 3542.

60. Aide memoire for Korean file, April 5, 1945, RG 226, entry A1 154, container 148, folder 149.

61. Clyde B. Sargent, Capt., AUS, to Maj. Gustav Krause, May 26, 1945, "Further on Colonel Stables' Visit Today," RG 226, entry A1 154, container 167, folder 2887. Also in container 201, folder 3414.

62. Memorandum from John T. Whitaker, Colonel, Inf., Intelligence Officer, to Commanding General, USF, China Theater, Attempted Penetration of OSS Operation, June 5, 1945, RG 226, entry A1 154, container 201, folder 3414.

63. According to Quentin Roosevelt, a major with SI in Chungking who later became a noted CIA operative, Yi Pomsok supported the Chinese training center while simultaneously serving as co-commander of Project Eagle. Quentin Roosevelt, Major, F.A., Chief, SI, Chungking, to Captain Clyde Sargent, "Activities of General Lee Bum-suk in Chungking," August 10, 1945, RG 226, entry A1 154, container 167, folder 2887.

64. Clyde B. Sargent, Capt., AUS to Major Gustav Krause, May 26, 1945, "A Visit

from the British Military Mission," RG 226, entry A1 154, container 167, folder 2887. Also in container 201, folder 3414.

65. Det. 202 Communications Outgoing, from Heppner to Krause, June 8, 1945, RG 226, entry A1 154, container 201, folder 3414.

66. Whitaker to Heppner, June 7, 1945; Det. 202 Communications Outgoing, from Heppner to Krause, May 28, 1945, RG 226, entry A1 154, container 201, folder 3414.

67. John V. Whitaker, Colonel, Inf., Intelligence Officer, to Commanding General, USF, China Theater, June 6, 1945, "Attempted Penetration of OSS Operation," RG 226, entry A1 154, container 167, folder 2887.

68. Incoming message from Sargent to Helliwell info Roosevelt & Krause, July 30, RG 226, entry A1 154, container 167, folder 2887.

69. Clyde B. Sargent, Capt., AUS to Lt. Col. Paul Helliwell and Maj. Quentin Roosevelt, July 16, 1945, "Recruiting Koreans in Ju-ch'eng"; Incoming message from Sargent to Helliwell info Krause and Roosevelt, Chungking 550, July 22, 1945, RG 226, entry A1 154, container 167, folder 2887.

70. Incoming message from Sargent to Helliwell info Krause and Roosevelt, Chungking 550, July 22, 1945; Outgoing message from Roosevelt to Bowdler, Krause for Sargent, Kunming 328/Hsian 57, July 28, 1945; Incoming message from Saginaw for Tango to Helliwell, Chungking 904, July 31, 1945, RG 226, entry A1 148, container 9, folder 129.

71. Northeastern Field Command, Headquarters, Hsian, Monthly Report, August 1945, September 1, 1945, RG 226, entry A1 154, container 208, folder 3544.

72. Sargent to Helliwell, August 10, 1945, RG 226, entry A1 154, container 201, folder 3413; Incoming wire from Hector to Heppner and Roosevelt, 349 Chungking, August 13, 1945, RG 226, entry A1 154, container 167, folder 2887.

73. Memorandum from Clyde B. Sargent, Capt., AUS to Maj. Gustav Krause, Mission of the Eagle Project, June 10, 1945, RG 226, entry A1 154, container 208, folder 3542.

6. Lost Crusade

1. The two colonels were Dean Rusk, a lawyer and reserve officer who later served as secretary of state (1961–69) under Presidents Kennedy and Johnson, and Charles Bonesteel, a regular officer who later became a full general and the Commanding General of U.S. Forces Korea between 1966 and 1969.

2. Cable from Heppner to Helliwell, August 10, 1945, RG 226, entry A1 154, container 192, folder 3285.

3. Cable from Heppner to Davis, August 10, 1945, RG 226, entry 90, container 3, folder 30.

4. Kim Ku, *Paekpom Ilchi*, 286.

5. Kim Woo Chun, *Kim Ku Sonsaengue Salmul Daraso*, 79.

6. Assessment, Eagle Project, RG 226, entry A1 154, container 199, folder 3379. This impartial review of the abilities of Project Eagle's Korean agents found that many, but not all, possessed the motivation, intelligence, and emotional stability for a mission isolated deep in enemy-controlled territory, and it found significant reservations about the majority. The results of the assessment were worse than expected, and it caused Sargent and Yi to delay the start of deployment to Korea until after a further phase of screening and retraining.

7. An Urgent Request to the United States Facing the Conclusion of the War, by Bum Suk Lee, Commander of the 2nd Detachment of the Korean Kwangbok Army; An Outline of a Plan, Operation, and Cooperation between OSS and This Detachment Right after the Japanese Imperialism Is Destroyed, Submitted by Bum Suk Lee, The Commander of the 2nd Detachment of the Korean Kwangbok Army, RG 226, entry A1 154, container 201, folder 3414.

8. Incoming wire from Helliwell to Roosevelt, 229 Chungking, August 10, 1945, RG 226, entry A1 154, container 167, folder 2887.

9. Outgoing radio message from Heppner to Bird, August 14, 1945, RG 226, entry A1 154, container 187.

10. Memorandum for the Eagle Project File by William P. Davis, Colonel, FA, Deputy OSS, August 11, 1945, RG 226, entry A1 148, container 9, folder 129. Sargent may have been long out of favor with Heppner and other officers at OSS China headquarters. Sargent had been left out of the officers accompanying Director Donovan during the August 7 meeting with Kim Ku, even though his direct counterpart, Yi Pomsok, accompanied Kim Ku. As a China hand who had been in China since the 1930s and with the COI/OSS since 1942, Sargent was an outsider to the officers at OSS China headquarters who had arrived in 1944-45, which may have contributed to him falling out of favor.

11. Outgoing radio message from Heppner to Bird for Sargent, August 14, 1945, RG 226, entry A1 154, container 201, folder 3414.

12. Memorandum from 2nd Lt. Hunter L. Fulford to Col. E. F. Connely, Subject: Major Willis H. Bird, January 29, 1944; Memorandum from Major Frank L. Ball Jr. to Security Office, Subject: Security Report on Major Willis Hesser Bird, O-91241, Ordnance, January 25, 1944, RG 226, entry 224, box 794, Personnel File of Bird, Willis.

13. For more information about Bird's negotiations with the Chinese Communists and the resulting controversy, see Yu, *The OSS in China*, 186-97.

14. A further problem with Bird, according to Chester Cooper, was that he was chronically drunk and rumored to have been sent to Xian to hide him after

embarrassing incidents in Chungking. Cooper remembered Bird's name incorrectly as "Walter Bride" and recalled other details about Operation Eagle incorrectly, however, so his description of Bird may not be accurate. Cooper, *In the Shadows of History*, 75–77. Chinese Communist accounts published after the war have described Bird as a security liability for the OSS, describing Chinese Communist intelligence operations that took advantage of an affair by Bird and his secretary in Chungking and used it to penetrate OSS operations in China, so there may be substance behind Cooper's memories. Yu, *The OSS in China*, 317n.

15. Outgoing radio message from Heppner to Bird, August 14, 1945, RG 226, entry A1 154, container 187.

16. Memorandum from Bird to Heppner, August 12, 1945, RG 226, entry A1 154, container 187.

17. Preliminary Report of Mission to Keijo, Korea, for the Relief of Prisoners of War Interned in That Country, by Willis H. Bird, Lt. Col., Ord., August 23, 1945, RG 226, entry A1 154, container 187.

18. Unaddressed message, Hsian 342, August 16, 1945, RG 226, entry A1 154, container 187.

19. Yi wore an unusual combination of uniform items that appeared to be an American uniform and web gear with a cloth-covered helmet that was either British or the identical American helmet used in the First World War. His three officers wore the Nationalist Chinese uniforms of the Korean Restoration Army instead of the American uniforms that they had been issued for Project Eagle, and each had a uniform and equipment belt that was the wrong size for him and did not match the others, suggesting that they had been hastily scrounged just before the mission.

20. Message from Bird to Heppner, Hsian 310, August 15, 1945, RG 226, entry A1 154, container 201, folder 3414.

21. Preliminary Report of Mission to Keijo, Korea, for the Relief of Prisoners of War Interned in That Country.

22. Outgoing message from Davis to Heppner info Krause, Kunming 636, August 17, 1945, RG 226, entry A1 148, container 9, folder 127. The OSS was skeptical about the OWI claim of authorization from the Pentagon to go on the mission, which may have been nothing more than War Department approval of OWI's general mission in China.

23. Preliminary Report of Mission to Keijo, Korea, for the Relief of Prisoners of War Interned in That Country.

24. Outgoing radio message from Heppner to 109, Davis, August 18, 1945, RG 226, entry A1 154, container 187.

25. Incoming message from Heppner to Bird info Krause and Chungking, Chungking 572/Hsian 343, August 19, 1945, RG 226, entry A1 148, container 9, folder 127.

26. Preliminary Report of Mission to Keijo, Korea, for the Relief of Prisoners of War Interned in That Country.

27. Japs Bring Up Tanks and Order American POW Relief Mission out of Korea, by Henry R. Lieberman (Representing the Combined Allied Forces), U.S. Office of War Information, August 22, 1945, RG 226, entry A1 154, container 187.

28. Preliminary Report of Mission to Keijo, Korea, for the Relief of Prisoners of War Interned in That Country.

29. Outgoing message from Davis to Heppner, Kunming 675/Hsian 98, August 19, 1945, RG 226, entry A1 148, container 9, folder 127.

30. Message from Fiser to Krause and Helm, Hsian 497, August 21, 1945, RG 226, entry A1 154, container 187.

31. Outgoing message from Davis to Peers, Kunming 717, August 21, 1945; Outgoing message from Davis to Krause for Bird info Heppner, Hsian 100/Kunming 690, August 20, 1945, RG 226, entry A1 148, container 9, folder 127.

32. Message from Duck to Helm and Opso, NAX 21, August 20, 1945, RG 226, entry A1 154, container 187.

33. Message from Heppner to Krause for Bird, Hsian 360, August 20, 1945, RG 226, entry A1 154, container 187.

34. Message from Heppner and Indiv to Bird info Krause, Hsian 367, August 20, 1945, RG 226, entry A1 154, container 187.

35. Outgoing message from Davis to Krause for Bird info Heppner, Hsian 100/Kunming 690, August 20, 1945, RG 226, entry A1 148, container 9, folder 127.

36. Bird also sent a message explaining himself ahead of his flight. It read, "Risked life of Eagle once. We failed. Requested internment and were ordered out at point of tank guns. Authorities refuse to recognize Wedemeyer's right to this mission until their government approves. We [are] lucky to have our heads. My judgement is that I report facts to you first hand unless peace actually signed. If peace signed want to go back at once but you are ordering 22 men to their death if we must buck their attitude now. Realize importance of getting in or would not have taken chance I did with mission. Also realize that *if* Russians are overrunning Korea they are doing so with armies. Japs say Russians standing pat. We can stay here on field and await peace or return Hsian but if latter, need new plane. . . . Please understand I want very much to go back as I have a few debts to pay off but not as a suicide mission." Memorandum from Bird to Heppner, RQA 2, August 21, 1945, RG 226, entry A1 154, container 187.

37. Outgoing message from Davis to Heppner and Indiv, Kunming 735, August 22, 1945, RG 226, entry A1 148, container 9, folder 127.

38. Japs Bring Up Tanks and Order American POW Relief Mission Out of Korea, by Henry R. Lieberman.

39. It is unclear from official records whether the allegation that Bird left behind food and medical supplies was true. It is possible that the allegation was only a rumor that began among General Wedemeyer's staff or in the OSS. Bird's report of the mission explicitly stated that the C-47's load included medical supplies for rescued prisoners of war. The report also made the possibly false statement that the addition of the AGAS officer and OWI war correspondent was made possible by dropping Koreans from the flight, though, so its statement about the medical supplies may have been false.

40. Message from Davis to Heppner, August 23, 1945, RG 226, entry 168, container 16, folder 221.

41. Message from Heppner to Donovan, August 23, 1945, RG 226, entry 168, container 16, folder 221.

42. Message from Heppner to Davis, August 23, 1945, RG 226, entry 168, container 16, folder 221.

43. Message from Heppner to Donovan, August 23, 1945, RG 226, entry 168, container 16, folder 221.

44. Message from Donovan to Heppner, August 24, 1945, RG 226, entry 168, container 16, folder 221. OSS China Theater headquarters asked Maj. Gustav Krause on September 5 to obtain reports from each member of the Eagle mission on what happened, how the mission was run, and any criticisms or good points. Message from Heppner and Helliwell to Krause, Hsian 636, September 5, 1945, RG 226, entry A1 154, container 187.

45. Heppner was apologetic in a message to Bird on August 25, stating, "Very regretful of situation which makes this move necessary. However, Theater is adamant." Outgoing radio message from Heppner to Bird, Chungking 821, August 25, 1945, RG 226, entry A1 154, container 201, folder 3414.

46. Message from Heppner to Donovan, August 26, 1945, RG 226, entry 168, container 16, folder 221.

47. Message from Heppner to Davis, Chungking 771, August 23, 1945, RG 226, entry A1 154, container 187.

48. Message from Helm to Duck, Hsian 538, August 17, 1945, RG 226, entry A1 154, container 187.

49. Message from Sargent to Helliwell, RQA 9, August 24, 1945, RG 226, entry A1 154, container 187.

50. Message from Stewart to Heppner, Hsian 593, August 28, 1945, RG 226, entry A1 154, container 187. This message indicated that a B-17 reconnaissance aircraft from Okinawa flew through Weihsien. It was probably an F-9 Flying Fortress

photo reconnaissance aircraft, redesignated the RB-17 after the war. Photographs taken in Weihsien show that the flight from Weihsien to Xian was on a C-47 equipped with the Rebecca direction finding system, used to home in on Eureka transponders laid by pathfinders to designate drop zones in airborne operations. The presence of these unusual aircraft in the Weihsien area is indicative of the aerial operations that the Fourteenth Air Force and other U.S. air forces were conducting during the OSS prisoner of war rescue missions in August 1945.

51. Yu, *The OSS in China*, 235–41.
52. The most complete account of the death of John Birch comes from the War Department report of its official inquiry into the incident. Report by War Department Office of Assistant Secretary of War, Strategic Service Unit, March 23, 1946, to Commanding General, AAF, China Theater, ATTN: military personnel officer, entry 168, box 16, folder 225 "Death of John Birch," cited in Yu, *The OSS in China*, 317n20.
53. Message from Davis to Heppner, Chungking 863, August 30, 1945, RG 226, entry A1 154, container 187.
54. Despite the failure of the mission, each U.S. serviceman who went to Seoul with Operation Eagle received the Soldier's Medal, awarded for heroism not involving actual conflict with the enemy.
55. Outgoing message from Stevens to Indiv and Fiser, Kunming 766, August 24, 1945, RG 226, entry A1 148, container 16, folder 237.
56. Incoming message from Heppner to 109, Chungking 824, 2269 Washington, August 26, 1945, RG 226, entry A1 148, container 16, folder 237.
57. Outgoing radio message from Headquarters, Office of Strategic Services, China Theater, to Fletcher, Wampler, and Krause, August 29, 1945, RG 226, entry A1 154, container 201, folder 3414.
58. Memorandum from William F. Davis, Colonel, FA, Deputy SSO, to Commanding General, United States Forces, China Theater, "EAGLE Project," August 31, 1945, RG 226, entry A1 154, container 167, folder 2887.
59. Message from Bird to Heppner, Hsian 706, September 1, 1945, RG 226, entry A1 154, container 201, folder 3413.
60. Message from Bird to Heppner, Hsian 706, September 1, 1945.
61. Outgoing message from Heppner to Davis, September 3, 1945, RG 226, entry A1 154, container 201, folder 3413; Outgoing message from Heppner to Davis, September 4, 1945, RG 226, entry A1 148, container 9, folder 127.
62. Lee Bum Suk to Lt. Col. Paul Helliwell, September 9, 1945, RG 226, entry A1 154, container 201, folder 3413.
63. Lee Bum Suk to Lt. Col. Paul Helliwell, September 9, 1945.
64. Memorandum from Paul L. E. Helliwell, Colonel, F.A., Intelligence Officer,

oss/ct, to Deputy Strategic Services Officer, oss/ct, September 21, 1945, RG 226, entry A1 154, container 201, folder 3413.

65. Memorandum from Silvio I. Bousquin, Lt. Col., ACD, Asst. Adj. Gen., to Strategic Services Officer, China Theater, September 13, 1945, RG 226, entry A1 154, container 167, folder 2887.

66. Outgoing message from Hepper to 109 info Helliwell (Kunming) and Oates (Hsian), September 15, 1945, RG 226, entry A1 148, container 9, folder 129.

67. Outgoing radio message from Headquarters, Office of Strategic Services, China Theater, to Fletcher, Wampler, and Krause, August 29, 1945, RG 226, entry A1 154, container 201, folder 3414. The order acknowledged that the end of the project would be a sensitive political issue and suggested that preliminary steps for liquidation be taken without formally notifying the Koreans, which would not occur until an officer arrived at the Project Eagle camp to discuss postwar actions with them. No record of the officer visiting the Project Eagle camp could be found. Clyde Sargent's September 17 letter to Colonel Helliwell indicates that he had taken on the task of discussing the end of the project and postwar actions with Yi Pomsok.

68. Willis Bird departed China for the United States on September 28 and was discharged from active duty in October. RG 226, entry 224, box 794, Personnel File of Bird, Willis. Bird's misadventures in Asia continued after the war. The former Sears, Roebuck employee from Chicago settled down in Bangkok, married a Thai woman, and started an import-export business that imported American products into Thailand, including McCormick spices—unlikely to have been a popular product in spice-rich Thailand. His cable address was "Eagle," possibly a reference to his moment of notoriety with Operation Eagle. In 1947 Bird wrote directly to William Donovan at his law firm after a coup in Thailand, offering his services to the newly formed Central Intelligence Agency. Willis H. Bird, Inc., to William J. Donovan, December 20, 1947, Donovan Collection, U.S. Army Heritage and Education Center, box 73A, book 40, file 680. Bird's firm did contract work for the Central Intelligence Agency but got him into more public embarrassments as well. In 1959 congressional testimony accused Bird of bribing a U.S. government official with $25,000 in order to gain a foreign aid construction contract in Laos. Yu, *The OSS in China*, 317n.

69. Kim Woo Chun, *Kim Ku Sonsaengue Salmul Daraso*, 80.

70. Memorandum from Clyde B. Sargent to Colonel Helliwell, Hsien, September 17, 1945, RG 226, entry A1 154, container 201, folder 3413.

71. Message from Eagle to Indiv, September 27, 1945, RG 226, entry A1 154, container 201, folder 3414.

72. Paul L. Helliwell, Colonel, F.A., Chief, Intelligence Division, to Kim Hak Kyu,

Commanding General, Third Detachment, The Korean National Army, September 25, 1945, RG 226, entry A1 154, container 208, box 3542.

73. Paul L. Helliwell, Colonel, F.A., Chief, Intelligence Division, to Lee Bum Suk, Commanding General, Second Detachment, The Korean National Army, September 28, 1945, RG 226, entry A1 154, container 208, box 3542.

74. The five enlisted men were Pvt. Marshall Shroyer, Pvt. 1st Class Dimitrious Matheos, Sgt. Richard Hill, Cpl. Guy Webb, and Technical Sgt. Alf Arnesen. Arnesen, the last man to join Project Eagle on August 21, was likely an exception among the five enlisted men in not welcoming the end of the war. A twenty-six-year-old from Brooklyn, New York, who had worked as a steamfitter after dropping out of high school, he had been activated with his National Guard unit in 1941 and volunteered for the OSS in 1943. With both American and British jump wings from training with the OSS and the British SOE, he had parachuted into France with a Jedburgh team for sabotage operations behind German lines in the Dijon area in September 1944. He then volunteered for further operations in the Pacific Theater, feeling that the Jedburgh teams "didn't do enough" in the European Theater. He would have been a key trainer and possibly a field agent for Project Eagle. RG 226, entry 224, box 22, Personnel File of Arnesen, Alf G.

75. Official Dispatch from CHAFX, Kunming to Office of Strategic Services, date August 18, 1945, RG 226, microcopy 1642, roll 25, frames 480–81.

76. Memo from William J. Donovan to Miss Rose Conway, August 18, 1945, RG 226, microcopy 1642, roll 66, frame 282.

77. The full message read: "Today in victory the people of Korea join the people of the United States in rejoicing with Japan's surrender and the end of the war throughout the world. Our enemy is defeated. Korea's freedom from Japanese oppression which we faithfully have resisted for 50 years is realized. America's freedom from the cruel attack of a powerful enemy is accomplished. Today in victory we celebrate the unconditional surrender of our common enemy. In victory and freedom, we the people of Korea express our genuine and deep appreciation to the Government and the people of the United States for their achievements in defeating our enemy. With freedom and peace the Korean people now begin their important work of building an independent state and a nucleus of democracy in the Far East. We have confidence in your guarantee of Korean independence and believe that Korea's independence is a key to peace in the Far East. In our endeavors to build an independent democracy we are relying strongly on the understanding and cooperative aid of the American Government and people. It is our hope that American Korean positive cooperation initiated in China during the last few months of the war against Japan

will continue and grow. We hope that the people of the United States and Korea eternally will guarantee the peace of a democratic world for which all freedom loving have sacrificed so much to win. We join you and your people in spirit and action to develop democracy and to maintain eternal peace. And to you, Mr. President, I send warm personal greetings." Memorandum for the President, William J. Donovan, Director, August 18, 1945, RG 226, microcopy 1642, roll 66, frames 283–84.

78. Harry Truman to General Donovan, August 25, 1945, RG 226, microcopy 1642, roll 66, frames 281.

79. Kim Woo Chun, *Kim Ku Sonsaengue Salmul Daraso*, 81–82.

80. Orders signed by Alfred D. Schiaffo, Captain, AGD, Ass't Adjutant, September 11, 1945; Letter Order #1235 signed by Cecil F Martin, Captain, Air Corps, Ass't Adjutant, September 17, 1945, RG 226, entry UD 92, container 289, folder 21.

81. There are several documents referencing claims by Weems that Director Donovan expressly requested preparation of the report. There are no surviving documents providing evidence of a request by Donovan, however, so if Donovan made such a request, he may have made it informally and verbally.

82. " Korea and the Provisional Government," Prepared by Clarence N. Weems Jr., Captain, AC, September 28, 1945, Donovan Collection, U.S. Army Heritage and Education Center, box 49, Korea Miscellaneous.

83. "Korea and the Provisional Government," 3–5.

84. "Korea and the Provisional Government," 5.

85. "Korea and the Provisional Government," 5.

86. "Korea and the Provisional Government," 7–8.

87. "Korea and the Provisional Government," 8.

88. "Korea and the Provisional Government," 10.

89. Statement of General Kim Hak Kyu of the Present Situation of Korea, September 27, 1945, 1, RG 226, entry UD 92, container 289, folder 21. The translator of the statement into English was Lt. Woon Sung Chung, who had departed Project Eagle on August 29. The full text read: "This is a brief statement to the American authorities as a reference material in dealing with the Korean question. It is written as a report on the outlook of Korea. I am grateful to the Allied nations for their forces of justice with which they have driven the Japanese forces from Korea and have given the Korean an opportunity to reestablish his freedom in Korea again. I feel it is very fortunate for Korea. The remaining question is how to establish the Korean Government in the future. If it is organized with the principles of democracy, it would not only be fortunate for Korea but also for the rest of the world. But, on the other hand, if the Korean Government should be organized with unjustifiable methods it

would not only be unfortunate for Korea, but also it would be very unfortunate for the peace of the world. There are two roads before Korea. One is to form a democratic government with the cooperation of and fulfilling the ardent desire of the large majority of the Korean people. The other is to establish a form of government which is inspired by Russian Communism. Russia is making every effort to make the world over to Communism. In other words, Russia has the ambition to make the world her own. Therefore, Russia uses every method to communize Manchuria and Korea because they are the most important areas to Russia in the Orient. After the Russian occupation of Korea north of latitude 38 degrees, Russia published no news as to her activity in Korea. The world is waiting for news from that area. We can only guess what the Russians are doing there. In my opinion, they are doing two things. The first is to make the Northern part of Korea a firm foundation of Communism toward the Southern part of Korea. How do they carry out these two objectives? Firstly, they buy or win over the heart of the Korean people with subtle methods of economic and political policy. Secondly, they organize strong communistic units in the occupied area. And thirdly, they send their men to the southern part of Korea to organize underground communist units. What is the counter measure against the policy of Russia's advancing toward South Korea? The first is to unify the Korean people in that area around the Korean democratic principles. The second is to establish a democratic government in the south and have the Korean people north of latitude 38 degrees join the democratic government with free will. The third is to withdraw the divided control of Korea in the north and south and to establish uniform policies all over Korea. The fourth is to reinforce the Korean Provisional Government and the Korean National Army, which have been the central force for democratic principles and have been the object of the belief of the Korean people, and to have these two agencies to control and lead the Korean people. The Korean Provisional Government stands for the democratic principle and has been fighting for the continuance of Korean independence for the last thirty years. Those leaders like Syngman Rhee and Kim Ku and others in the government are the most respected leaders of the Korean people. At the beginning of Korean national liberation it would be hard to concentrate the democratic political ideology unless the leaders of the government get into Korea and have them the symbol of the democratic ideological concentration among the Korean people. By this method it will be possible for the Koreans to check the rush of communism from the north toward the south. The Korean people are eagerly expecting the return of the Korean Provisional Government to Korea. It has been reported in the newspapers and radio communications from Korea, that a leader of the democratic party in Korea proper, Mr. Song Chin-Woo, is said to have made a statement. Among other things Mr. Song stated that the complicated political question in Korea could be straightened out only by having the Korean Provisional Government in Chungking come into Korea in the shortest possible time and the return of the Provisional Government was the desire of tens of thousands of the Korean people. If we don't relieve the yearning of the people in due time, it would make the Korean people doubtful and despairing and it would make the Korean people much harder to concentrate the people ideology and it would give a wonderful chance to spread Communism to the south. If Korea should be conquered by Communism, it would be unfortunate not only to Korea but to China as well as to the national policy of the United States toward the Far East and to the peace of the world. America, China, and the other allied democratic nations should give this close consideration. The Chinese government of Chiang Kai-shek has realized this principle. Therefore, China asserts that the Korean Provisional Government in Chungking should get into Korea. There are two conditions necessary for the proper functioning of the Korean Government. The first is the international recognition and backing of the United States, China, USSR, and England. The second is an armed force which can protect and support the Government. China is assisting in the reinforcement of the Korean National Army. She will do this by releasing the Korean soldiers in the Japanese Army in China and turning them over to the authority of the Korean National Army when they disarm the Japanese soldiers in China. The number of the Korean nationality in the Jap Army in China is reported to be about two hundred thousand. The occupation of Korea by the Korean National Army would not only be necessary for Korea itself but also would be helpful to the United States, China, and England and would be fortunate for the peace of the world. I believe this because the firm independence of Korea would check the rearmament of Japan and could check the southward movement of the northern Red. Therefore, it is necessary for the United States, China, England, and Russia to help the Korean National Army getting into Korea. I am sure the Korean people want to cooperate with America. The reasons for this are: the relation between Korea and America has been very good in the last hundred years; America has given help to Korea by means of religion, education, and social work in the past. The Korean people remember these relations. The Korean people know that America has no territorial ambition over Korea because they know what America intends to do with the Philippine Islands. I believe that America is against aggression and Korea will need the help of America when she reorganizes her economy, industry, etc. There are several reasons why I would like to have full cooperation between Korea and America."

90. Significance of the Korean Independence Army in Relation to American Objectives in China, by Captain Clarence N. Weems Jr., Former Chief, R&A Korea Desk, OSS—China Theater, October 11, 1945, RG 226, entry UD 92, container 289, folder 21.

91. Significance of the Korean Independence Army in Relation to American Objectives in China, 3, 5.

92. Weems estimated that an initial advance of $500,000 would be necessary, to provide $5 each for the expenses of 100,000 men, out of whom the initial 50,000 would be selected. He stated that the final amount necessary would be difficult to estimate, as Yi Chong Chon and Kim Hak Kyu had not provided him with firm estimates during his last meeting with them a month earlier. Significance of the Korean Independence Army in Relation to American Objectives in China, 4. Weems stated that aid "should be handled by an American who has an intimate knowledge of the Provisional Government and the Korean Independence Army and has their confidence; such an individual should also have a background of knowledge of Chinese politics and of the general workings of the Russian diplomatic service in China. Significance, 2.

93. Significance of the Korean Independence Army in Relation to American Objectives in China, 5.

94. Significance of the Korean Independence Army in Relation to American Objectives in China, 5.

95. Clarence N. Weems Jr., Captain, AC, to Lt. Col. Duncan C. Lee, Divisional Deputy, Far East, SI, October 11, 1945, RG 226, entry UD 92, container 289, folder 21.

96. Clarence N. Weems Jr., Captain, AC, to Colonel Lee, October 20, 1945, RG 226, entry UD 92, container 289, folder 21

97. Duncan C. Lee, Lt. Col., AUS, DIv. Dep., Far East, SI to Director, SSU, October 31, 1945, RG 226, entry UD 92, container 289, folder 21.

98. John Magruder, Brigadier General, USA, Director, to Colonel Alfred McCormack, Special Assistant to Secretary of State, October 1945, RG 226, entry UD 92, container 289, folder 21.

99. Note to Lt. Col. Duncan C. Lee, November 3, 1945, RG 226, entry UD 92, container 289, folder 21.

100. A copy of Weems's report is in the files of the XXIV Corps, and its presence appears to have confused some historians, who assumed mistakenly that the report was requested by General Hodge, not OSS Director Donovan. Kim Ku, *Paekpom Ilchi*, 283–84 n14.

7. End of Innocence

1. Boose, "Portentous Sideshow." Military maps of Korea used by XXIV Corps planners would have been the maps made by Evelyn McCune for the Army Map Service.
2. Boose, "Portentous Sideshow."
3. Boose, "Portentous Sideshow." For the State Department directive, see "Basic Initial Directive to the Commander in Chief, U.S. Army Forces, Pacific, for the Administration of Civil Affairs in Those Areas of Korea Occupied by U.S. Forces," transmitted October 17, 1945, in *Foreign Relations of the United States, 1945*, 4:1074–93.
4. Memorandum to Chief, Special Funds, from Chief, Division Z, Branch Z, Subject: Captain Hahm, June 26, 1946, RG 226, entry 224, container 304, folder Hahm, Ryong C.
5. Clarence N. Weems Jr., Captain, AC, to Major Swain, Personnel Officer, CAD, Washington DC, October 25, 1945; Memorandum for the Director, Strategic Services Unit, War Department, Subject: Captain Clarence N. Weems Jr., October 30, 1945, RG 226, entry UD 92, container 289, folder 21.
6. Sargent published a translation and analysis of the official biography of Emperor Wang Mang that he had completed in 1940 as a doctoral thesis at Columbia University, but could not defend and publish before the war interrupted. J. J. L. Duyvendak, "'Wang Mang, a Translation of the Official Account of His Rise to Power as Given in the 'History of the Former Han Dynasty' by Clyde Bailey Sargent," *T'oung Pao*, 2nd ser., vol. 40, nos. 1–3 (1950): 216–27. The book was published in China in 1947 and later reprinted in the United States in 1977. See Clyde Bailey Sargent, *Wang Mang: A Translation of the Official Account of His Rise to Power as Given in the "History of the Former Han Dynasty"* and Gu Ban, Pan Ku, Biao Ban, Zhao Ban, and Clyde Bailey Sargent, *Wang Mang: A Translation of the Official Account of His Rise to Power*.
7. Moon and Eifler, *The Deadliest Colonel*, 234.
8. Messages from Commanding General, U.S. XXIV Corps to Senior Japanese Military Commander in Korea South of 38 Degree North Latitude, August 31, 1945; Messages from Commanding General, XXIV Corps to Commanding General, Seventeenth Japanese Army Group, Keijo, Korea; Messages to Commanding General of the XXIV Corps of the United States Army Okinawa, September 1, 1945, RG 554, container 33, folder Repatriation and Transfer of Control to US (Creation of Trusteeship).
9. G-2 Report, RG 554, box 22, folder Military Government Activities: Political Parties.
10. Message to Commanding General of the U.S. Twenty-Fourth Army, Okinawa,

September 1, 1945, RG 554, container 33, folder Repatriation and Transfer of Control to US (Creation of Trusteeship).

11. After his release from prison in Taejon in 1932, Yo Un Hyong ran the newspaper *Choson Ilbo* in Seoul, with an agenda of passively resisting Japanese rule. The newspaper's most noteworthy moment was in 1936, when it reported the Olympic gold medal and new world record of Korean marathoner Son Ki Jung at the 1936 Berlin Summer Olympics, when he competed as part of the Japanese team. The front-page photograph deleted the Japanese flag from So Ki Jung's uniform, and Japanese authorities responded by arresting Yo Un Hyong and banning the newspaper. Sports were a significant part of Yo's life; he had coached the Fudan University soccer team in Shanghai in 1929 and had been arrested by Japanese agents that year while watching a baseball game. He continued his involvement in sports in Seoul after his release.

12. "United States Policy regarding Korea, Part II, 1941–1945," 65–66, declassified unpublished research paper by the Division of Historical Policy Research, State Department, May 1950, printed by the Institute of Asian Culture Studies, Hallym University, Chunchon, Korea, 1987.

13. For the Press, no. 763, October 16, 1945, RG 554, box 22, folder General U.S. Policy towards Korea, 1945–46.

14. They landed at a former Chinese airport and Japanese military airbase that today is Shanghai's Hongqiao International Airport, which Kim Ku mistakenly believed was built on the site of Hongkou Park, the site of the bombing of Imperial Japanese leaders in Shanghai by Yun Ponggil that he had ordered in April 1932. He admitted that he had never set foot in Hongkou Park during his fourteen years in Shanghai and that someone else had told him that the airport was in Hongkou Park. Kim Ku, *Paekpom Ilchi*, 291.

15. Kim Ku, *Paekpom Ilchi*, 292.

16. A scheme to fund the Korea Restoration Army by issuing bonds in China that would be redeemable in Korea apparently existed in Tianjin and possibly other cities. The USAMGIK liaison officer overseeing the evacuation of Korean refugees in Tianjin in 1946–47, 1st Lt. Shamil H. Ibragimoff, reported in May 1946 that he had discovered bonds, declared to be redeemable in Seoul by an article in a Korean newspaper in Tianjin, which apparently were illegally issued to raise funds from Koreans in China for the Korea Restoration Army. Letter of Ibragimoff, May 11, 1946, RG 554, box 34, folder Repatriation from China. The presence of Ibragimoff as a U.S. Army officer in Tianjin in 1946–47 was an unusual coincidence in history, as he had been raised in Tianjin in the city's Russian exile community, where his parents still lived in 1946, and based on his name his ancestry was likely to have been Chechen and Muslim. Letters

written by Ibragimoff relate discoveries about situations in Tianjin that could have come only from someone familiar with the city and its communities. For example, he reported the attitude of White Russians in Tianjin toward the Soviet Union, commenting favorably on his own "Turko-Tartar" people, writing on March 14, 1946, "I don't have the exact figures, but at least 80% of former white Russians have voluntarily or otherwise changed the color of their complexion. The same is true in Peiping [Beijing] and Shanghai. However, I might remark in passing that the Turko-Tartar people as a whole have displayed some courage, and even if their future is pretty dark, so far only 2 families out of approximately 50 in Tientsin have changed their allegiance." Letters of Lt. Shamil Ibragimoff, February 7, 1946, March 14, 1946, March 28, 1946, May 4, 1946, May 11, 1946; Memorandum to Repatriation Section, Communications Group, Executive Headquarters, Peiping, China, December 2, 1946, RG 554, box 34, folder Repatriation from China.

17. An investigation by the Sixth Infantry Division in Pusan in March 1946 found that all 1,010 Koreans repatriated on one ship, LST 897, which arrived in Pusan from Shanghai on March 8, 1946, LST 897, were former Korea Restoration Army recruits who had quit. They had been recruited in September 1945, but after not receiving food, clothing, and shelter that the Korea Restoration Army had promised them, they revolted in December 1945 and asked U.S. military authorities in China to repatriate them to Korea. 6th Div G-2 Periodic Report no. 142, 1900I, March 9, 1946, RG 554, box 34, Refugees from China.

18. CG 24 Corps to COM GEN China info SCAP, 6th Inf Div, USAMGIK, TFGCT 2126, March 18, 1946, RG 554, box 34, Refugees from China.

19. Korean repatriation teams with Chinese- and English-speaking Koreans sent by the USAMGIK assisted in supervising the evacuations of refugees from Shanghai, Tianjin, and Qingdao. They worked out of the headquarters of the U.S. Forces China Theater (Shanghai), First Marine Division (Tianjin), and Sixth Marine Division (Qingdao). SCAP to CG USAFIK info CG China Theater, CG Third Amphib Corps, January 18, 1946; To SCAP info CG China Theater, CG Third Phib Corps, CG USAMGIK, January 20, 1946; CG China to USAFIK, For Foreign Affairs Section, January 28, 1946, RG 554, box 34, Refugees from China.

20. Memorandum, October 8, 1945, RG 554, box 33, folder Repatriation and Transfer of Control to US (Creation of Trusteeship).Despite his initial unfamiliarity with Korea, Benninghoff had done a creditable job of identifying and assessing the major political factions in Korea before the end of September, with the assistance of the XXIV Corps G-2 (intelligence) section. Subject: Political Movements in Korea, September 29, 1945, RG 554, box 22, folder General U.S. Policy towards Korea, 1945-46.

21. Trusteeship (Radios) (Outgoing), CG USAFIK to SCAP, TFGCG 144, 100927/I, November 10, 1945, RG 554, box 33, folder Repatriation and Transfer of Control to US (Creation of Trusteeship).
22. Radio, Korean Situation (Outgoing), CG USAFIK to SCAP, TFGCG 144, 100927/I, November 10, 1945.
23. Trusteeship (Radios) (Outgoing), CG USAFIK to SCAP, TFGBI 20, 201200/I, November 20, 1945, RG 554, box 33, folder Repatriation and Transfer of Control to US (Creation of Trusteeship).
24. Trusteeship (Radios) (Outgoing), CG USAFIK to SCAP, TFGBI 20, 201200/I, November 20, 1945.
25. Korean Situation (Incoming), Washington State Dept SGD Byrnes to CG USAFIK (for Langdon), November 29, 1945, RG 554, box 33, folder Repatriation and Transfer of Control to US (Creation of Trusteeship).
26. CG USAFIK to SCAP (Please inform Atcheson and pass to WARCOS for State), TGYMG 459, December 11, 1945, RG 554, box 33, folder Repatriation and Transfer of Control to US (Creation of Trusteeship).
27. CG USAFIK to SCAP info CINCAFPAC ADV, TFGCG 190, December 14, 1945, RG 554, box 33, folder Repatriation and Transfer of Control to US (Creation of Trusteeship).
28. Department of State, Communique on the Moscow Conference of the Three Foreign Ministers, no. 965, December 27, 1945, RG 554, box 22, folder General U.S. Policy towards Korea, 1945–46.
29. By December 1945, Capt. Ryong Chun Hahm and several Korean American enlisted men from Project Eagle were working at U.S. military government headquarters. They may have sympathized with the Korean Provisional Government and Kim Ku, but there is no evidence of it.
30. Washington to CINCAFPAC ADV info CINCAFPAC, December 30, 1945; WARTAG to CINCAFPAC ADV info XXIV Corps, December 31, 1945; Radios, Korean Situation (Outgoing), CG USAFIK to SCAP, TFGCG 212, January 2, 1946, RG 554, box 33, folder Repatriation and Transfer of Control to US (Creation of Trusteeship).
31. Soviet propaganda also announced that the United States had decided to make Korea use the same currency as Japan, a U.S. military occupation yen. TCGCG 255 (from Hodge personally), January 26, 1946, RG 554, box 33, folder Repatriation and Transfer of Control to US (Creation of Trusteeship).
32. Hodge appears to have been thoroughly frustrated with Korea as well at around this time. He apparently considered leaving Korea, as on January 28 he had offered in a personal message to MacArthur that he would "gladly accept relief" to serve as a scapegoat. Radio: January 28, 1946, Hodge to General MacArthur

personally TFGCG 262 281320/I, RG 554, box 33, folder Repatriation and Transfer of Control to US (Creation of Trusteeship).

33. State Department to Langdon, November 29, 1945.

34. Hodge issued angrily worded demands for advance notice from the State Department of trusteeship-related developments on January 2 and 26, 1946, after the reactions in Korea to the Moscow Conference declaration on trusteeship and to the Soviet news radio broadcasts on January 25. CG USAFIK to SCAP, TFGCG 212, January 2, 1946; TCGCG 255 (from Hodge personally), January 26, 1946.

35. Radios, Korean Situation (Outgoing), CG USAFIK TO SCAP, TFGCG 272, 0123191, February 1, 1946, RG 554, box 33, folder Repatriation and Transfer of Control to US (Creation of Trusteeship). Hodge's official report to the State Department was far tamer in its comments. To SCAP from CF USAFIK (Hodge for Benninghoff pass to State Department, Washington, copy to Atcheson Tokyo), TFGBI 190, February 7, 46, RG 554, box 33, folder Repatriation and Transfer of Control to US (Creation of Trusteeship).

36. "United States Policy regarding Korea, Part III, December 1945-June 1950," 5-7, declassified unpublished research paper by the Division of Historical Policy Research, Department of State, December 1951, printed by the Institute of Asian Culture Studies, Hallym University, Chunchon, Korea, 1987.

37. A U.S. Army intelligence officer learned in April 1946 about a possible assassination attempt sent from the south against Kim Il Sung and Kim Tu Bong, chairman of the New People's Party in North Korea, who was Kim Il Sung's party leader and superior. According to an informant who had been a policeman in Pyongyang and was in Seoul as an organizer for the New People's Party, a group of fourteen men had been arrested in Pyongyang with letters from the Korean Provisional Government, allegedly planning the assassinations. Whether the U.S. military government was able to confirm the existence of this particular assassination plot was not apparent from the accompanying records. Letter from John D. Evans Jr., Major, MI, Chief, Bureau of Public Opinion, Report of a plot to assassinate Kim, Du Bong, and Kim, Il Sawng, North Korean political leaders, April 14, 1946, RG 554, box 33, folder Public Opinion Trends.

38. CG USAFIK to CG China info SCAP pass to Atcheson, TFGBI 154, January 23, 1946, RG 554, box 34, Refugees from China.

39. *Who's Who in Korea*, 3rd rev., October 15, 1947, RG 554, box 76, folder Who's Who in Korea 15/Oct. 1947.

40. Cumings, *The Origins of the Korean War*, 2:197-98.

41. Hodge to SCAP, TFPOL 40, September 21, 1946, RG 554, box 22, folder Military Government Activities: Political Parties.

42. Radios, Korean Situation (Outgoing), CG USAFIK TO SCAP TFGCG 333, 022313,

April 2, 1946, RG 554, box 33, folder Repatriation and Transfer of Control to US (Creation of Trusteeship).

43. Radio, CG USAFIK TO SCAP, TFGCG 352, April 27, 1946, RG 554, box 33, folder Repatriation and Transfer of Control to US (Creation of Trusteeship). Public opinion polls conducted in April 1946 by the Opinion Sampling Section of the USAMGIK's Department of Public Information and analyzed in May 1946 indicate that there was a basis for Hodge's belief that American political principles and U.S. interests would prevail under a Korean government. These polls indicated that the general population in the south overwhelmingly favored American political principles and living in the south over Soviet Communism and living under the northern regime. In a survey of 651 persons, one-third urban and two-thirds rural, 77 percent viewed living in the north unfavorably, and over three times as many preferred "American democracy" than preferred "Soviet Communism." Effectiveness of Japanese and Soviet propaganda in the Provinces and in Seoul, May 20, 1946, RG 554, box 29, folder Records of Provisional Government.

44. Hodge also had to spend his time and attention dealing with a domestic political controversy after a congressman on the House Committee on Military Affairs (a predecessor to the House Committee on Armed Services), John Sheridan from Pennsylvania, complained in committee about the quality of mess hall food and Post Exchange goods in Korea and called for Hodge to be relieved of command, after a congressional delegation visit to Korea on August 31 and September 1, 1946. News of this development reached Korea and undermined Hodge's authority at a time when he was dealing with significant unrest in Korea, and Hodge sent a personal request to MacArthur on September 26 for reassurance of administration confidence in his command. Reflecting his exasperation after a year of crises in Korea, he commented regarding his continuing in Korea, "That I leave to you and the War Department though personally I do not oppose being relieved." Hodge received such reassurances from House members, the War Department, and MacArthur on September 28, and the issue ended. Message from J. R. Hodge to CINCAFPAC (For General MacArthur personally), TFGCG 497, September 26, 1946; Washington (WDGPO) to CINCAFPAC (Pass to Gen Hodge), September 28, 1946; Incoming message from CINCAFPAC to CG USAFIK (Gen Hodge), September 28, 1946; Hodge to CINCAFPAC (Personal to General MacArthur), TFGCG 501, September 29, 1946, RG 554, box 33, folder Repatriation and Transfer of Control to U.S. (Creation of Trusteeship).

45. After a period of house arrest in the Koryo Hotel, Cho Man Sik went to prison. He disappeared in 1950, reportedly executed along with other political prisoners by North Korean soldiers in October 1950, while the North Korean regime was

evacuating Pyongyang ahead of the arrival of UN forces during the UN offensive into North Korea after the amphibious landing at Inchon and recapture of Seoul in September 1950. For his struggles for Korean independence against both Japan and the Soviet Union, the Republic of Korea awarded Cho the Order of Merit for National Foundation in 1970.

46. The Soviet and North Korean Communist Parties considered Cheondogyo to be ideologically tolerable as a peasant movement against common ideological enemies, and the Friends Party continues to exist as a powerless figurehead controlled by the Workers' Party of Korea.

47. For a detailed description of the Soviet leadership in northern Korea, the biography of Kim Il Sung, and the process of forming the North Korean regime, see Lankov, *From Stalin to Kim Il Sung*, 1-76.

48. Cumings, *Korea's Place in the Sun*, 238-43.

49. Jon Jordan Weems is buried in the infant section of Yanghwajin Foreign Missionary Cemetery in Seoul. Posted on October 28, 2011. Find A Grave. Accessed on April 6, 2016. http://www.findagrave.com/cgi-bin/fg.cgi?page=gr&gsln=weems&gsiman=1&gscid=2213616&grid=79469495&.

50. "George McAfee McCune (1908-1948) and His Works," *Journal of Modern Korean Studies* 2 (December 1985): 42-44.

8. After the Mission

1. As his home and office in Seoul, Kim Ku used the Gyeonggyojang (Capital Bridge) House, originally built in 1938-39 by Korean gold magnate Choe Changhak, who was one of the wealthiest men in Korea under Imperial Japanese rule from ownership of a gold mine that ended up in North Korea after 1945. Choe offered the house after Kim Ku's arrival in Seoul in November 1945. After Kim Ku's assassination, the house went through multiple owners and uses, serving as the embassy of Taiwan and becoming part of Samsung Kangbuk Medical Center in 1967. In 2005 it finally received designation as a national historic site.

2. At his trial Ahn Du Hui stated that he had acted alone in assassinating Kim Ku, and he was convicted and sentenced to death. Syngman Rhee commuted the sentence to fifteen years in prison, and Ahn served less than a year before being released and reinstated in the ROK Army after the Korean War broke out in June 1950. After the war he lived under an assumed name for his protection. In 1992 Ahn stated in an interview with the Dong-A Ilbo that he had acted on the orders of Syngman Rhee's chief of intelligence. In 1999 a bus driver beat him to death with a club to avenge the death of Kim Ku.

3. Kim Ku's burial occurred at a site in Seoul's Hyochang Park that he himself had selected as the final resting place for the remains of leading patriots who had

died during the independence struggle. Korean patriots interred at Hyochang Park include Yun Ponggil and Yi Pongchang, whom Kim Ku had selected and sent on the bombing missions against the emperor of Japan in Tokyo and the Imperial Japanese command in Shanghai in 1932. A space has been reserved for Ahn Chunggun, whose remains have not been found.

4. See, e.g., Cumings, *Korea's Place in the Sun*. Cumings's ideological bias is apparent in his treatment of countless events and issues. For example, he barely mentions Korea's March First Movement and refuses to call it by its commonly accepted name, following the line of Korean Communists who denounced it as an action by bourgeois ideological enemies.

5. Clyde Sargent made an effort to educate people in his local community in Newport about China as well. He founded the Chinese Room in the Newport Public Library, which is now the Sargent Special Collections Room, and donated his personal collection of Chinese books and artifacts to it. He also began the compilation of photographs of China by his father, R. Harvey Sargent, a project that his son Robert Sargent completed and made into the traveling exhibition *China: Exploring the Interior, 1903–04*.

6. The only published accounts of Project Eagle are in Maochun Yu's *The OSS in China*, which describes Project Eagle and Operation Eagle briefly without mentioning Yi Pomsok or anyone else except Sargent and Willis Bird, and in Chester Cooper's *In the Shadows of History: Fifty Years behind the Scenes of Cold War Diplomacy*, which has a chapter about Project Eagle and Operation Eagle written from memory almost sixty years after the events. They appeared after the declassification of all OSS operations in China in 1996 and 2005, respectively. Project NAPKO appeared in a publicly released work earlier in 1975, in Carl Eifler's autobiography, *The Deadliest Colonel*, but it appears not to have received any further attention aside from the GIMIK boats.

7. For more information about the Human Resources Research Institute, see Robin, *The Making of the Cold War Enemy*.

8. Clarence N. Weems Jr., "The Korean Reform and Independence Movement (1881–1898)," submitted in partial fulfillment of the requirements for the degree of Doctor of Philosophy in the Faculty of Political Science, Columbia University, June 1954.

9. Homer Hulbert visited Korea at the invitation of Syngman Rhee and died a week after his arrival. He was buried in Yanghwajin Foreign Missionary Cemetery in Seoul in the first state funeral for a foreign citizen in Korea. For more about Hulbert's life and passing, see the website of the Hulbert Memorial Society in Korea, http://www.hulbert.or.kr/.

10. Weems, *Hulbert's History of Korea.* Weems's publications during the early 1960s also included a handbook, *Korea: Dilemma of Underdeveloped Country.*
11. The author assisted Kim Woo Chun and Hulbert Memorial Society founder Kim Dong Jin with the award nomination for Clarence Weems.
12. One of the last survivors was Evelyn McCune, widow of George McCune. She left her own mark on U.S.-Korea relations in a life that lasted more than half a century after George's passing. She earned her own master's degree and continued George's work at the University of California, including completing and publishing his book *Korea Today*, which became a best-seller when its publication in 1950 coincided with the outbreak of the Korean War and it provided the only comprehensive and up-to-date survey of the history, politics, and economic situation of Korea. During the war, she almost single-handedly saved Korea's main collection of its cultural heritage, on a special mission from General MacArthur to find artifacts looted by North Korea from the National Museum of Korea in Seoul. She entered Seoul immediately behind the soldiers and marines fighting their way into the city after the Inchon landing in September 1950, with only a single soldier as an escort, and found and preserved the museum's treasures in the city's ruins. In Washington she founded and headed the Korea unit at the Library of Congress in 1951–52, educating members of Congress on the little-known country where the United States was at war. She worked in Korea for the U.S. government and the United Nations from 1952 to 1954 and then taught at universities in Korea, Japan, and California for decades, authoring numerous books and articles on Korean art and culture. Her works on the arts and culture of Korea include *The Arts of Korea: An Illustrated History*, *The Inner Art: Korean Screens*, and *Kim Rides the Tiger: A Story of Korea*. Evelyn McCune passed away in California in 2012 at the age of 105.
13. The Hulbert Memorial Society, founded in 1999, has promoted the memory of Homer Hulbert in Korea. Its founder, Kim Dong Jin, published the biography *Homer Hulbert: Crusader for Korea* in 2010.
14. Kim Kwon Jung, "George McCune Stood by Koreans under Japanese Colonial Rule," *Korea Herald*, November 30, 2015, http://www.kpopherald.com/view.php?ud=201511301623559159432_2.

BIBLIOGRAPHY

Manuscripts and Archives

Donovan, William J. Collection. U.S. Army Heritage and Education Center, Carlisle PA.

Donovan, William J. Papers. Buffalo History Museum Research Library, Buffalo NY.

Korean Missionary Files. United Methodist Archives and Historical Center (UMAHC), Drew University, Madison NJ.

Record Group (RG) 226, the declassified records of the Office of Strategic Services, and RG 554, the records of General HQ, Far East Command, Supreme Commander Allied Powers and United Nations Command. National Archives and Records Administration (NARA), College Park MD.

Record Group (RG) 160, box 16. Presbyterian Historical Society, Philadelphia.

Progress Report, October 24, 1944. Georgia Tech Archives, Atlanta.

Roosevelt, Franklin D. Papers as President, President's Secretary's File, 1933–45. Franklin D. Roosevelt Presidential Library and Museum, Hyde Park NY.

Sargent, Clyde. Letter Extracts, 1941–47, and Goodfellow, Millard Preston, Papers, 1942–67. Hoover Institution Library and Archives, Stanford, California.

Vanderbilt University yearbook, 1930. Vanderbilt University Archives, Nashville.

Weems, Clarence N., Jr. Master's thesis. Vanderbilt University Archives, Nashville.

Weems, Clarence N., Jr. Dissertation. Columbia University Archives, New York.

Weems family genealogy. Weems-Botts Museum, Dumfries VA.

Weems matriculation cards. Emory University Archives, Atlanta.

Published Works

Avery, Pat McGrath, and Joyce Faulkner. *Sunchon Tunnel Massacre Survivors*. Bridgeville PA: Red Engine, 2008.

Boose, Donald W., Jr. "Portentous Sideshow: The Korean Occupation Decision." *Parameters*, Winter 1995, 112–29.

Brown, Anthony Cave. *Wild Bill Donovan: The Last Hero.* New York: Times, 1982.

Brown, Arthur Judson. *The Korean Conspiracy Case.* Northfield MA: Northfield, 1912.

Buswell, Robert E., Jr., and Timothy S. Lee, eds. *Christianity in Korea.* Honolulu: University of Hawaii Press, 2006.

Chung, David. *Syncretism: The Religious Context of Christian Beginnings in Korea.* Albany: State University of New York Press, 2001.

Clark, Donald H. *Living Dangerously in Korea: The Western Experience, 1900-1950.* Norwalk CT: Eastbridge , 2003.

Cooper, Chester L. *In the Shadows of History: Fifty Years behind the Scenes of Cold War Diplomacy.* Amherst NY: Prometheus, 2005.

Coursey, O. W. *Who's Who in South Dakota.* Vol. 5. Mitchell SD: Educator Supply, 1925.

Cumings, Bruce. *Korea's Place in the Sun: A Modern History.* New York: W. W. Norton, 1997.

———. *The Origins of the Korean War.* Vol. 2, *The Roaring of the Cataract, 1947-1950.* Princeton: Princeton University Press, 1991.

Dae Young Ryu. "Understanding Early American Missionaries in Korea (1884-1910): Capitalist Middle-Class Values and the Weber Thesis." *Archives de sciences sociales des religions* 113 (2001): 93-117.

Fitch, George A. *My Eighty Years in China.* Taipei: Mei Ya, 1974.

Foreign Relations of the United States, 1945. Vol. 4. Washington: Government Printing Office, 1969.

Gale, Esson M. *Salt for the Dragon: A Personal History of China, 1908-1945.* East Lansing: Michigan State College Press, 1953.

Gale, Rev. James G. "Count Terrauchi, Governor of Chosen." *New York Independent,* February 29, 1912, 438-40.

Gale, Sarah Anne H. "My Recollection of a Korean-English Dictionary in Preparation." *Journal of Modern Korean Studies* 2 (December 1985): 47-52.

"George McAfee McCune (1908-1948) and His Works." *Journal of Modern Korean Studies* 2 (December 1985): 34-46.

Gu Ban, Pan Ku, Biao Ban, Zhao Ban, and Clyde Bailey Sargent. *Wang Mang: A Translation of the Official Account of His Rise to Power.* China Studies from Confucius to Mao. New York: Hyperion, 1977.

Hulbert, Homer B. *The History of Korea.* Seoul: Methodist, 1905.

———. *The Passing of Korea.* New York: Doubleday, Page, 1906.

Kim Dong Jin. *Homer Hulbert: Crusader for Korea.* Seoul: Cham Choun Chingu, 2010.

Kim Han-Kyo. "Shannon McCune and His Korean Studies." *Journal of Modern Korean Studies* 4 (May 1990): 9-12.

Kim Ku. *Paekpom Ilchi: The Autobiography of Kim Ku.* Trans. Jongsoo Lee. Lanham: University Press of America, 2000.

Kim Kwon-jung. "George McCune Stood by Koreans under Japanese Colonial Rule." *Korea Herald,* November 30, 2015. http://www.kpopherald.com/view.php ?ud=201511301623559159432_2.

Kim Woo Chun. *Kim Ku Sonsaengue Salmul Daraso.* 1998.

Lankov, Andrei. *From Stalin to Kim Il Sung: The Formation of North Korea, 1945-1960.* New Brunswick NJ: Rutgers University Press, 2002.

McCune, Evelyn. *The Arts of Korea: An Illustrated History.* Rutland VT: Charles Tuttle, 1962.

———. *The Inner Art: Korean Screens.* Berkeley CA: Asian Humanities, 1983.

———. *Kim Rides the Tiger: A Story of Korea.* New York: John Day, 1951.

McCune, George. "The Exchange of Envoys between Korea and Japan during the Tokugawa Period." *Far Eastern Quarterly* 5 (May 1946), 305-25.

———. "The Japanese Trading Post at Pusan." *Korea Review,* June 1948, 11-15.

———. *Korea Today.* Cambridge: Harvard University Press, 1950.

McCune, George McAfee, and John Arnold Harrison, eds. *Korean-American Relations: Documents Pertaining to the Far Eastern Diplomacy of the United States.* Vol. 1, *The Initial Period, 1883-1886.* Berkeley: University of California Press, 1951.

McCune, George Shannon. *American Support of Presbyterian Missions in Korea.* Gainesville FL, May 1, 1984.

———. "Fifty Years of Promotion by the Home Board and Home Church." Jubilee Papers, Korea Mission, Presbyterian Church, USA. Reprinted in *American Support of Presbyterian Missions in Korea.* Gainesville FL, May 1, 1984.

———. "The Yi Dynasty Annals of Korea." *Transactions of the Korean Branch of the Royal Asiatic Society* 29 (1939): 58-82.

McCune, Shannon. *Korea: Land of Broken Calm.* Princeton: Van Nostrand, 1966.

———. *Korea's Heritage, a Regional and Social Geography.* Rutland: Charles E. Tuttle, 1956.

———. "The Mansei Movement, March 1, 1919." Colloquium Paper no. 5, Center for Korean Studies, University of Hawaii, Honolulu, 1977.

———. "The Testing of a Missionary: George Shannon McCune and the Korea Conspiracy Case of 1910-1913." In *Essays and Papers,* 7:263-77. Seoul: Soong Jun University, 1977.

Moon, Thomas, and Carl Eifler. *The Deadliest Colonel.* New York: Vantage, 1975.

"Obituary: Benjamin Burch Weems (1914-1986)." *Journal of Modern Korean Studies* 3 (December 1987): 148-49.

Park Eun-sik. *The Bloody History of the Korean Independence Movement.* Seoul: Somyŏng Ch'ulp'an, 2008.

Robin, Ron Theodore. *The Making of the Cold War Enemy: Culture and Politics in the Military-Intellectual Complex.* Princeton: Princeton University Press, 2001.

Sargent, Clyde Bailey. *Wang Mang: A Translation of the Official Account of His Rise to Power as Given in the "History of the Former Han Dynasty."* Shanghai: Graphic Art Book, 1947.

Thompson, Heather McAfee McCune, and Darlene McAfee Blackwood. *A Daughter's Journey: Evelyn Becker McCune.* Lulu.com, 2007.

"United States Policy regarding Korea, 1834-1941." Declassified unpublished research paper by the Division of Historical Policy Research, State Department, May 1947. Chunchon, Korea: Institute of Asian Culture Studies, Hallym University, 1987.

"United States Policy regarding Korea, Part II, 1941-1945." Declassified unpublished research paper by the Division of Historical Policy Research, Department of State, May 1950. Chunchon, Korea: Institute of Asian Culture Studies, Hallym University, 1987.

"United States Policy regarding Korea, Part III, December 1945-June 1950." Declassified unpublished research paper by the Division of Historical Policy Research, Department of State, December 1951. Chunchon, Korea: Institute of Asian Culture Studies, Hallym University, 1987.

U.S. War Department, General Staff, G-2 Division. *A History of the Military Intelligence Division, 7 December 1941-3 September 1945.* Washington: Military Intelligence Division, 1946.

Van Tassel, David D. "The Legend Maker." *American Heritage*, February 1962, 58-59, 80-92.

Weems, Benjamin B. *Reform, Rebellion, and the Heavenly Way.* Tucson: University of Arizona Press, 1964.

Weems, Clarence N. "Benjamin Burch Weems: May 28, 1914-January 31, 1986." *Korean and Korean-American Studies Bulletin* 2, no. 3 (Fall/Winter 1986): 6-7.

——. *Hulbert's History of Korea.* New York: Hillary House, 1962.

——. *Korea: Dilemma of Underdeveloped Country.* Headline series, no. 144. New York: Foreign Policy Association-World Affairs Center, 1960.

Weems, C. N. "Building a Church in Korea." *World Outlook*, September-October 1933, 4-5, 34.

——. "Centenary Days in Korea." *World Outlook*, August 1933, 8-9, 34.

——. "Early Days in Korea." *World Outlook*, July 1933, 8-9, 32-33.

Who Was Who in America. Vol. 2. Chicago: A. N. Marquis, 1950.

Wichtrich, A. R. *MIS-X Top Secret.* Raleigh NC: Pentland Press, 1997.

Woo Sung Han. *Unsung Hero: The Story of Colonel Young Oak Kim.* Riverside CA: University of California Young Oak Kim Center for Korean American Studies, 2011.

Yu, Maochun. *The OSS in China: Prelude to Cold War.* Annapolis MD: Naval Institute Press, 1996.

Yu, P. H., and C. K. Lee. "The Biography of Rev. C. N. Weems." In *In Commemoration of Thirty Years of Missionary Service of Rev. C. N. Weems*, 1-6. Wonsan, Korea, 1939.

INDEX